Social Assistance in Developing Countries

The rapid spread of large-scale and innovative social transfers in the developing world has made a key contribution to the significant reduction in global poverty over the last decade. Explaining how flagship anti-poverty programmes emerged, this book provides the first comprehensive account of the global growth of social assistance transfers in developing countries. Armando Barrientos begins by focusing on the ethical and conceptual foundations of social assistance, and he discusses the justifications for assisting those in poverty. He provides a primer on poverty analysis, and introduces readers to the theory of optimal transfers. He then shifts the focus to practice, and introduces a classification of social assistance programmes to help readers understand the diversity in approaches and design in developing countries. The book concludes with an analysis of the financing and politics of the emerging institutions and of their potential to address global poverty.

ARMANDO BARRIENTOS is Professor and Research Director at the Brooks World Poverty Institute at the University of Manchester. His research interests focus on the linkages between welfare programmes and labour markets in developing countries, and on policies addressing poverty, vulnerability and population ageing. His most recent books are *Just Give Money to the Poor: The Development Revolution from the Global South* (2010, with Joseph Hanlon and David Hulme), *Demographics, Employment and Old Age Security: Emerging Trends and Challenges in South Asia* (2010, edited with Moneer Alam) and *Social Protection for the Poor and Poorest: Concepts, Policies and Politics* (2008, edited with David Hulme).

Social Assistance in Developing Countries

ARMANDO BARRIENTOS
BWPI, University of Manchester

CAMBRIDGE
UNIVERSITY PRESS

CAMBRIDGE
UNIVERSITY PRESS

University Printing House, Cambridge CB2 8BS, United Kingdom

Published in the United States of America by Cambridge University Press, New York

Cambridge University Press is part of the University of Cambridge.

It furthers the University's mission by disseminating knowledge in the pursuit of education, learning, and research at the highest international levels of excellence.

www.cambridge.org
Information on this title: www.cambridge.org/9781107039025

© Armando Barrientos 2013

First published 2013

Printed in the United Kingdom by Clays, St Ives plc

A catalogue record for this publication is available from the British Library

Library of Congress Cataloguing in Publication data
Barrientos, Armando.
Social assistance in developing countries / Armando Barrientos, BWPI, University of Manchester.
    pages   cm
Includes bibliographical references and indexes.
1. Transfer payments – Developing countries.   2. Public welfare – Developing
countries.   3. Poverty – Developing countries.   I. Title.
HC59.72.P63B37   2013
362.5′82091724–dc23

2013010586

ISBN 978-1-107-03902-5 Hardback

For
Michael Brecker (1949–2007)
Zim Ngqawana (1959–2011)

Contents

Figures

Tables

Acknowledgements

This book is the product of over a decade's research and study on the emergence of anti-poverty transfer programmes in developing countries. Engagement with national and international policymakers has provided me with many additional insights and an understanding of the important role of policy and politics. The motivation for embarking on writing the book came from a realisation that a comprehensive account of the growth of anti-poverty transfer programmes, firmly grounded in theory, was sorely needed. I offer this book as contribution to filling this gap.

I have received help, support and inspiration from countless people – too many to list individually. I would like to thank all those with whom I have engaged through individual discussions, workshops and conferences over many years. A great many colleagues and friends have helped shape my approach and ideas. This is a very long list, but I would especially like to thank Moneer Alam, Francisco Ayala, Stephanie Ware Barrientos, Jonathan Bradshaw, Francesca Bastagli, Tony Bebbington, Fabio Bertranou, Simone Cecchini, Jiandong Chen, Michael Cichon, Sarah Cook, Guillermo Cruces, Mark Davies, Stephen Devereux, Richard Disney, Jasmine Gideon, Mark Gorman, Ian Gough, Margaret Grosh, Anthony Hall, Joe Hanlon, Amanda Heslop, Sam Hickey, David Hulme, Katsushi Imai, Naila Kabeer, Peter Lloyd-Sherlock, Lutz Leisering, Francie Lund, Anna McCord, Juliana Martinez Franzoni, Santosh Mehrotra, Carmelo Mesa-Lago, Maxine Molyneux, Valerie Møller, Lauchlan Munro, Miguel Niño-Zarazúa, Truman Packard, Sony Pellisery, Martin Powell, David Robalino, João Saboia, Rachel Sabatés-Wheeler, Bernd Schubert, Esther Schüring, Helmut Schwarzer, Kunal Sen, Fabio Soares, Sudarno Sumarto, Jenn Yablonski and the late Peter Townsend. Two reviewers and several colleagues provided extensive comments on drafts of this book, in particular Stephanie Ware Barrientos, Simone Cecchini, Guillermo Cruces, Indranil Dutta, Moritz von Gliszczynski, Sam

Hickey, David Hulme, Alma Kudebayeva, Paul Mosley, Esther Schüring, Kunal Sen, Juan Miguel Villa and Katrin Weible. I have benefited hugely from their comments and suggestions. I am solely responsible for the errors and omissions that remain. Clare Degenhardt and Roo Griffiths helped to edit the manuscript.

My understanding of the challenges involved at the country level would have been significantly poorer but for the insights provided by many researchers and policymakers in developing countries. I would especially like to acknowledge Nuno Cunha (Mozambique); Neo Symutani and Donald Woods (Zambia); Fabio Bertranou (Chile and Argentina); Guilherme Delgado, Helmut Schwarzer and Fabio Soares (Brazil); Gulsana Turusbekova (Kyrgyzstan); colleagues from the Chronic Poverty Research Centre; the Department for International Development (in particular Catherine Arnold, Katie Fawkner-Corbett, Matthew Greenslade and Sonya Sultan); HelpAge International; the International Labour Office and UNICEF; and especially Charles Lwanga-Ntale (Uganda and east Africa). Collectively, they opened for me several windows into the realities of building anti-poverty transfer programmes.

Without the support and encouragement of my colleagues at the Brooks World Poverty Institute at the University of Manchester this book would not have been completed successfully. A three-month research fellowship at the Zentrum für interdisziplinäre Forschung of the university of Bielefeld, in Germany, between April and June 2011 provided me with the opportunity to complete the manuscript. I am particularly grateful to the members of the FLOOR (Financial assistance, Land policy, and glObal sOcial Rights) group there, Lutz Leisering, Ulrike Davy and Benjamin Davy, for their hospitality and many productive discussions.

To all the above, and many more, I owe a deep gratitude for making this book possible.

PART I

Introduction

1 | *The emergence of social assistance in developing countries*

The eradication of poverty is arguably the world's greatest challenge for the twenty-first century. In a sense, this has been the case for the past three centuries; the difference today is that its eradication has become a distinct possibility. The past two decades, but especially the first decade of the twenty-first century, have seen large reductions in world poverty. The World Bank has estimated that the share of the population living below US$1.25 stood at 52.2 per cent in 1981, falling to 40.9 per cent in 1990 and 22.4 per cent in 2008. The number of people living below this extreme poverty line fell from 1.9 billion in 1990 to 1.2 billion in 2008 (Chen and Ravallion, 2012).[1]

Several factors have contributed to the fall in poverty rates in developing countries in the past decade. These include democratisation, sustained economic growth, investment in basic services, rising commodity prices and the emergence of large-scale anti-poverty transfer programmes. This book focuses on the last of these. Anti-poverty transfer programmes – or social assistance, to use a more precise term – provide direct transfers in cash and/or in kind to individuals or households experiencing poverty or vulnerability, with the aim of facilitating their permanent exit from poverty. In the first decade of this century such programmes spread rapidly to the majority of developing countries. This book provides a comprehensive analysis of their role and significance in reducing poverty across the world and demonstrates that permanent and sustainable poverty eradication is not achievable without them.

---

[1] The United Nations (UN) Economic Commission for Latin America and the Caribbean (ECLAC) has estimated that, in 1999, 37.2 per cent of Latin Americans lived in poverty, while 18.7 per cent could not meet basic food requirements. By 2009 these shares had fallen to 27.8 and 13.3 per cent, respectively (ECLAC, 2010).

What is new?

A strong motivation for writing this book has been the staggering growth of anti-poverty transfer programmes in developing countries since the middle of the 1990s. A conservative estimate of their reach indicates that between 0.75 and 1 billion people in developing countries are currently receiving transfers.[2] In the mid 1990s this figure would have been insignificant, which is probably why no one considered measuring it. The growth of anti-poverty transfer programmes in the South has taken most development researchers and international organisations by surprise.

A handful of examples of the growth of social assistance in the South will help illustrate this point. In the mid 1990s China introduced an anti-poverty transfer programme in urban areas to assist people in extreme poverty and vulnerability. The 'Minimum living standards guarantee' scheme, referred to as the *Dibao*, was intended to provide transfers in cash and in kind to older people or people with disabilities lacking regular income, family support or assets. Typical of such initiatives, the national programme grew out of a pilot programme, this one developed in Shanghai in 1993. The restructuring of state enterprises at the end of that decade led to rapidly rising unemployment, and the *Dibao* was extended to assist retrenched workers. Programme coverage rose from 2.6 million in 1999 to over 20 million by 2002 and over 22 million in 2004 (Chen and Barrientos, 2006; Wang, 2007).

Around the time that the authorities in Shanghai began experimenting with the *Dibao*, progressive municipalities in Brazil were considering how to respond to persistent poverty and vulnerability, which recurrent crises had made worse. In 1995 a handful of municipalities designed and implemented guaranteed income programmes tied to schooling and directed at households in extreme poverty. The thinking behind *Bolsa Escola* was that income transfers by themselves would not be effective in improving the longer-term productive capacity of these households. Other municipalities rapidly adopted the *Bolsa Escola* approach, aided from 1997 by federal subsidies. In 2001 *Bolsa Escola* became a federal programme, reaching around 9 million households. It

---

[2] This estimate is based on the 'Social assistance in developing countries' database (Barrientos, Niño-Zarazúa and Maitrot, 2010).

provided the core of *Bolsa Família*, introduced in 2003, and now reaches in excess of 12 million households (de Castro and Modesto, 2010).

In South Africa, the African National Congress government, which came to power in 1994 under the leadership of Nelson Mandela, set up a commission to consider the reform and expansion of social assistance in the country (Lund, 2008). Social assistance in the country had traditionally relied on transfers in cash or grants to groups in acute poverty or vulnerability. Among these, the old age grant focused on older people and people with disabilities and was widely perceived to be effective in reaching the poorest households. The commission came to the conclusion that an extension of the grants to children in households in poverty would help address worryingly high levels of child malnutrition. The child support grant came into existence in 1998 for children below seven years of age, and it was gradually extended to children below the age of eighteen over the next decade. It currently reaches in excess of 9 million children in South Africa (Woolard and Leibbrandt, 2010).

The examples from these three countries provide striking illustrations of the rapid growth in social assistance programmes, but similar developments can be observed in the great majority of developing countries (Barrientos, Niño-Zarazúa and Maitrot, 2010). Overall, the expansion of transfer programmes amounts to a significant step towards building the institutions needed to successfully eradicate extreme poverty in the world.

The focus of this book is on direct transfers to households in poverty and in extreme poverty. These constitute a small proportion of all government transfers and are best described as social assistance or anti-poverty transfer programmes. They are tax-financed transfers to individuals and households aimed at addressing poverty (Barrientos, 2007),[3] described as programmes because the actual transfers are often part of a set of interventions grounded in a particular understanding of poverty. In most cases they are formulated and managed by government agencies, although they can involve a variety of providers and non-governmental organisations (NGOs), and, across developed and developing countries, they typically absorb between 1 and 2 per cent of gross

---

[3] Where transfers are financed using international aid, they are also tax-financed, but the taxes are collected in a different jurisdiction.

domestic product (GDP). Social assistance transfers should be distinguished from humanitarian and emergency transfers.

In developing countries, social transfer programmes show considerable innovation and diversity. This diversity serves as a reminder of the fact that domestic factors have largely shaped programme design and implementation. Regional clusters of programmes – employment guarantees and social pensions in south Asia; human development conditional programmes in Latin America; social assistance grants in southern Africa – hint at localised policy diffusion (Barrientos and Hulme, 2009).

The influence of poverty research is directly observable in the scale and innovation in anti-poverty transfer programmes over the past decade.[4] The strength of this influence is striking in the design of human development conditional transfers and employment guarantees (Fiszbein and Schady, 2009; Morley and Coady, 2003; Skoufias, 2005), but also in approaches and techniques applied to beneficiary selection,[5] transfer composition and levels and monitoring and evaluation (Ravallion, 2005) and in their acknowledgement of the role of social risks and dynamic processes in generating poverty traps.[6] Most importantly, research influence can be seen in the focus of transfer programmes on households, as well as on groups in extreme or persistent poverty. Increasingly, multidimensionality is feeding into programme development (Azevedo and Robles, 2009).

Given the diversity in programme design, it will be helpful to develop a classification of anti-poverty transfer programmes to enable a discussion of 'ideal types'.[7] This classification identifies three ideal types. The first consists of social assistance programmes providing *pure income transfers*. These provide regular cash or in-kind transfers to individuals or households facing poverty or vulnerability, including social pensions and child grants. The second type includes programmes providing

---

[4] For a recap on advances in poverty analysis and their impact on policy, see Kanbur (2009).

[5] On the variety and effectiveness of selection techniques on the ground, see Coady (2004) and Coady and Skoufias (2004). It is instructive that, as recently as 1990 and in the context of a discussion on targeting, Besley and Kanbur could write that the 'administrative capacity to do this simply does not exist in many (perhaps most) developing countries' (1990: 6).

[6] The social risk management literature emphasises the role of risks; see Holzmann and Jorgensen (1999) and Morduch (1998a).

[7] This classification is discussed in detail in Chapter 5.

transfers combined with asset accumulation. Here, cash transfers work side by side with interventions aimed at human, financial or physical asset accumulation. The third type includes *integrated poverty reduction* programmes. Integrated poverty reduction programmes not only combine a wider range of interventions than the previous type but also have the distinctive feature that the income transfer is not the dominant component. A case is made below that this classification provides a good entry point into the conceptual underpinnings of social assistance programmes. The three programme types reflect distinctive understandings of poverty: poverty as lack of income; poverty as deficiencies in income and assets; and poverty as multidimensional deprivation.

Why social assistance?

Social assistance has until recently been conspicuous by its absence in development thinking and debate. The 1991 volume *Social Security in Developing Countries* (Ahmad *et al.*, 1991) offers a stocktake on thinking on this issue at that time. There are very few references to social assistance or to direct transfers to households in poverty, but, in the context of discussing strategies for developing countries, it makes a distinction between 'growth-mediated security' and 'support-led security'. The latter strategy has a role for wide-ranging public support, including 'social assistance in order to remove destitution without waiting for a transformation in the level of general affluence' (Drèze and Sen, 1991: 22). The 1995 Copenhagen Declaration contains a commitment to poverty eradication, but focuses mainly on social insurance and service provision.[8] It makes reference to 'safety nets' but solely in the context of structural adjustment and as a short-term emergency intervention.[9] The Millennium Development Goals, adopted in 2000, make no mention of social assistance or social protection, although the 2010 review discussions did consider them in some detail.

Taking a longer perspective on development, it is pertinent that the origins of welfare provision in European countries in the sixteenth,

---

[8] 'The eradication of poverty requires universal access to economic opportunities that will promote sustainable livelihoods and basic social services, as well as special efforts to facilitate access to opportunities and services for the disadvantaged' (UN, 1995: 42).

[9] 'Short term by nature, safety nets must protect people living in poverty and enable them to find productive employment' (UN, 1995: 53).

seventeenth and eighteenth centuries are to be found in social assistance schemes. The Poor Laws in the United Kingdom, for example, constituted an early attempt at institutionalising basic living standards in rural areas (Szreter, 2007). The Speenhamland scheme, instituted in 1795, provided for direct subsidies to families affected by unemployment, as recounted by Polanyi (1957). Other European nations gradually followed suit during the eighteenth and nineteenth centuries, extending provision for groups in extreme poverty or destitution. Lindert (2004) estimates that disbursements ranged between 0.5 and 2 per cent of GDP in the early nineteenth century. Social insurance schemes began with the implementation of Otto von Bismarck's disability and old age pension in Germany, enacted in 1889.

The development of European welfare states, with comprehensive protection 'from the cradle to the grave', dates only to the period since World War II.[10] Financed by a significant hike in payroll taxation and buttressed by corporatist political settlements – engaging the government, trade unions and employers – and a macroeconomic framework of sustained growth, the emerging welfare states *appeared* to have done away with the need for social assistance.[11] Researchers prepared to ignore all prewar poverty policy could have concluded that the eradication of absolute poverty did not require a large contribution from social assistance. Barry (1990: 503) captures the moment perfectly:

Should any decent welfare state relieve poverty? Of course it should. But in a well-ordered welfare state almost all the jobs of relieving poverty will be done by policies whose objectives and rationales are quite different. For all except a few unfortunates who fall through the cracks, the relief of poverty is a by-product of a system of cash benefits founded upon principles that do not include the relief of poverty.

The golden age of welfare provision in European countries achieved considerable success in almost eradicating absolute poverty, but the wish that this could be done without social assistance was never realised. A survey of social assistance in Organisation for Economic Cooperation and Development (OECD) countries in the 1990s found that, far from having disappeared, social assistance provision was growing

---

[10] In fact, the old age pension introduced by Bismarck did not achieve 60 per cent coverage until the 1960s.

[11] Beveridge's welfare model also foresaw the gradual elimination of social assistance, but failed to achieve it.

(Gough *et al.*, 1997). At any rate, countries such as Australia and New Zealand always relied on means-tested benefits as the core of their social security, very much like South Africa. High and persistent unemployment in the 1980s led to renewed interest in the working of social assistance and, in particular, active labour market policies.[12] The number of OECD studies published on social assistance and related subjects in the past decade suggests that it remains a core component of welfare states, albeit extensively rebuilt and redesigned (Adema, 2006). The impact of the 2008 financial crisis on developed nations, especially in the United States, has forced a stocktake of their social assistance institutions, with a view to strengthening them (Bitler and Hoynes, 2010).

Historically, Latin America and the Caribbean is the one developing region where Barry's take on poverty reduction without engaging social assistance became the orthodoxy. Social insurance institutions emerged in Latin America in the 1920s in the shape of insurance funds covering life course contingencies for specific groups of workers, especially the armed forces and other public sector workers and railway workers (Mesa-Lago, 1991). In the 1960s and 1970s social insurance funds expanded to include other contingencies and other groups of workers in formal employment. Governments in the region got involved, attracted in large part by the savings accumulated in the funds, and proceeded to integrate and consolidate the occupational funds. This facilitated an expansion of coverage, encouraged by strong advocacy from the International Labour Organization (ILO) (Usui, 1994).[13] Uruguay and Argentina reached almost full coverage of the labour force in the early 1970s, in Argentina's case through the creation of a subsidised insurance fund for self-employed workers. In other countries, gains in coverage were modest and social insurance funds weaker, but the expectation was that social insurance would gradually expand to cover more vulnerable workers until universal coverage was achieved. Social assistance institutions were surplus to requirements. Moreover, direct transfers to low-income households were often

---

[12] In part, the focus was on ensuring that social assistance did not undermine work incentives (OECD, 2003).

[13] For an insightful account of the role of the ILO in the underestimation of social assistance in developing countries' social protection policy, see Seekings (2008b).

blatantly used by political elites searching for short-term electoral advantage.[14]

Social assistance programmes in the Latin America and Caribbean region remained small, residual, fragmented and highly clientelistic. The structural adjustment and financial crises in the 1980s and early 1990s punctured expectations on the expansion of social insurance. The 1980s are often described as Latin America's 'lost decade', as unemployment and poverty climbed in the face of de facto labour market liberalisation (Altimir, 1997; Barrientos, 2004). The reform of social insurance funds on the one hand and labour market liberalisation on the other conspired to produce a sharp reduction in social insurance coverage in the region. By 2006 coverage of the economically active population by social insurance funds in Argentina had fallen to less than 40 per cent, and to 13 per cent among workers in the bottom income quintile (Rofman, Lucchetti and Ourens, 2008).[15] For the region as a whole, only one in every four economically active workers contributes to a pension plan. The recent emergence of social assistance in Latin America is an important indication that crucial components were missing in the version of the European model transplanted to the region.[16]

To sum up, social assistance is an essential component of a global poverty reduction and eradication strategy. The contribution of social assistance has been severely downplayed in development thinking and debates, as well as in those on social security and social policy. The underestimation of the role of social assistance in development strategies has a great deal to do with the spell on development researchers cast by the 'golden age' European model, which presumes that poverty can be eradicated without engaging with poverty reduction, that it will be a by-product of other policies.[17] The expansion of social assistance in the South suggests otherwise.

---

[14] Latin Americans use the term *asistencialismo* to describe the use of transfers in this context.

[15] Social insurance coverage for the labour force has improved since 2006.

[16] See, among others, Barrientos (2009b), Barrientos and Santibañez (2009a), Ferreira and Robalino (2010), Fiszbein (2005) and Levy (2008).

[17] It is remarkable how isomorphic this social policy perspective is with the Washington consensus approach. The latter proposes that poverty reduction is a by-product of economic growth and argues that direct transfers to households in poverty might be detrimental to growth and therefore dysfunctional for poverty reduction.

Why now?

What explains the sudden expansion in social assistance in the first decade of this century? Why have governments reconnected with poverty? There are several possible explanations. These are discussed in their respective settings in the following chapters, but it is helpful to introduce them here.

The last two decades of the previous century were punctuated by crises, structural adjustment and liberalisation. Reference has already been made to the crisis in the early 1980s, and the structural adjustment that followed, leading to a 'lost decade' in the Latin America region. The 1997 financial crisis in Asia appeared to bring to an end the 'Asian miracle'. Structural transformations raced across the socialist bloc, ushering in barely fettered market forces. One of the outcomes of these large structural shocks was a sustained rise in poverty and vulnerability in developing countries. Liberalisation, and labour market liberalisation in particular, engendered a sharp rise in vulnerability, sustained through the recovery phase. Public sector cuts and extensive reforms undermined the capacity of governments to address rising poverty. These processes created what Latin Americans aptly refer to as 'social debt' – *deuda social*: very large and structural deficits in protection and well-being, especially among the most vulnerable sections of the population. Recovery, and a reassessment of the role of the state in society, began to create the conditions in which this social debt could be addressed.

Two key processes have shaped effective demand for policies addressing poverty and vulnerability: democratisation and domestic revenue generation. Democratisation processes have strengthened the political voice and influence of low-income groups. Growth led to rising tax/GDP ratios, which enhanced fiscal space.[18] The tax mix shifted towards consumption taxes and natural resource revenues, the former in particular bringing low-income groups within fiscal representation (Daude and Melguizo, 2010). Complementing these processes at the national level, international policy has given priority to poverty reduction. The Millennium Development Goals have helped enforce and coordinate the poverty reduction efforts of multilateral and bilateral donors, in

---

[18] For an analysis of these trends in Latin America, see Cornia (2010). For Africa, see African Development Bank (AfDB) and OECD Development Centre (2010).

ways that could have contributed to the stronger focus on poverty reduction in many developing countries (Hulme, 2010). The international policy environment has encouraged a greater focus on poverty among developing countries.

The role of poverty research in securing an improved understanding of poverty and in developing the very practical tools to provide the building blocks for effective programmes and strategies has also been an important influence. Political and public support for poverty reduction strategies is more likely to be forthcoming if there are practicable and effective interventions that can demonstrably reduce poverty. The confluence of democratisation, growth, stronger effective demand for poverty reduction at national and international levels and improved knowledge and practice has contributed to the expansion of social assistance in the South.

What to expect from anti-poverty transfers?

The rapid growth in anti-poverty transfer programmes in developing countries risks raising unfounded expectations regarding their contribution to poverty reduction and to social and economic development more generally. The growing interest in anti-poverty transfers in international development policy circles has largely followed, not led, developing country initiatives. There is a risk that, in the hands of the aid industry, anti-poverty transfers will be transformed into a 'silver bullet', capable of solving all development problems. There is a pattern to development discourses, whereby otherwise sound policies (but also concepts and theories) are extended in all directions to cover all possible problems and domains until they break down under the weight of hyped-up expectations. An understanding of what anti-poverty transfers can do is crucial to avoiding this fate.

Social assistance is one of several interventions that, combined, can help address poverty. Sustained poverty reduction requires, at the very least, economic growth capable of enhancing economic opportunity for groups in poverty; basic services supporting the accumulation of productive capacity by households in poverty; and social protection and social assistance able to raise and stabilise basic living standards among groups in poverty. Conventionally, and in the context of developed countries, social protection is understood to include social insurance, social assistance and labour market policies. In the context of developing countries, social protection is often understood in a narrower sense, as including direct transfer programmes addressing poverty and vulnerability. In this book, the broader sense is conveyed by the term 'social protection', and 'social assistance' describes social protection in the narrower sense. Social assistance is likely to be effective in reducing poverty in combination with growth and basic service provision.[19] There are few trade-offs available to policymakers committed to poverty reduction. In the absence of economic opportunity and access to basic services, social assistance is unlikely to make a significant contribution to sustained poverty reduction.

The main objective of social assistance programmes is to address poverty and vulnerability. Vulnerability in this context is understood as the (high) probability that households will find themselves in poverty in the future. In most anti-poverty transfer programmes, this core objective is linked to intermediary or proximate objectives, such as asset protection, asset accumulation, nutrition or service utilisation. Programme design and implementation follow from programme objectives. Knowledge about the influence of transfers on household behaviour and decision-making underlies these linkages (Barrientos, 2012).

Economic models of households' decision-making provide the starting point for examining the impact of transfers. Take a modest, but regular, income transfer. Households faced with a rise in income will consider how best to employ this to improve their welfare. A middle-income household, perhaps reasonably satisfied with its living standards, would probably use additional income to buy a bit more of the same, and perhaps save a little. For households in poverty, the additional income provides them with the opportunity to address their many deficits. As their consumption is constrained by their income, they will give strong consideration to improving their nutrition. In cases of acute deprivation, perhaps the main use of the additional income will be to increase food consumption. Regular transfers to households in extreme poverty can also influence how they manage their scarce resources in a longer-term perspective. Reliable transfers make possible small investments in human and other productive assets. Therefore, moderate but regular income transfers can be expected to have an impact on

---

[19] Other conditions and interventions are required too, especially political voice and participation and a significant reduction in gender discrimination.

household consumption, especially food consumption, and also on households' ability to invest in their own productive capacity.

Given favourable economic conditions and access to basic services, anti-poverty transfers can be expected to lead to improvements in household consumption and productive capacity, which in turn lead to poverty reduction and, over time, facilitate exit from poverty. There is diversity across programmes and countries in terms of their precise objectives, but these two constitute the core effects of social assistance. The level and design of the transfers are important to determine how these effects unfold. Implementation is important too. It is very likely that social assistance programmes will generate secondary or indirect effects, and, indeed, there is a growing literature on indirect effects, which the following chapters review. However, these depend on the interaction of programme design and implementation, on the one hand, and environmental conditions, on the other.

The end game: institution building and poverty eradication

The rapid growth of anti-poverty transfer programmes in developing countries signals an important shift in the configuration of their welfare institutions – the set of interlinked institutions producing welfare. Esping-Andersen coined the term 'welfare regimes' to describe the way that households and state and market institutions in high-income countries combine to produce welfare (1990). In his view, the relative weight and significance of these institutions determine the achieved levels of welfare in different societies.[20] The key insight emerging from the analysis of welfare regimes is the fact that welfare is produced, and that it is to an important extent the outcome of the interplay of core institutions. The growth of social assistance in the South signals an important addition to welfare production institutions in developing countries. In many countries, especially low-income ones, it adds a component of welfare production that was absent. In other countries, primarily middle-income ones, the growth of social assistance will lead to a reconfiguration of existing welfare institutions. In middle-income countries with large-scale social insurance welfare institutions, the nature of this reconfiguration can turn out to be far-reaching and

---

[20] Extending this approach to developing countries would need to account for the role of international organisations, multilaterals and bilaterals; see Gough (2004).

complex. Broadly, the growth of social assistance enhances the role and responsibilities of the state in producing welfare, perhaps at the expense of the relative contributions of the family and markets.

Another important insight from welfare regime analysis is a focus on institutions as opposed to short-term interventions. The latter have tended to dominate practice in international development. There are few gains from approaching social assistance programmes as self-standing and short-term development projects, such as delivering malaria nets or water pumps. The point about the rise of social assistance programmes is that it reflects institution building in developing countries. In some countries this process is at an embryonic stage, with social assistance programmes implemented as pilot programmes, or with a predefined time window. In other countries institutionalisation is at a more advanced stage, marked with constitutional or legal changes and with the creation of ministries of social development, including social assistance agencies. The progression from embryonic to mature forms of institutionalisation is by no means guaranteed or straightforward, but it is under way in many countries. A more appropriate understanding of emerging social assistance programmes will materialise only if they are studied as a first stage in the development of long-term and stable institutions charged with the reduction, prevention and eradication of poverty.

The focus of anti-poverty transfer programmes in developing countries has been on reducing the incidence of poverty. The scale and persistence of poverty in the South risk making references to poverty eradication sound aspirational and futuristic. In this book, the term 'poverty eradication' has a different sense and a specific context. It is intended to emphasise that poverty eradication implies a sustained effort to reduce poverty where it exists and to prevent its recurrence. It follows from this that social assistance needs a more or less permanent institutional base. This is confirmed by the continued presence of social assistance institutions in advanced countries. It is to be hoped that social and economic development will reduce the role and significance of social assistance institutions, but is unlikely to eliminate them altogether.

Breaking new ground

The aim of this book is to provide a systematic and comprehensive account of social assistance in developing countries. In doing so, it breaks new ground in important respects.

The book opens with a discussion of the ethics of assistance. This is foundational to any analysis of why societies assist groups in poverty. The available literature on social assistance in developing countries rarely touches on these fundamental issues, yet an ethical framework is essential in order to understand the role and scope of social assistance.

There is a large and growing literature on transfer programmes, most of it extremely valuable. The largest share of this literature focuses on specific programmes in specific countries, often investigating their design and impact. In the project approach, which dominates development research, the questions posed are often of an instrumental kind. Does a particular programme achieve its objectives? Should transfers be conditional or unconditional? Should they rely on categorical targeting or means testing? What programme features are appropriate for countries with poor implementation capacity? Are the main features of programme design justified, given the programme objectives? The approach this book takes breaks new ground because it attempts to address these important questions after introducing and discussing a conceptual framework for anti-poverty transfers. A framework linking the ethics of assistance, poverty analysis, the economics of social assistance and the evolution of institutions is the main focus of the first part of the book.

The considerable diversity in programme design in developing countries is often presented as a menu of features from which programme designers can extract their favourite combination. This literature is valuable in clarifying the options opened to policymakers (Grosh *et al.*, 2008), and the relative advantages of specific types of programmes, human-development-conditional transfers, social pensions, public works, etc. The discussion in this book takes this approach one step further by developing a typology of anti-poverty programmes, grounded in understandings of poverty. This approach enables a deeper understanding of the diversity of anti-poverty transfer programmes in the South.

The book pays close attention to three dimensions of social transfers rarely considered in the literature. It underlines the importance of politics, especially in the context of the financing of anti-poverty transfers; it pays attention to issues of implementation to a greater extent than the existing literature does; and it emphasises the importance of institutional dynamics in explaining the future evolution and impact of new forms of assistance in developing countries. A large share of the literature on anti-poverty transfer programmes, and especially the impact evaluation literature, sticks to a 'black box' approach. The impact evaluation literature has yielded important insights into the effectiveness or otherwise of social transfer programmes, including their effectiveness in achieving outcomes, both intended and unintended. However, it is in the nature of this approach that the political and policy processes associated with anti-poverty transfers are not given sufficient attention. Nonetheless, these are important processes. At their core, social assistance programmes embed shared solidarity values informed by epistemic political processes. This book pays appropriate attention to political and policy processes with a view to securing a rounded understanding of anti-poverty transfers in developing countries.

The motivation behind this book is to provide a systematic and comprehensive analysis of social assistance in developing countries. It intends to take the reader beyond project or instrumental approaches and to examine and assess the role of social assistance as a welfare production institution.

Structure of the book

The book divides into two parts. The first part develops a conceptual framework for social assistance, linking through the ethics of assistance, poverty analysis and the economics of optimal transfers. Together, these three chapters develop a perspective on the theory of social assistance in developing countries. The second part focuses on current practice. It offers a typology of anti-poverty transfers grounded in poverty understandings; considers lessons from the incidence, implementation and impact of anti-poverty transfers in developing countries; and examines the key issues of budgets, finance and politics associated with social assistance. Readers will notice that the book strives to cover experiences and findings from social assistance programmes from all developing regions. However, a Latin American 'bias' is unavoidable. The early introduction and spread of anti-poverty programmes in that region, and the breadth and depth of research generated around Mexico's *Progresa/Oportunidades* and Brazil's *Bolsa Escola/Família*, for example, mean that they figure prominently in the discussions below.

A summary of the main topics of individual chapters follows. Chapter 2 discusses the ethics of assisting groups in poverty, as the only appropriate starting point for any serious discussion on anti-poverty transfers. It draws on philosophical discussions of the institutions of social justice and cooperation that locate the foundations of assistance in a 'political conception of justice'. The chapter addresses three fundamental questions: why should individuals and societies assist the worst off? What is the value of assisting those in poverty? What are the limits of assistance? The ethics of assistance is seldom addressed explicitly in the literature, yet it is fundamental. The conclusions emerging from the discussion of these questions in this chapter help guide and organise the discussion in the rest of the book.

Chapter 3 is intended to provide readers with a basic grounding in the poverty concepts and measures essential to an understanding of the objectives, design and impact of anti-poverty transfer programmes. This chapter provides the key building blocks needed to understand the features of these programmes, and to help make sense of and assess their expected effects. Social assistance consists of a set of programmes, policies and institutions whose primary functions are to reduce, prevent and eradicate poverty. An understanding of poverty concepts and measures is therefore essential. Two main questions organise the materials in this chapter: what is poverty? How should it be measured? Some of the materials covered in this chapter belong to a largely technical literature. The presentation is aimed at a well-informed, interested readership. Additional notes at the end of the chapter, and references throughout the text, offer an entry point for readers interested in following up on the more technical literature.

Chapter 4 links the materials and conclusions of the preceding two chapters to the analysis of optimal transfer programmes. This is a very important chapter. The literature on optimal transfers is highly technical and grounded in economics, but this chapter strives to make the findings from this literature accessible to well-informed and interested readers. The chapter is built in three main stages. The first considers the following question: assuming an insufficient budget, what would be the best way of allocating this budget so as to maximise its poverty reduction impact? In brief, the answer to the question depends on policy-makers' poverty reduction objectives. This approach is restrictive, because it does not take account of the role of incentives and information, especially as it assumes the distribution is a one-off. The second stage introduces and examines a basic model of optimal transfers capable of accommodating these two issues within a more general framework. It asks the question: what parameters need to be considered to ensure effective anti-poverty transfer programmes in the presence of identification and incentive requirements? An examination of the role of work requirements in transfer programmes, for example, discusses their potential to address information deficits by enabling beneficiaries to self-select into transfer programmes while maintaining full work incentives. The third stage examines the literature on tax transfer schemes, with the aim of providing an insight into the kind of framework needed to integrate transfers and their financing. This addresses the question: what should the size of an anti-poverty budget be?

The study of optimal anti-poverty transfers in Chapter 4 brings together the ethical perspectives on assistance in Chapter 2 and the poverty concepts and measures in Chapter 3 to form a comprehensive analytical framework for the study of social assistance. It also provides a bridge to the study of existing social assistance programmes in developing countries in Chapters 5, 6 and 7.

The core objective of the discussion in Chapter 5 is to develop a typology of social assistance programmes, based on the understanding of poverty underlying them. The classification generates a small number of programme types ('ideal types') and facilitates an understanding of key design features and expected effects. It also provides a means of comparing and assessing transfer programmes. The classification provides insights into the three main areas of programme design innovation. Social assistance programmes in developing countries pay a great deal of attention to incentives, rather than relying solely on income effects. They increasingly aim to address multidimensional poverty by packaging a set of interventions around the transfer. They also show a growing awareness of the need to strengthen the productive capacity of households, especially through interventions aimed at asset accumulation, particularly human asset accumulation. This chapter includes an examination of programme objectives, beneficiary selection, transfer levels and modalities, co-responsibilities and conditions, as well as the important issues around the duration of support and exit strategies. The discussion ensures a systematic understanding of the core features of current anti-poverty transfer programmes in developing countries.

Chapter 6 examines in more detail three key areas of existing anti-poverty transfer programmes: their incidence, implementation and impact. Establishing the reach of social assistance programmes is essential to the task of assessing their effectiveness in reducing world poverty. The literature has been dominated by 'targeting' studies, which largely focus on determining the extent to which transfers leak to non-eligible groups. The limitations of this approach are well known, and have stimulated research on more comprehensive measures of incidence. This chapter focuses on these and on the processes of beneficiary selection and registration that determine the reach of social assistance. Comparative and analytical literature on the implementation of anti-poverty transfers in developing countries is scarce: the chapter identifies knowledge gaps around implementation and discusses the importance of institutionalisation and information. Meanwhile, there is a large and fast-growing literature on the impact of anti-poverty transfers in developing countries. The last section of this chapter assesses the main findings emerging from this literature on the impacts on consumption, poverty and productive capacity. The chapter ends with a consideration of the long-term effects of anti-poverty transfers.

Chapter 7 focuses on issues of financing and politics in the context of anti-poverty transfers in developing countries. It addresses the following three questions: what resources are required to support assistance programmes in developing countries? Where are these resources going to come from? How can public support be generated for assistance programmes? Taking sequentially a positive and a normative approach to the question of the required size of the budget, the chapter provides some rough estimates. Developing countries with more advanced assistance programmes allocate between 1 and 2 per cent of their GDP to social assistance. Low-income countries spend a fraction of this figure, normally with a significant contribution from international aid. Normative approaches start instead from a needs assessment, and suggest that a much larger budget is required. The chapter then turns to the financing of this budget. International policy discussions to date have been dominated by a resource mobilisation approach to the financing of anti-poverty transfer programmes in developing countries. The limitations of this approach mean that a more comprehensive framework is recommended. Financing social assistance is not just a matter of generating additional resources, and it is not primarily about aid. It is essential to study the incentive and legitimacy implications of alternative financing mixes. Moreover, it is crucial to see the issue of financing as 'politics by other means'. This is the approach this chapter adopts, and it links up to the discussion of optimal anti-poverty transfers in Chapter 4.

The concluding chapter begins by outlining the main factors explaining the growth of social assistance in developing countries, paying attention to regional dynamics. It also considers longer-term factors associated with demographic trends, globalisation and migration. The discussion looks ahead to the future of assistance in developing countries and considers the potential for further extension of the scale of assistance, and its institutionalisation. It identifies and discusses knowledge gaps and policy challenges, and draws out the main lessons for global poverty eradication emerging from the analysis in the book.

These are the main themes of the book. As noted above, its objective is to provide a systematic and comprehensive understanding of emerging social assistance in developing countries. Readers will judge whether or not it has achieved this aim.

PART II

Foundations

2 | *Ethical foundations*

Research and policy discussions on social assistance programmes often begin by addressing issues of design and implementation efficiency. This is an important area, which this book covers in some detail later on, but it is not an appropriate starting point. The ethics of assistance is seldom addressed explicitly in the literature, yet it is foundational to the processes and choices that determine the scope and nature of social assistance. Three important questions take us to the core of the ethics of assistance. Why should individuals and societies assist the worst off? What is the value of assisting those in poverty? What are the limits of assistance? This chapter tackles these questions, in search of a firm foundation on which to support the analysis that follows.

There is a large literature relevant to the ethics of assistance; the literature on egalitarianism, for example, is vast, and in parts extremely complex. It is beyond the scope of this book to provide a comprehensive review of this literature; the discussion focuses instead on selected key contributions that throw light on the three questions identified above. The chapter assesses justifications for assisting those in poverty based on morality and on political conceptions of justice. The value of assistance is covered by introducing and discussing the priority view, while the limits of assistance are considered through a discussion of sufficiency. Other perspectives are referred to as the discussion proceeds, but the hope is that the main contributions selected for examination provide firm footholds for the subsequent analysis in the book.

The chapter begins by examining two main approaches to the foundations of assistance. One provides a justification of assistance on the basis of individual morality. The core question underlying this approach is: why should I help those in poverty? Appropriate answers to this question are to be found in an assessment of reasonable rights and duties pertaining to individuals. An alternative approach is to provide a justification for assistance based on a 'political conception of justice', in the Rawlsian sense. Here the underlying core question is:

what are the appropriate institutions of social justice and cooperation, and why should they include assistance to those in poverty? These two approaches throw light on the justifications for assistance.[1]

The chapter then discusses priority and sufficiency views on assisting those in poverty. The priority view argues that there is greater value in assisting the worst off in society; the sufficiency view argues that the priority of assisting the worst off applies only up to a point, a threshold. These views provide important insights into the value and limits of assistance. The insights of the priority and sufficiency views carry over to the analysis of poverty and of the economics of assistance, the subjects of the following chapters. They also inform the examination of the design and implementation of social assistance programmes, which is the focus of the later part of the book.

Justifications for assisting those in poverty

This section discusses in turn two approaches, each providing a separate justification for assisting those in poverty. The first focuses on individual rights and duties and shows under which circumstances a duty to assist people in poverty arises. The second approach does not start from individual conduct but, instead, focuses on social arrangements consistent with justice. In this approach, a political conception of justice entails assisting the poor.

Individual morality and assistance

Most people would agree with the view that we have a duty to assist others in need. Assistance can be justified by referring to negative duties or positive duties. An example will help distinguish between these two. Imagine that a child lies at the side of the road, having sustained an injury to his or her leg from a passing car. A bystander is in a position to help the child be taken to hospital, and can be said to have a duty to do this. The duty of assistance can be justified by the fact that helping the child to hospital will secure him or her prompt medical attention and will reduce the harm caused by the injury. Generalising from this case,

---

[1] In the discussion that follows, I make a distinction between morality and ethics, the first pertaining to individual rights and duties, the second to social arrangements and institutions.

we could say we have a positive duty to improve the welfare of others, and especially those who are in need.

Now let us suppose that, instead of being a bystander, the person in a position to assist the child is in fact the driver of the car who caused an otherwise avoidable injury to the child. It is straightforward to conclude that the driver has a duty to assist the child. However, in this case the duty of assistance is grounded on the car driver's responsibility for the accident that led to the child being injured. Generalising from this situation, we could say that we have a negative duty not to cause harm to others, and therefore to minimise as far as possible any adverse effects that our actions have on others. In this latter case, we could also say that the duty of assistance is grounded on both negative and positive duties. The car driver has a specific duty to help the child to hospital, in order to minimise the harm for which he or she is responsible, but he or she also has a general duty to take action to improve the child's welfare. Intuitively, the negative duty feels stronger and more compelling than the positive duty.

Positive and/or negative duties can be used to support assistance to individuals and households in poverty. They provide a justification, and explanation, for the myriad forms of support that individuals provide within their families and communities.

It will be helpful to follow up on the role of positive and negative duties as possible justifications for international assistance. Singer's principle of benevolence states that, if it is possible to prevent some significant bad from occurring to others, without sacrificing anything of comparable value to ourselves, then we have a moral duty to do so (Singer, 1972). It follows from this principle that we have a duty to assist those in poverty to overcome their situation, because their situation is dire and ours is not, and by helping them we make their situation better, requiring at worst a less than proportionate sacrifice on our part. The principle of benevolence justifies assisting those in poverty, on the basis that there is moral value in improving the welfare of others and that this moral value exceeds the sacrifice of donors. Importantly, Singer argues eloquently that the duties that flow from the principle of benevolence apply globally (Singer, 2002).

It can be argued that, in certain circumstances, the principle of benevolence may be too demanding (Arneson, 2004). Without reference to practical or financial limits, the duty of assistance could involve very large-scale transfers to the global poor, perhaps entailing significant sacrifices for donors. Singer and Pogge swiftly reject this complaint on empirical grounds. Singer points to the gap that exists between what citizens of the United States believe their government allocates to international assistance (an amount equivalent to 15 per cent of US GDP), what they perceive to be a fair allocation (5 per cent) and the actual allocation (0.15 per cent) (Singer, 2002). Pogge points to the World Banks's *World Development Report 2000/ 2001: Attacking Poverty*, which calculated that the amount required to lift the global poor to the US$2-a-day poverty line was then equivalent to 1.13 per cent of the incomes of the developed economies (Pogge, 2004). It is hard to describe a 1.13 per cent additional tax on developed economies as a hugely demanding sacrifice, especially when this is set aside for the eradication of income poverty in the South. Other factors also come into play in assessing both sacrifices and benefits. International assistance can be so ineffective, given, say, corruption or incompetence, as to make the duty of assistance uncompelling.

In several important contributions, Pogge has developed a justification for international assistance based primarily on a negative duty on the part of the North (Pogge, 2001; 2002; 2004). His argument is that developed countries are under a strong obligation to help the global poor because they are responsible for the incidence of severe poverty in the South. To the extent that developed countries have established and shaped international economic institutions to suit their own interests, often to the detriment of developing countries, their populations could be held responsible for the conditions that give rise to global poverty. In his view, severe poverty in developing countries is directly attributable to the actions of developed countries. The populations of developed countries have benefited from the unjust global economic architecture and therefore have a duty to help the global poor. As Pogge puts it, citizens of developed countries 'should reduce severe harms we will have caused, and. . .should not take advantage of injustice at the expense of its victims' (2004: 278).

Grounding assistance on negative duties has several advantages. Negative duties to assist the global poor are seen to be more compelling and powerful than positive duties. Positive duties are circumscribed by group membership, to an extent that negative duties are not. In our example above, say the bystander is a foreign tourist unable to understand the language of the child or hospital staff. His or her positive duty to assist can be argued to be weaker than that of the mother or father of the child. In the context of poverty-related assistance, it is straightforward to imagine situations in which the duty of assistance is substantially watered down.[2] At the same time, negative duties as a basis for assistance can be problematic. Pogge's critics point to the difficulties involved in establishing an appropriate empirical basis for determining the level of compensation from the North sufficient to discharge negative duties towards the South (Patten, 2005; Risse, 2005).

Assistance within a political conception of justice

An alternative route to justifying assistance to those in poverty focuses on a political conception of justice. This approach is not circumscribed to individual morality and personal duty but, instead, focuses on social institutions. It asks what social arrangements – institutions in a broader sense – best advance justice, and what the role of assistance is within them. Following up on this approach leads to a discussion of the ethical basis for assistance, located in notions of justice arrived at through political processes. Rawls' political notion of justice is the foremost example of this approach.[3]

Rawls' political notion of justice is motivated by an acknowledgement of two main parameters of modern liberal democratic societies.[4] First, these societies contain a plurality of world views, each with a distinctive view of the good. Their coexistence requires a measure of political agreement and tolerance. Second, the core structure and institutions of society[5] – especially its economic institutions, such as markets and occupational choice – generate inequalities that, if unchecked, render them unstable. In these conditions, it is inescapable that notions

---

[2] For a discussion of the role of distance in assisting the global poor, see Chatterjee (2004).

[3] Rawls developed and refined this notion of justice over time; see Rawls (1971; 2001).

[4] Rawls includes here societies with a range of economic systems: capitalist, social democratic and property-owning socialist systems.

[5] By the basic structure of society, Rawls means 'society's main political, constitutional, social and economic institutions and how they fit together to form a unified scheme of cooperation over time', comprising 'first the institutions that define social background and includes as well those operations that continually adjust and compensate for the inevitable tendencies away from background fairness'. He emphasises that this 'structure lies entirely within the domain of the political' (2005: xli).

of justice must be public, agreed by all and understood as a shared value. Rawls is led to the conclusion that only political notions of justice can meet these requirements. Politics enables members of a society with a plurality of life plans to agree on shared notions of justice capable of facilitating economic cooperation under fair terms. A political notion of justice is not 'perfectionist', in the sense of bringing about an ideal conception of the good, but 'constructivist', in the sense of building an overlapping consensus around basic principles.[6]

What are these basic principles? Rawls argues that reasonable people, operating under a veil of ignorance regarding their eventual status in society, would agree on a political notion of justice based on two main principles: (a) that 'each person has an indefeasible claim to a fully adequate scheme of basic equal liberties, which scheme is compatible with the same scheme of liberties for all'; and (b) that 'social and economic inequalities are to satisfy two conditions: first that they are to be attached to offices and positions open to all under conditions of fair equality of opportunity; and second, they are to the greatest benefit of the least advantaged members of society' (Rawls, 2001: 42; 2005).

The second part of (b), the difference principle, has resonance for discussions on poverty and assistance. In Rawls' approach, a person's advantage is measured by an index of primary goods. Primary goods are not goods in the usual sense of the word but, instead, all-purpose means of achieving one's life plans. Rawls discusses five kinds of primary goods: basic rights and liberties; freedom of movement and occupation in a context of opportunity; powers and prerogatives of offices and positions of authority and responsibility; income and wealth; and the social basis of self-respect. It is contingent on the institutions of a society operating under this political conception of justice to ensure that the index of primary goods is maximised for the least advantaged members of the community.

It is important not to read a concern with the least advantaged as referring directly to poverty (Freeman, 2007).[7] In a highly prosperous society, the least advantaged – that is, households at the bottom of the distribution of the index of primary goods – might not necessarily be in

---

[6] For an alternative assessment of this point, see Sen (2009). Pogge (1989) provides a good introduction to and discussion of Rawls.

[7] The index to Rawls' *A Theory of Justice* contains no entry for poverty.

poverty in the sense of also being at levels of welfare below a socially acceptable minimum.[8]

The social minimum is one of the institutions embedding the difference principle, but it has the most relevance for issues of poverty and assistance.[9] Rawls notes the essential role of commitment in lending continuous support, and therefore stability, to the basic structure. A political notion of justice requires that the members of society be prepared to endorse its basic structure. However, the inequalities generated by the working of the basic structure imply that sustaining this commitment to economic cooperation and institutions can be problematic. What guarantees that those who are disadvantaged, even severely disadvantaged, remain committed to the basic structure? Rawls' answer is a social minimum, a floor capable of ensuring that the strains of commitment never become excessive and undermine the stability of the overlapping consensus.

The characterisation of the social minimum evolved through Rawls' work, providing along the way many valuable insights into the context of alternative justifications for assisting those in poverty. The original characterisation of the social minimum in Rawls' 1971 *A Theory of Justice*, referred to above, linked the social minimum directly to the difference principle. The social minimum is guaranteed by the government 'either by family allowances and special payments for sickness and employment, or more systematically by such devices as a graded income supplement (a so-called negative income tax)' (Rawls, 1971: 243). The social minimum is presented as a background institution needed to achieve distributive justice, ensuring that the least advantaged are able to 'identify with interests broader than their own' (155). As such, the social minimum is distinguished from institutions of assistance motivated by prudential objectives.[10]

---

[8] This opens up a deeper set of issues about what is meant by poverty, to be considered later in this chapter and in the next chapter. In developing countries, poverty is normally understood in absolute terms, as indicating a deficiency in welfare below a socially acceptable minimum. In developed countries, poverty is usually understood in relative terms, as indicating a position at the bottom of a distribution of welfare.

[9] The social minimum is part of a package. Other policies are important, too, such as ensuring basic liberties and fair equality of opportunity and preventing monopolies. See Rawls (1971).

[10] 'The idea is not simply to assist those who lose out through accident or misfortune (although this must be done), but instead to put all citizens in a position to

Rawls' original characterisation of the social minimum was subject to an insightful critique by Waldron. Waldron's main point was that Rawls had justified the social minimum in terms of the requirements of distributive justice, but in fact its main justification was as a means of addressing need. A needs-based social minimum, 'a certain minimum. . .necessary for people to lead decent and tolerable lives' (Waldron, 1986: 21), could be argued to fit better with the aim of ensuring that the strains of commitment do not become excessive. Deprivation, as Waldron eloquently writes (30), 'in the despair that characterises it, the defiance it excites, and the single minded violence it may occasion, . . .poses a simmering threat to the viability of the societies it afflicts. There is therefore a prima facie reason why any society should avoid the situation in which significant numbers of people are in need.'

Rawls' response to Waldron's criticism is interesting in the way it reinforces and clarifies his approach to the social minimum. The subsequent revisions to *A Theory of Justice*, and the restatement in the 2001 *Justice as Fairness*, further define and develop the social minimum concept. In *Justice as Fairness*, Rawls distinguishes two different ways in which the strains of commitment can be experienced as excessive. The first follows Waldron's needs-based justification for the social minimum, and arises in a situation in which 'our share of resources does not permit us to lead a decent life' (Rawls, 2001: 128). The social minimum in this context can be defined as the minimum considered to be 'politically prudent' to preclude unrest. Rawls describes this approach to the social minimum as restricted utilitarianism, in the sense that it combines utilitarianism with the need to preserve a basic floor.

The second way the strains of commitment can become excessive has less to do with resources and more to do with political participation, with growing 'distant from political society' and feeling 'left out'. In this approach, consistent with justice as fairness, the social minimum is intended to ensure that 'the least advantaged feel they are a part of political society' (Rawls, 2001: 129). This is in line with Rawls' earlier statement to the effect that 'the minimum is to be set at that point which, taking wages into account, maximises the expectations of the least

manage their own affairs and to take part in social cooperation on a footing of mutual respect under appropriately equal conditions' (Rawls, 1971: xv).

advantaged group. By adjusting the amount of transfers, . . .it is possible to increase or decrease the – *life* – prospects of the more disadvantaged, their index of primary goods' (1971: 252, emphasis added).

According to Rawls, restricted utilitarianism remains a limited approach because improving the resources of the least advantaged to prevent unrest might well not be sufficient to address the second way in which the strains of commitment become excessive, namely when the least advantaged cease to feel that they have a stake in the basic structure.[11]

The justification of assisting those in poverty emerging from a political conception of justice is rich in scope and detail. In liberal democratic societies with pluralistic values and a basic social structure that inescapably generates large inequalities in welfare, preventing the strains of commitment from becoming excessive requires a social minimum. Assistance to those in poverty through the social minimum is not justified purely as a means to prevent social unrest and ensure basic levels of need satisfaction. Its substantive role is to ensure that the least advantaged can participate fully in political life, as equal citizens. Furthermore, the institutions embedding the principles under a political conception of justice need to ensure that the sacrifices experienced by the least advantaged work to secure justice as fairness.

Why should we assist those in poverty? This section has provided two different answers. The first is that we have a duty to assist groups in poverty because they are in a difficult situation and we are not. It is important that lives go as well as they might, and, if we accept this principle, we are duty-bound to bring this about. The duty of assistance is stronger if we are responsible for the situation of groups in poverty. However, there are important limitations to the duty of assistance, some of which have to do with the relative weight of sacrifice and gain and the extent of responsibility. There are few mechanisms ensuring duty compliance. A second approach might prove superior. Instead of relying on individual conduct, a focus on social arrangements consistent with a political conception of justice provides a stronger justification for

---

[11] The idea of an *overlapping consensus* makes this point most clearly. The 'idea is not that of satisfying needs as opposed to mere desires, nor is it that of redistribution in favor of greater equality. The constitutional essential here is rather that below a certain level of material and social well-being, and of training and education, people simply cannot take part in society as citizens, much less as equal citizens' (Rawls, 2005: 166).

assisting those in poverty. In a liberal democracy with a plurality of world views and a basic social and economic structure generating significant inequality, assisting groups in poverty is necessary to ensure their continued commitment to economic cooperation and political processes. A social minimum is needed to ensure that those in poverty are persuaded to participate in political life, and can do so in conditions of equality.

The value and limits of assistance

The previous section focused on justifications for assisting those in poverty, seeking to identify moral and ethical frameworks that could provide foundational justifications for assistance. It led to the conclusion that the ethical foundations of assistance to those in poverty are to be found in political conceptions of justice. The discussion in this section takes this argument forward by examining approaches that throw light on the value and limits of assistance to those in poverty. It might be helpful to signpost the argument that follows. The section begins by outlining the priority view. It argues that an improvement in the welfare of the worst off has priority, in the sense of having greater value. The priority view applies more or less directly to assessing the value of assisting those in poverty. Some find the priority view too demanding and propose instead a sufficiency variant. The sufficiency view argues that what matters is that the worst off have enough. The section then assesses the strength of these views, and draws implications for understanding the value and limits of assisting those in poverty.

Priority

Prioritarians argue that priority should be given to helping the worst off because an improvement in their welfare, say as a result of a transfer, has greater value. A focus on the worst off is shared by alternative notions of justice. It is therefore important to identify and evaluate their justifications for embracing the priority view. Some egalitarian approaches share a priority view to the extent that they seek to level up, starting from the worst off. Restricted utilitarianism, to use Rawls' terminology, can also have a focus on the worst off if their utility is weighted appropriately. Even contractarian approaches can develop a focus on the worst off (Scanlon, 1998). Egalitarians, utilitarians and contractarians can also be prioritarians. In what follows, the priority view is presented as providing a distinct justification for attaching priority to the worst off. The distinctiveness of the priority view comes not only from its focus on the worst off but also from the fact that this focus is not grounded in relational concerns. Parfit (1997; 1991) provides a compelling discussion of the priority view.[12] He writes, '[O]n the priority view, we do not believe in inequality. [...] We do of course think it is bad that some people are worse off. But what is bad is not that these people are worse off than *others*. It is rather that they are worse off than *they* might have been' (1991: 22, emphasis in original).

At the risk of repeating the quotation, it is important to underline that there are two related claims here. The first is that priority does not rely on egalitarianism to justify a focus on the worst off. The second claim is that priority is grounded on the fact that people are worse off than '*they* might have been' – a non-relational justification. The weight of the literature on priority has focused on assessing the first claim; this is reviewed briefly below. For our purposes in this chapter, the second claim holds the greater interest. It encapsulates priority as a distinctive approach to valuing assistance to those in poverty.

Given its significance, it will be helpful to flesh out this point a bit more. Parfit (1991: 23, emphasis in original) suggests it

may help to use this analogy. People at higher altitudes find it harder to breathe. Is this because they are higher up than other people? In one sense, yes. But they would find it just as hard to breathe even if there were no other people who were lower down. In the same way, on the Priority View, benefits to the worse off matter more, but that is only because these people are at a lower *absolute level*. It is irrelevant that these people are worse off *than others*. Benefits to them would matter just as much even if there *were* no others who were better off.

Some counter that Parfit's reference to the 'worst off' and/or 'worse off' smuggles back in a comparative element, but he disputes that this comparative element necessarily entails a relational interpretation. 'On this view, if I am worse off than you, benefits to me are more important. Is this because I am worse off than you? In one sense, yes. But this has nothing to do with my relation to you' (Parfit, 1991: 22–3). This

---

[12] It should be noted that Parfit does not endorse the priority view.

assertion can be transposed to a poverty context in an uncontroversial way (Barrientos, 2010b). Absolute poverty reflects substantial deficits in well-being, independently of whether others are richer, or, indeed, poorer.

Returning to the first claim, a literature has developed assessing the claim that priority need not rely on egalitarianism.[13] It is well beyond the scope of this discussion to review this literature in detail, but reprising some of the main points may be useful for the argumentation below.

Making a case for the priority view without reference to egalitarianism strengthens a focus on the worst off. This is because of the 'levelling down' objection to egalitarian approaches. 'Intrinsic' egalitarians believe that social states in which people are equal are better. Egalitarians who find equality to have intrinsic value will be persuaded that a social state in which everyone's welfare is at the level of the worst off is better than one in which inequalities prevail. A society in which everyone is equally poor will be more desirable to them than one in which some, even a majority, are prosperous but others are in poverty.[14] The 'levelling down' objection is less problematic for 'instrumental' egalitarians. Instrumental egalitarians are persuaded that equality has an instrumental value – believing, for example, that greater equality ensures better governance, happier workers or lower crime rates. They will reject levelling down because the instrumental advantages of equality may then not materialise.[15] However, 'instrumental' egalitarians will

---

[13] See Broome (forthcoming), Brown (2006), Fleurbaey (forthcoming), Hausman (forthcoming), Holtung and Lippert-Rasmussen (2007), McKerlie (2003), Petersen and Hansson (2005), Tungodden (2003) and Vallentyne (2000).

[14] 'Equality at a lower level of well-being might seem as preferable to inequality at a higher level of well-being for everyone. Imagine an egalitarian community at a fairly low level of economic development whose numbers, though not experiencing great hardship or absolute poverty, have a simple life style. Given the opportunity of economic development which would make them all better off but introduce substantial inequality, they might prefer to remain less prosperous but equal' (Norman, 1988: 51).

[15] Some have argued that an instrumental version of egalitarianism requires the context of a single community, to enable the effects of inequality to be transmitted. The priority view has no such requirement. Suppose that citizens in the United States are unaware of the existence of a group of developing countries, and vice versa. The former have a very high standard of living, whereas the latter have a very low standard of living. An instrumental egalitarian, with a relational perspective on poverty, would have no grounds for complaining about the existing inequalities, but a prioritarian would. The priority view has universal

need another principle or value, in addition to equality, to reject the 'levelling down' objection.

Instrumental egalitarians are in favour of equality, but they are also in favour of other things, such as maximising welfare, which enables them to reject the 'levelling down' objection. Inescapably, this implies the presence of potential trade-offs between equality and maximising welfare, and/or other values. Instrumental egalitarians would unquestionably agree with the priority view in circumstances in which the improvement of the worst off leaves others unaffected. Taking social states X and Y, instrumental egalitarians would argue that *if the worst off are better in X than in Y, while everyone else is the same in X as in Y, then X is better than Y.*[16] Improving the well-being of the worse off in these circumstances can be justified by the priority view and the egalitarian view. It gets more complicated in circumstances in which the improvement in the well-being of the worst off comes at the expense of others. This is because, in this situation, the two principles, equality and welfare maximisation, might not move in the same direction. Instrumental egalitarians could find that a small improvement in the welfare of the worst off comes at the expense of a large loss in welfare for others, and come to the conclusion that the reduction in inequality does not justify the welfare loss. In these circumstances, prioritarians and instrumental egalitarians will go separate ways. The priority view avoids the 'levelling down' objection, which affects egalitarianism.

We can now turn to the second claim, that the informational basis of the prioritarian view is non-relational. Parfit takes up, and rejects, alternative informational bases for judgements about the value of assisting those in poverty. Utilitarian views could recommend helping the worst off in circumstances in which doing so maximises the sum of utility, for example when income has rapidly diminishing marginal utility. In Parfit's description, '[u]tilitarians claim that we should give these people priority when, and because, we can help them *more*, [whereas the priority] view claims we should give them priority, even when we can help them less' (1991: 19, emphasis in original).

Others recommend justifying a focus on the worst off on an assessment of the greatest or more urgent need (Nagel, 1991). Parfit points out

scope: 'It is irrelevant whether these people are in the same community, or are aware of each other' (Parfit, 1997: 214).

[16] This is Broome's version of the Pareto principle, the principle of the personal good, which replaces utility with well-being (1995).

that this view 'implies that we should give priority to needs rather than persons. The more urgent needs of someone who, on the whole, is better off take priority over the less urgent needs of someone who is worse off' (1991: 21).[17] Priority places value directly on assisting the worst off, instead of on the benefits (utilitarianism) or the satisfaction of urgent needs. The informational basis for the valuation is the welfare of the persons involved.

A crucial – but often ignored – point about welfare, as the informational basis used in notions of justice, is that welfare applies to whole lives, not to segments of lives (childhood, old age) or spells (unemployment, sickness or poverty) (Barrientos, Gorman and Heslop, 2003). The basis for evaluation is not people's welfare today or tomorrow but people's welfare throughout their whole lives (McKerlie, 2002; 2003). A focus of notions of justice is that people's whole lives go as well as they might. This applies to the priority view too.

Several objections have been raised against the priority view. Some find priority to be too demanding. The priority view demands that priority be given to the worst off, even when this requires that substantial benefits to the better off be forgone. Sen (1976b) objects to maximin versions of Rawls' difference principle, even in its lexicographic version. Arneson voices this concern in the context of international assistance: 'The priority view appears much too demanding and open ended in the obligations it imposes on us to improve people's lives around the globe' (2002: 177–8). Some of these objections can be addressed if care is taken to define the appropriate informational basis for priority.[18] To an extent, these complaints simply highlight the fact that the priority view

---

[17] The urgent needs view can also be undermined by the problems involved in adjusting for the influence of 'expensive tastes' (rich people who desperately need caviar at breakfast) and 'cheap tastes' (poor people who can make do with cornflakes). The point about differentiating *current urgent needs* from *badly off lives* is discussed below. The prioritarian value attaches to whole lives.

[18] Moreno-Ternero and Roemer interpret the priority view as operating between two egalitarian spaces: resources and outcomes. Equal resource allocations ignore the 'differential ability of individuals to convert the resource into the desired outcome', while an equal outcome allocation 'seems too extreme: it may require giving the lion's share of the resource to very "handicapped" individuals, ones with poor outcome functions' (2005: 2). This interpretation voices widely shared concerns about the apparent 'demandingness' of the priority view, but it wrongly identifies the informational basis of the priority view – that is, what lives might have been. Moreno-Ternero and Roemer redefine priority as the principle that no one should dominate in both the resources and the outcomes spaces.

keeps to a single focus on welfare, and rejects the possibility of trade-offs with alternative values.

In response to these objections, some have focused on establishing limits to the value of assisting those in poverty. This is discussed below in the context of the sufficiency view.

Sufficiency

Sufficiency proposes a limit to assisting those in poverty. Frankfurt encapsulates the core sufficiency view as follows: what 'is important from the point of view of morality is not that everyone should have the *same* but that each should have *enough*' (Frankfurt, 1987: 21–2, emphasis in original). The moral[19] concern can therefore be restricted to assisting those who are below a basic threshold, and the implication for policy is the use of 'available resources in such a way that as many people as possible have enough or, in other words, to maximize the incidence of sufficiency' (31). Sufficiency is often billed as a more moderate form of the priority view (Tungodden, 2003), especially as giving priority to those below a minimum threshold could be read as a weaker version of the priority view. In fact, as the discussion below demonstrates, there are important differences between the sufficiency and the priority views.

Central to the sufficiency view is the claim it makes on the ethical uniqueness of the basic threshold. Whether people are above or below this threshold has special significance. The sufficiency view maintains the focus on welfare as the informational basis for assessing the moral value of benefits. It implies a welfare function that is discontinuous at the threshold. Assisting those at or above the threshold holds no ethical value.

How can the particular significance of the threshold be justified? Some variants of sufficiency justify the threshold by reference to some *substantive level*. Crisp argues that '80 years of a good quality life' defines a reasonable threshold (Crisp, 2003: 762).[20] Arneson justifies

---

[19] Note that 'moral' in this context describes more appropriately social arrangements (pertaining to ethics), rather than individual rights and duties (pertaining to morality proper).

[20] How we interpret the sufficiency view in the context of a whole life is an interesting and important issue. According to Arneson (2002: 192), 'One judges whether someone is at the sufficiency level by assessing that person's entire life.

a threshold by reference to the resources needed to ensure full participation in society, as suggested by Walzer: '[A] person has enough when poverty does not block her from being a full member of a democratic society' (cited by Arneson, 2002: 173). Waldron discusses a variant of this basic threshold in Rawls' work, as the level necessary to ensure continued commitment to cooperation in economic and social life (Waldron, 1986). Frankfurt defines the threshold as the point at which people are contented with their lives – that is, the level of well-being above which there is no reason to complain (Frankfurt, 1987). Nussbaum describes a capabilities-based threshold as the capability to function at an acceptable level in all the ways that are individually necessary and together sufficient for a decent quality of human life (cited by Arneson, 2002). A substantive threshold can also be defined in terms of self-respect.[21] In poverty analysis, nutritional requirements are often used to define a monetary poverty line (Ravallion, 1996). Thresholds can also be defined by reference to a *point in the distribution* of well-being, such as the two-thirds of median earnings used by the European Union (identifying those at risk of poverty), or the ILO's decent work standards. Some define the basic threshold by reference to a *legitimating process*. Nagel, for example, suggests that the threshold should be arrived at by discussion leading to unanimity on the least acceptable outcome, whereas Crisp is prepared to rely on an impartial observer (Crisp, 2003; Nagel, 1991).

As can be seen from this trawl, definitions of the basic threshold abound. If anything, the issue is how to discriminate between the different thresholds. A grounded approach could look for a justification of alternative thresholds in underlying ethical frameworks. For example, it is possible to trace the substance of Nussbaum's threshold to the underlying capability approach. However, an ethical justification for the thresholds themselves is problematic.

In a sense, this could well be an impossible, or misplaced, task to attempt. If it is better that lives go as well as they might, how could a threshold be justified? There is a large measure of arbitrariness to the

---

The aim that is proposed is that the person's life, taken as a whole, should meet the sufficiency level.' There are, of course, alternative interpretations of what this implies in practice. It could be argued that the principle implies that at no time in someone's life should welfare be allowed to fall below the threshold. Alternatively, it could be proposed that, averaging good and bad times, the principle implies that lives on average should reach the threshold.

[21] For Hegel, a measure of self-respect is the defining threshold; see Moon (1988).

thresholds proposed. Why is eighty years of good-quality life the threshold and not seventy-nine years, or eighty-one years? Recognising the inherent ethical arbitrariness of the thresholds proposed, Arneson suggests that sufficiency can be better understood as an unavoidably rough and ready guide to policy, rather than as an ethically grounded threshold. As later chapters discuss, this applies with some force to poverty lines in common use.

Sufficiency and priority

The sufficiency view has been described as a moderate version of the priority view (Arneson, 2000; Brown, 2006; Fleurbaey, forthcoming; Holtung, 2007). From the standpoint of priority, the ethical arbitrariness of the threshold is not the only problematic aspect of sufficiency. There are substantive differences between priority and sufficiency, especially in a poverty context.

Sufficiency denies that the well-being of those above the threshold has moral value. This assessment might coincide with priority under certain circumstances, such as when the worst off are precisely those below the threshold, and the difference in welfare existing between those below and those immediately above the threshold is sufficiently large for there to be no moral value in helping the latter. In this particular case, giving priority to the worst off and giving priority to those below the threshold appear to be the same thing. The sufficiency view has much in common with poverty approaches, for example in the use of the poverty line as the threshold for poverty status and entitlement to assistance. This is especially true when poverty status is based on a discrete poverty head-count measure. However, these are limiting cases.

In contrast with priority, sufficiency attaches no significance to changes in well-being among those below the threshold, as long as they remain below it. Whereas priority will attach value to improvements in the welfare of the worst off that leave them worst off, sufficiency denies any significance to these changes, as positive moral value gains attach only to changes in well-being that ensure people cross the threshold.[22] This difference between priority and sufficiency is very

---

[22] This complication has led to further differentiation in the sufficiency view. Brown (2006) develops several variants of the sufficiency view that aim to incorporate more explicitly some dimensions of the priority view. For example, a variant of

important in the context of assessing alternative schemes for assisting people in poverty. The sufficiency view has nothing to say on a scheme of assistance that benefits people in poverty who nevertheless remain in poverty; the priority view does.

In view of the extensive use of thresholds in poverty analysis, perhaps a more interesting question to address is whether sufficiency constitutes a reasonable restriction on the priority view, and whether adding a sufficiency threshold to the priority view is helpful. The priority view does incorporate thresholds, namely 'what life might have been'. In the priority view, there is no moral value in assisting those whose lives have gone as well as they might have done. However, this threshold is of a different quality from the threshold in the sufficiency view. The threshold in the priority view is not intrinsically relational. It is unlikely to be the same across different individuals or households. Unless we assume 'cloned' individuals, there is no guarantee that a unique threshold will describe 'what life might have been' for all individuals in the worst-off group. Indeed, one of the main difficulties involved in setting a sufficiency level is the fact that it must apply uniformly to a community.[23] Setting a minimum common welfare threshold, as proposed by the sufficiency principle, can fit with the priority view only in the case of 'cloned' individuals.

In sum, the priority view attaches value to assisting people in poverty, and the value reflects their welfare, defined in terms of the deficit with respect to what they might have achieved. In the priority view, people are in poverty not because their lifetime welfare is lower than that of a reference group or individual but because it is significantly less than it

---

sufficiency could apply weights across the full distribution of a well-being measure, rising for levels of well-being further away from, and below, the threshold. Applying weights to those above the threshold could also allow for some trade-off in terms of the benefits to the worse off and the better off. However, sufficiency lacks a clear ethical foundation, and the ad hoc nature of these hybrid sufficiency specifications fails to make good this deficiency.

[23] It is well understood in poverty analysis that poverty lines in welfare terms may require different individual-specific resource levels. This applies, for example, in the context of population heterogeneity in converting income into capabilities. 'If we wish to stick to the income space, these variations in the conversion of incomes into capabilities would require that the relevant concept of poverty be that of inadequacy (for generally minimally acceptable capabilities) rather than absolute lowness (independently of the circumstances that inform the conversion). The poverty line income can be then specific to a community, or a family, or even a person' (Sen, 1997b: 213).

might have been. Sufficiency sets a limit to the value of assisting those in poverty. In the sufficiency view, there is no value in assisting those above the threshold, nor in assisting people in poverty who remain poor in spite of assistance. The threshold in the sufficiency value is ad hoc. Sufficiency is not necessary to priority, and it can be rejected as a reasonable restriction of the latter.

The ethical foundations of assisting those in poverty

The chapter started by noting that most research and policy discussion of poverty reduction programmes begins by discussing issues of design and effectiveness, but pointed out that this is not the appropriate start-ing point. The ethical foundations of assistance are fundamental. Why should individuals and societies assist the worst off? What is the value of assisting those in poverty? What are the limits of assistance? Looking for answers to these questions ought to take precedence over issues of design and effectiveness. The introduction was careful not to promise a comprehensive review of the vast literature relevant to these questions. Instead, the approach was to focus on selected contributions capable of providing firm footholds for the analysis in the rest of the book.

Why should we assist those in poverty? Perhaps because we have a duty to assist people when they are in a difficult situation and we are not; and the moral imperative is stronger if we are responsible for the situation experienced by those in poverty. Even if this is not the case, upholding the principle that lives should go as well as they might entails a duty of assistance. However, there are few mechanisms that ensure compliance, and, at the same time, myriad potential limitations to this duty. The discussion in this chapter has focused on international aid, but the main arguments also apply at the domestic level. It makes sense to seek instead to justify assistance to those in poverty less on the grounds of individual conduct and more on the basis of the nature of appropriate social arrangements. A political conception of justice pro-vides a stronger and richer justification for assisting those in poverty. This is in part because it takes on board the nature of the institutions within which we give shape to our lives – the basic structure, to use Rawls' term – but also in part because a political notion of justice best reflects the rationale for existing social protection institutions.

What is the value of assisting those in poverty? The priority view argues that there is value in assisting the worst off, not because they are worse off than others but because their lives have not gone as well as they might have done. Some consider the priority view too demanding. They ask what the limits to assistance are. The sufficiency view makes a case for not valuing assistance beyond a threshold, a poverty line. However, the justifications for thresholds or poverty lines are ad hoc, even when the bases for ordering people along a (welfare) dimension are accepted.

The discussion in this chapter intended to provide firm footholds for the analysis of social assistance in developing countries. The above summary of the main findings identifies these footholds. The analysis has also raised some important issues in the context of existing studies of social assistance, perhaps the most significant being the need to ground social assistance in deeper notions of justice. This has two implications and one challenge for the analysis of assistance. The first implication is the need to examine the growth of social assistance as emerging institutions reflecting and embedding notions of justice. The second is that the poverty focus of social assistance can be best studied and evaluated with a priority perspective. The challenge, in line with the conclusion that priority does not entail sufficiency, is to limit the role of poverty lines in the discussion of poverty reduction that follows in later chapters. The ethical footholds discussed in this chapter help illuminate the road ahead, but they also raise important issues. The analysis in the following chapters comes back to these footholds, tests them, applies them and adapts them.

3 | *Poverty concepts and measures for social assistance*

The main objective of this chapter is to familiarise readers with the basic tools of poverty analysis needed to examine social assistance in developing countries. Social assistance consists of a set of programmes, policies and institutions whose primary functions are to reduce, eradicate and prevent poverty. An understanding of poverty concepts and measures is therefore essential to study the growth of social assistance in developing countries. Two main questions organise the materials in this chapter: what is poverty, and how should it be measured?

There are many notions of poverty in the literature, often emphasising one or other dimension or approach. This chapter reviews the main poverty concepts and measures used in the theory and practice of anti-poverty transfers. In developing countries, social assistance is focused on absolute poverty. Poverty is identified with significant deficits in well-being considered unacceptable in a given community. Poverty is a state, in the sense that individuals, households or communities can be said to be 'in poverty'. English-language work on poverty is littered with references to 'the poor', which gives a sense that poverty is a characteristic of some people.[1] Increasingly, poverty is understood as intrinsically multidimensional,[2] and duration is a key dimension. In international poverty policy discussions, reference is often made to global poverty. This is in contrast

---

[1] Early studies of poverty in the eighteenth and nineteenth centuries sometimes identified a class of people as 'the poor', as 'vagrants' or as 'paupers'; see Davis (1979). Modern approaches to poverty are instead premised on poverty as a state 'that can be greatly reduced with the right economic and social policies [, which are] in no small measure a public responsibility' (Ravallion, 2011: 7).

[2] 'Poverty has various manifestations, including a lack of income and productive resources to ensure sustainable livelihoods; hunger and malnutrition; ill-health; limited or lack of access to education and other basic services; increased morbidity and mortality from illness; homelessness and inadequate housing; unsafe environments and social discrimination and exclusion' (UN, 1995: 57).

with the definition of absolute poverty mentioned above, suggesting that poverty is defined primarily at the level of the polity. Households in poverty in Kenya are, on average, likely to have levels of well-being different from those experienced by households in poverty in Uruguay. The notion of global poverty suggests instead a 'cosmopolitan' standard of well-being, which requires further consideration.

Measuring poverty, and especially changes in poverty over time, is essential to poverty analysis, anti-poverty policy and social assistance.[3] The task of designing, refining and implementing effective social assistance is dependent to an important extent on our capacity to measure poverty with accuracy. Identifying potential beneficiaries, determining the size of anti-poverty budgets and assessing the impact and effectiveness of transfer programmes all require relatively sophisticated poverty measurement. The growth of social assistance programmes in developing countries has been made possible in large part through advances in poverty analysis.

These are the main themes of this chapter. The literature on poverty concepts and measurement is vast and growing, and the materials in this chapter provide a selective take on these.[4] The interest in this chapter is in what these notions of poverty entail for social assistance programmes in developing countries. Some of the materials are highly technical, but the presentation is aimed at a well-informed, interested readership. The additional notes in the Annex, and the references throughout the text, provide an entry point to readers interested in following up on the more technical literature.

What is poverty?

Poverty describes significant deficits in well-being considered unacceptable in a given polity. Well-being, or welfare, is what makes our lives go well. There are competing perspectives on the informational basis of well-being. Some find it in the resources at the disposal of individuals or

---

[3] On the importance of poverty measurement more broadly, the following is illuminating: 'Booth's description of poverty in a completely statistical way was, in a sense, conceptually liberating. His definition of poverty as an inadequate number of calories per day, based on a scientific analysis of the average adult's daily energy need, allowed poverty to be identified, measured and possibly alleviated' (Davis, 1979: 96).

[4] For comprehensive treatments of poverty concepts and measurements, see Atkinson (1987), Chakravarty (2009), Duclos and Araar (2004), Haughton and Khandker (2009) and Sen (1997a).

households, or their monetary equivalent. Wealthier households are those with command over large quantities of resources or income. Households in poverty are those with low incomes. Some argue that the informational basis of well-being is utility – what people themselves consider to be valuable or to bring them happiness; this is usually referred to as a welfarist perspective (Sen and Williams, 1982). Rawls suggests that the informational basis of well-being consists of the 'primary goods' that people command, understood as all-purpose tools enabling them to realise their life plans (Rawls, 1971). Sen makes the case that the informational basis of well-being can be found in capability – the 'beings and doings' that people value (Sen, 1985). It is beyond the scope of this book to examine these different perspectives in any detail. In a sense, deficiencies in well-being can be specified in terms of any, or all, of these perspectives. In the rest of the chapter, it is taken for granted that a focus on, say, income or consumption could be redefined in terms of alternative informational bases. It is interesting that anti-poverty policy usually falls back on resources as the informational basis of well-being (Streeten, 1984). What matters is that people considered to be in poverty reach a particular level of income, or consumption, or that they have access to specific goods and services.

Theories of well-being are strongly evaluative. Their main function is to assess and evaluate levels of well-being across people in a given population. 'Poverty' is a description applied to people at the bottom of the distribution of well-being. Conventionally, poverty applies to points in the distribution of well-being below the poverty line. The previous chapter discussed the fact that poverty lines reflect a sufficiency approach and the limitations of such an approach. To an important extent, the poverty line is arbitrary. It can be slightly higher or slightly lower without undermining the substantive meaning of poverty. It is therefore difficult to endow the poverty line, as a single point in the distribution of well-being, with a unique value. The discussion below makes it clear that poverty lines have a limited role in social assistance programmes. In fact, the extent to which people are in poverty, and differences in well-being between them, are of greater practical and conceptual significance.

The introduction made the important point that poverty is not a characteristic of individuals or households but a state in which they may find themselves. Households are not poor, they are in poverty. In fact, for many households, poverty is transient: it lasts for a short period of time or for a spell. For another group, poverty is of longer duration: it is chronic or persistent. Duration is therefore one of the many dimensions of poverty, but it has great importance in the context of anti-poverty policy. There are other dimensions of poverty too. Being in poverty is often associated, among other things, with poor nutrition, limited engagement in economic activity, discrimination, limited voice and limited access to basic services.

A distinction is often made between absolute and relative poverty. Absolute poverty describes people's deficiency in well-being with respect to a particular level of well-being. Relative poverty, on the other hand, identifies people in poverty as those who are in the lower segments of the distribution of well-being. A generalised improvement in well-being in the population will reduce absolute poverty but could leave relative poverty unaffected. This chapter focuses largely on absolute poverty, as it is this conceptualisation that has driven theory and practice in social assistance in developing countries.

Measuring poverty: how much poverty is in. . .?

Measuring poverty involves addressing the question 'How much poverty is in a household/community/country?'.

Anti-poverty programmes are the outcome of political processes acknowledging a shared responsibility to assist households in poverty, but it is undeniable that research and knowledge play a part in shaping the political and policy processes that lead to the adoption and extension of transfer programmes. Public and elite perceptions of the feasibility and effectiveness of social assistance programmes, crucial to mobilising political support, are themselves influenced by research and knowledge. Substantive advances in the analysis of poverty in developing countries, at the theoretical and applied levels, have greatly facilitated the expansion of social assistance programmes in developing countries.[5] Three developments are especially important in this context: improvements in knowledge about the properties of poverty indexes and their application; the spread of household survey data collection in developing countries; and advances in computer and information technology, which have eased the operationalisation of poverty analysis.[6] These developments have ensured a shorter lag from theory to practice.

[5] For a discussion, see Kanbur (2009).
[6] For an example, see Duclos and Araar (2004).

The challenge for this section lies in reviewing the main building blocks of poverty measurement, while providing insights and links to the more technical and detailed applications. The section covers two main topics: well-being indicators and thresholds; and the identification of people in poverty and their aggregation.

Well-being indicators and thresholds

Traditionally, the analysis of poverty has focused on single indicators of well-being: income or consumption. It makes sense to focus on income as an indicator of well-being, because, in market economies, households use their income to buy the goods and services they need. In this context, income is an all-purpose tool deployed in order to achieve particular levels of well-being, obviating the more difficult task of establishing households' needs and preferences. For the purposes of poverty analysis, a focus on household income is common. In practice, this variable aggregates at the household level information provided across income sources and household members.[7] There are well-known measurement errors applying to the income variable arising from imperfect information on the part of the survey respondent; survey gaps of particular income sources; and the variability of income over time. In a developing country context, income, even if measured without error, may have limitations as a proxy for well-being if services and goods are not available or are not fully marketised. Using household consumption instead of household income as a well-being indicator could in principle address some of these issues, while raising another set of measurement issues. In practice, measures of consumption are based on survey respondents' information on household expenditures, normally aggregated over a number of items (including food and non-food expenditure). Household consumption is likely to be less variable over time than income, and, arguably, can provide a more direct measure of household well-being. At the same time, care should be taken to assess the way that large expenditures, especially housing, are accounted for. In rural areas,

---

[7] Strictly, income is defined as the monetary flows that leave one's wealth intact. Income equals expenditure plus changes in net worth. Household surveys rarely attempt to measure wealth, and concentrate instead on measuring after-tax income flows from specific sources such as labour, private and public transfers, interest from saving and profit from businesses.

production for one's own consumption can be a large fraction of total household consumption.[8]

Income and consumption indicators are measured at the household level. This raises the issue of how to compare households of different size and composition. Suppose we are interested in measuring child poverty or old age poverty. We need to work out a way of allocating household well-being to individual members. The simplest approach is to divide household income or consumption by the number of household members, arriving at a measure of per capita income or consumption. This is problematic as a measure of household well-being. First, there are economies of size in household well-being production. Second, some of the goods and services that households consume have the property that several people can consume them at the same time; they are public goods. A household of three needs one stove and three meals whereas a household of five needs one stove and five meals. The implication is that the larger household requires marginally less income or consumption than a smaller household to achieve the same level of well-being. Differences in household composition are important too. It is likely that a household of three adults has a different set of needs and preferences from a household of one adult and two children. Providing children require less expenditure than adults, the latter household could, in principle, achieve the same level of well-being as the former household with marginally less income or consumption. Adjustments may be required to compare the well-being of households of different size and composition. Applying equivalence scales to household income or consumption yields adult equivalent measures that can be compared across households.[9] Inequalities in intra-household resource allocation imply that adult equivalent measures of well-being need to be considered with care (Haddad and Kanbur, 1990).

Proponents of a multidimensional approach to poverty argue that single indicators of well-being are unable to provide a full and comprehensive account of poverty. They suggest that poverty analysis should instead focus on several dimensions at the same time. The

---

[8] For a detailed discussion of the relative advantages of income and consumption as well-being indicators, see Deaton (1997).

[9] An equivalence scale is an index used to convert nominal household well-being for heterogeneous households into a comparable measure of well-being. See additional note A3.1 in the Annex and, for a more detailed discussion, Lanjouw and Ravallion (1995).

multidimensional approach imposes greater complexity on the analysis and measurement of poverty, but raises important issues associated with the informational basis of well-being, as briefly mentioned at the start of the chapter. In the capability approach, to take one of the perspectives reviewed above, single indicators provide at best a limited insight into a person's capability; multidimensional indicators stand a better chance of capturing capability, reflecting a more comprehensive view of the informational basis of well-being.

In the single-dimension case, a single poverty threshold is often employed to identify households in poverty. A specific level of income or consumption acts as the poverty line. With varying levels of sophistication, poverty lines in developing countries are constructed by referring to a basket of goods and services required for basic subsistence, defined in monetary terms.[10] Food poverty lines are constructed by converting a basket of locally consumed foodstuff, sufficient to ensure minimum daily subsistence for a person of average needs and health, into a monetary value by using local prices. This is often referred to as the food or 'extreme' poverty line. In some cases, non-food subsistence components are added, taking account of the costs of accessing education and health care and other basic services. This is often referred to as a 'moderate' poverty line. There is considerable variation in practices across countries, and some lack any official poverty line.[11]

Identification and aggregation

Having selected appropriate indicators of well-being, whether single or multidimensional, and appropriate poverty lines, it is now possible to identify households in poverty. This requires a comparison of the level of their well-being – adult equivalent income, say – and the poverty threshold. Households with well-being levels at or below the threshold are considered to be in poverty.[12]

---

[10] See, among others, Kakwani (2003) and Ravallion (1996).

[11] South Africa, for example, lacks an official poverty line. Brazil uses the official minimum wage to determine the value of social assistance benefits. Mexico has three poverty lines: a food poverty line; a capability poverty line, which includes food and basic services; and an assets poverty line, which includes housing and other assets.

[12] Technically, this requires an identification function p(.) mapping from the well-being indicator y and the poverty threshold z to an indicator variable, such that $p(y;z) = 1$ if a household is in poverty and $p(y;z) = 0$ if the household is not in poverty. See the Annex to this chapter.

The next task is to aggregate poverty at the community, region or country level. This exercise is important, because it enables policy-makers and researchers to ask how much poverty is in a community, region or country, and also to compare poverty across units and across time. This assessment is essential to designing and implementing effective anti-poverty programmes. At the same time, this is a complex exercise, because it involves, implicitly or explicitly, weighing up the poverty experienced by different households and communities. This involves ethical values that unavoidably influence policy priorities.

The poverty headcount rate – the proportion of households in poverty – usually dominates policy discussions. Millennium Development Goal 1 Target 1A, for example, commits the international community to halving, between 1990 and 2015, the proportion of people whose income is below US$1 a day. In many ways, the poverty headcount rate is a very limited measure of poverty. It pays no attention to how much poverty is in each household: a household on US$0.20 and a household on US$0.99 count the same. As importantly, if a household previously on US$0.99 falls to US$0.20, this is not reflected in the measure. From an anti-poverty perspective, and in a context of limited budgets, a country that focuses policy on the US$0.99 households will be 'more successful' in reaching Target 1A than a country that focuses policy on the US$0.20 households.

Poverty gap measures of poverty address some of the limitations of the headcount rate. They focus on the gap in well-being, the difference between the well-being indicator across households and the poverty threshold. A household at US$0.99 will have a poverty gap of US$0.01, whereas a household at US$0.20 will have a poverty gap of US$0.80. Household poverty gaps can be aggregated at the community level, and then standardised to enable comparison. The aggregate poverty gap provides information on the total budget needed to take all households in poverty up to the poverty line. In order to compare communities with different population size, it will be necessary to divide the poverty gap by the population, to yield an average poverty gap comparable across communities. Comparison across time will often be complicated by changes in the level of the poverty line, but standardising the average poverty gap as a proportion of the poverty line enables comparison of the poverty gap measure across time. However, the poverty gap measure is also a limited tool. Compared with the poverty headcount measure, it weights the poverty of each household by its dollar poverty gap. If a household previously on US$0.99 falls to US$0.20, the poverty gap measure reflects this. Reliance on dollar amounts can be problematic. A household previously on US$0.99 falling to US$0.79 is counted as the same change in the measure as a household on US$0.20 falling to zero. From an anti-poverty policy perspective, a country that distributes a fixed insufficient budget will demonstrate the same policy effectiveness whether it focuses on households in extreme or moderate poverty, or whether it randomly distributes its budget among households in poverty.

The poverty gap squared measure addresses the limitations of the poverty gap measure by weighting the poverty in each household by the household's own poverty gap. This has the effect of giving greater priority to households with the greatest poverty. A household on US$0.20 will have a poverty gap squared of US$64, whereas a household on US$0.99 will have a poverty gap squared of US$0.01. If a household previously on US$0.99 falls to US$0.79, the aggregate poverty gap will increase by US$4.40 (US$4.41 – US$0.01), whereas, if a household on US$0.20 falls to zero, the aggregate poverty gap will increase by US$36. The poverty gaps of households in poverty can be aggregated for a particular community and standardised by population and the poverty line to enable comparisons across communities and across time. In policy terms, using the poverty gap squared measure to assess the effectiveness of anti-poverty policy will enforce a priority on the poorest – the households with the greatest poverty gaps. A disadvantage of the poverty gap squared measure is its opaqueness to policymakers, for whom the poverty headcount and the poverty gap measures are more accessible and directly interpretable (Myles and Picot, 2000).

Commonly used poverty indexes

The poverty reduction objective of social assistance programmes can be specified further as the minimisation of a particular poverty index.[13] Selected poverty indexes are introduced below.

---

[13] See additional note A3.2 in the Annex on the technical basis of poverty functions.

The Foster–Greer–Thorbecke measure

The measure introduced by Foster, Greer and Thorbecke (1984) provides a flexible index aggregating households' poverty gaps in ways that make explicit the ethical assumptions behind the measure. The Foster–Greer–Thorbecke measure nests the poverty headcount, poverty gap and poverty gap squared measures. The Foster–Greer–Thorbecke measure P_α is easily implementable and group-decomposable, which has ensured its wider used in empirical and policy work. The basic ingredient of this measure is the poverty gap, commonly used in its normalised version – that is, as a fraction of the poverty line. The P_α poverty function can be written, for the discrete case, as

$$P_\alpha(y; z, \alpha) = \frac{1}{N} \sum_{i=1}^{q} [(z - y_i)/z]^\alpha, \alpha \geq 0 \qquad (3.1)$$

Here, y is a welfare indicator, z is the poverty line and α is a parameter. The normalised poverty gaps $(z - y_i/z)$ are raised to the power α, and then aggregated for all units in poverty q, and divided by the population N.

In this measure, α plays a very important role. It is the power applied to the poverty gap, and can be interpreted as reflecting ethical preferences concerning poverty in a particular community, as a measure of that community's 'aversion to poverty'. When $\alpha = 0$, the poverty function yields the poverty headcount (by definition $x^0 = 1$, so that, for $\alpha = 0$, $P_0 = q/N$). When $\alpha = 1$, the poverty function yields the per capita poverty gap, the aggregate of the poverty gaps of the poor, standardised as a fraction of the poverty line, normalised by the population N. When $\alpha = 2$, the poverty function delivers the poverty gap squared. When $\alpha > 1$, the poverty function is increasingly sensitive to the size of the poverty gaps among the poor, which is why α is interpreted to reflect 'aversion to poverty'. As α approaches infinity, the poverty function converges into a Rawlsian maximin measure, in which the poverty gaps of the poorest unit alone determine the value of $P\alpha$.

The Watts measure

In an early contribution, Watts (1968) develops a poverty index grounded in an understanding of poverty as a severe constraint on the choice set of households. He is at pains to demonstrate that poverty is not a characteristic of individuals (a view held by the 'culture of poverty' approaches then dominant) but a factor of the situation faced by some households. Households' consumption is determined by their preferences and the resources they command – their 'choice set'. For Watts, 'poverty is associated with severe constriction of the choice set' (321). This is best measured by comparing the income y_i^* of a household with the poverty threshold z. For households with $y_i^* > z$, their income is replaced by z, resulting in a censored distribution of income y_p^*. The fact that 'poverty becomes more severe at an increasing rate as successive decrements of income are considered' (326) suggests the use of a logarithmic function, as in

$$Pw\left(y_p^*; z\right) = \frac{1}{N} \sum_{i=1}^{q} \left(\ln z - \ln y_{ip}^*\right) \qquad (3.2)$$

The Watts measure has not been used extensively in poverty analysis, despite the fact that it has many useful properties (Zheng, 1993). It has been employed in the analysis of pro-poor growth (Ravallion, 2003; Morduch, 1998b).[14] Chakravarty *et al.* (2008) employ it in the context of multidimensional poverty analysis.

The Sen measure

Sen's poverty measure is also worth considering, because it does two things rather differently. Sen argues that the poverty line is important. Crossing the (poverty) line has particular significance and ought therefore to influence the measure. He also argues that a relational dimension of poverty is important, and should also influence poverty aggregation. Sen (1976a) proposes the following poverty index:

$$P_{Sen}(y; z) = HI + H(1 - I)G_p \qquad (3.3)$$

The Sen measure combines the poverty headcount rate H, the income gap rate I and a measure of distribution of the well-being indicator among those in poverty G_p (Sen, 1997a). The Foster–Greer–Thorbecke measure and the Watts measure are examples of

---

[14] Given a constant positive rate of economic growth g per year, current income relates to the poverty line as in $z = y_i(1 + g)^t$, and therefore the expected time for an individual i to exit poverty can be written as $t_g^i \approx (\ln z - \ln y_I)/g$ – that is, the Watts index divided by g. See Morduch (1998b).

non-relational poverty indexes, whereas the Sen measure is an example of a relational poverty index.[15]

Multidimensional indexes

Measuring poverty in a multidimensional setting involves a multiplicity of well-being indicators and thresholds. These can be approached in the same way as single-dimension indicators. The additional complication arises from the need to establish the relative weight of the indicators in an aggregate index, and the underlying relationship between indicators. For example, what is the relative weight of education and health well-being indicators in determining the overall well-being of an individual? Is it appropriate for education outcomes to compensate for health outcomes? Consensus on these two issues is absent in the literature.

Chakravarty (2009) discusses extensions of the Foster–Greer–Thorbecke and Watts measures to the multidimensional well-being indicator case. The aggregation now takes place along dimensions and units. The multidimensional extension of the Foster–Greer–Thorbecke measure can be written as

$$P_{\alpha Multid}(Y; Z, \alpha) = \frac{1}{N} \sum_{i=1}^{N} \sum_{j=1}^{d} \hat{b}_j \left[\left(z_j - y_{ij} \right) z_j \right]^{\alpha j}, \alpha \geq 0 \qquad (3.4)$$

Here, Y represents the row vector of achievements for a specific unit – individual, household or community. The column vector of dimensions thresholds is represented by Z, and b_j denotes the weights associated with each dimension j, with $\Sigma_{j=1} b_j = 1$. In turn, the multidimensional extension of the Watts measure can be written as

$$Pw_{Multid}\left(Y_p^*; Z\right) = \frac{1}{N} \sum_{i=1}^{N} \sum_{j=1}^{d} \hat{b}_j \, \log\left(z_j / y_{pi}^*\right) \qquad (3.5)$$

The multidimensional poverty measures described above have been applied in contexts in which the dimensions are measured cardinally.

Given that many examples of multidimensional poverty analysis rely on ordinal variables, it will be useful to make reference to poverty

---

[15] See additional note A3.4 for a more detailed coverage of non-relational poverty indexes.

measures appropriate in this context. Let us consider the case in which d dimensions are converted into 0/1 deprivation indicators c_i by applying dimension-specific thresholds to the ordinal variables. Each individual's well-being will therefore be represented by a row vector of d zeros and ones. A second threshold is required to identify individuals in poverty. Denote this threshold by k, with $1 \leq k \leq d$, so that the two polar cases are the union case, in which individuals are in poverty if they are deprived in one dimension – that is, $|c_i| = 1$; the intersection case, in which individuals are in poverty if they are deprived in all dimensions – that is, $|c_i| = d$; and intermediate points, when individuals are in poverty if they are deprived in k dimensions or more – that is, $|c_i| \geq k$. The ratio of the number of deprivations experienced by an individual to the maximum possible number of deprivations experienced is $(|c_i| \geq k) / d$. From this basis, Alkire and Foster (2011) propose the following aggregate measures of poverty:

$$P_{AFMultid}(Y, Z, k) = HA, \text{ where } H = q^k N \text{ and } A = (|c_i| \geq k)/q^k d \tag{3.6}$$

This multidimensional poverty measure combines the headcount poverty ratio, given k, with a measure A of the average deprivation share across people in poverty.

Axioms and dominance

Uncertainty prevails over appropriate methods in the following two areas of poverty analysis: choice over poverty lines and choice over poverty measures.

The discussion on the limitations of sufficiency in the previous chapter and the discussion on poverty thresholds in this chapter concluded that poverty lines can be an arbitrary threshold.[16] It is therefore advisable to test whether estimated poverty measures are robust to variations in the poverty line, say between a minimum level $zmin$ and a maximum level $zmax$. This is essential in the context of comparing poverty estimates across time or communities. Stochastic dominance tests are now commonly applied to poverty estimates, with precisely this objective in

---

[16] Public debates on whether poverty lines are too high or too low are common at country level.

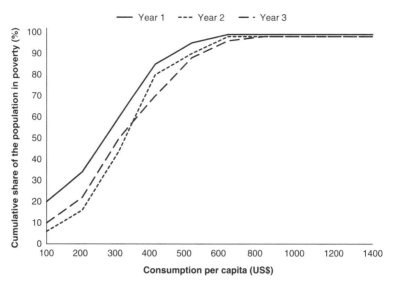

Figure 3.1 Poverty incidence curves and stochastic dominance
Source: Author.

mind.[17] They work by comparing the cumulative distribution function
of poverty estimates for all z such that *zmin* $< z <$ *zmax*. Figure 3.1
shows the cumulative distribution function for country X in year 1 to
year 3 of the poverty headcount rate for a range of incomes, with each
income point considered as a possible poverty line. As can be seen, the
poverty headcount rate for year 2 is below the year 1 rate for all levels of
income. This can support the conclusion that poverty has fallen unam-
biguously in year 2 with respect to year 1, independently of where the
poverty line is set. The distribution of poverty estimates for year 1
'dominates' the distribution of poverty estimates for year 2. Nowhere
is it lower in year 1. In the context of the Foster–Greer–Thorbecke P_α
measure below, the poverty headcount is equivalent to P_0 and the figure
shows 'first-order' dominance. First-order dominance establishes that
dominance also applies to higher integrals of the Foster–Greer–
Thorbecke measure – P_1 and P_2, for example. In situations in which
the cumulative poverty functions for different years or groups cross at
some point, such as year 2 and year 3 in Figure 3.1, it is possible to

---

[17] See additional note A3.4. The application of stochastic dominance to poverty was
     pioneered by Atkinson (1987). Zheng (2000) has a detailed treatment.

implement second-order dominance tests for P_1; and, in the event that curves cross here, higher-order dominance tests will provide additional information.

The second area of uncertainty over appropriate methods concerns the variety of poverty indexes available. Three were discussed in the previous section in the context of single-dimension indicators of well-being and a further two for the multidimensional case. In fact, many more poverty measures are currently available, and new ones are being introduced. How should we discriminate between the different poverty indexes? Sen (1976a) was the first to introduce an axiomatic approach to identifying the properties of different poverty measures. This is equivalent to establishing plausible conditions that poverty measures are expected to meet.

The extent to which poverty measures comply with proposed axioms has been the subject of detailed discussion.[18] It is not possible to provide a full discussion of axioms and poverty indexes here, but it might be useful to discuss three axioms in the context of the poverty measures presented above.[19] The focus axiom establishes that poverty measures should not be influenced by changes in the well-being of non-poor households. This suggests an exclusive focus on households in poverty.[20] All poverty measures comply with this condition. The subgroup decomposability axiom requires that poverty measures be aggregated accurately from the poverty measures of component groups. This is important for poverty policy, as it guides geographic or categorical selection of beneficiaries, for example. The Foster–Greer–Thorbecke measure and the Watts measure are subgroup-decomposable, but the Sen measure is not. The strong transfer axiom requires that the poverty measure reflect transfers from a poor household to a less poor household. Measured poverty should increase if a transfer programme requires that a household in extreme poverty transfers a small sum of

---

[18] For a detailed discussion of the axiomatic approach to single-dimension poverty measures, see, among others, Foster (1984), Seidl (1988) and Zheng (1997). For a discussion of the axiomatic approach to multidimensional poverty measures see, among others, Alkire and Foster (2011), Chakravarty and Silber (2008), Foster (1984), Seidl (1988) and Zheng (1997).

[19] A formal definition of the axioms discussed here can be found in additional note A3.5.

[20] In the context of social assistance transfers, poverty measures satisfying the focus axiom would not be sensitive to the gains in well-being associated with anti-poverty programmes for paternalistic and altruistic taxpayers.

income to a household in moderate poverty. The Sen measure and the poverty headcount and poverty gap measures (P_0 and P_1) fail to satisfy the strong transfer axiom.[21]

The axiomatic approach to poverty measures and the application of stochastic dominance contribute to an assessment of the robustness of poverty estimates, and throw light on the implications of choices on poverty lines and poverty measures.

Poverty dynamics and vulnerability

It is important to reflect on the time dimension of poverty. The estimates of poverty derived from the application of poverty indexes to household survey data provide a measure of poverty at a point in time. From the perspective of anti-poverty policy, an understanding of poverty dynamics is essential.[22] The objective of social assistance is to reduce, and help eradicate and prevent, poverty. Persistent or chronic poverty is often associated with a reduced productive capacity, owing to cumulative deficits in health and nutrition, asset and network depletion and increased vulnerability (Chronic Poverty Research Centre (CPRC), 2005). Chronic or persistent poverty deepens the harm caused by poverty, and is itself a factor in maintaining households in poverty. Preventing and eradicating poverty involves adopting a prospective approach to poverty. Vulnerability can be defined as the probability that individuals or households will find themselves in poverty in the future. Reducing vulnerability (to poverty) is essential to poverty prevention and eradication.

Panel data surveys, in which sampled households are followed over an extended period, are increasingly becoming available in developing countries.[23] This makes it possible to study changes in the socioeconomic status of households over time, through careful comparison of

---

[21] The implications for the choice of poverty measures to evaluate social assistance transfers are obvious.

[22] In determining the target population of *Bolsa Família in Brazil*, the Brazilian government measured the number of households with per capita incomes below one-quarter of the poverty line at 11 million in 2006, using the national household survey dataset. However, over a three-month period 15 million households fell below this threshold at one point in time. See Soares, Ribas and Soares (2009).

[23] For a listing of developing countries with panel data, see Baulch (2011); see also Baulch and Hoddinott (2000).

observations at given intervals. Studies have shown that there is considerable variation in poverty status over time, with some households exiting poverty, others falling into poverty and some remaining in poverty.

Three main approaches to the study of the duration dimension of poverty provide a basis for estimating persistent poverty and vulnerability.[24] The shortfall approach focuses on measuring a 'permanent income' component in household income. Following standard consumption theory in economics, this approach is grounded on the proposition that households have some target standard of living, given their resources and preferences (Ravallion, 1988). With observations on household consumption over time, it becomes possible to identify a mean level of consumption over the span of the observations, which is taken to reflect an approximation of household's 'permanent income'. Households whose mean income over time is below the poverty line can be considered to be structurally in poverty. This is in contrast with other households that may be in poverty at some point in time – owing to variations in market conditions, for example – but whose mean consumption is above a poverty threshold (Jalan and Ravallion, 2001).

Another approach focuses on counting the poverty spells observed for households (Baulch and Hoddinott, 2000). With the benefit of a panel data set that contains observations at, say, four points in time, it becomes possible to establish how many times the sampled households are observed to be in poverty. Households observed in poverty in all spells are indisputably persistently poor, but there may be grounds for stating that households observed to be in poverty for three out of four points in time are also in persistent poverty.

Finally, another approach focuses on measuring vulnerability, understood as the probability that a household will find itself in poverty in the future. At its core, this is a predictive, ex ante approach. From information on the current situation of households, this approach assesses the likelihood that they will experience poverty in the future. Chaudhuri (2003) provided the initial impetus for the application of this approach. He developed a methodology based on the assumption that the cross-section variance in household consumption could proxy for the cross-time variation, and on that basis support a predictive approach to the likelihood of future poverty without the need for panel data. An

---

[24] Additional note A3.6 contains a definition of the three approaches.

intrinsic difficulty with the notion of vulnerability, as a forward-looking approach to poverty, is the fact that it seeks to predict ex ante the likelihood of poverty, which can be done only stochastically, if at all. At the same time, this is its greatest advantage, especially when the prevention of poverty or its persistence is the key objective.[25]

Recent research has focused on extending single-dimension poverty measures to the many time periods case.[26] This literature has so far concentrated on the spells approach above.

Global poverty?

The international policy focus on poverty associated with the Millennium Development Goals has stimulated interest in the notion and measurement of *global* poverty. As indicated at the beginning of this chapter, poverty is defined to apply at the polity level. It follows from this that a notion of global poverty is, at best, an advocacy tool (Deaton, 2001). However, alternative approaches are available. Pogge (2008) argues that economic interdependence provides a basis for a notion of global poverty, understood as the deficits in well-being that are a direct consequence of globally integrated markets and institutions. In this context, global poverty helps place a spotlight on the responsibility of developed countries towards developing countries. This responsibility is indivisible, and therefore requires a global poverty notion.[27] The indivisibility of effects would also recommend a notion of global poverty to guide and coordinate global poverty reduction, and to measure the effectiveness of international organisations focused on poverty reduction (Chen and Ravallion, 2004; 2009).

The World Bank measure of global poverty on the basis of US$1 and US$2 has been the subject of considerable controversy. The US$1-a-day poverty line[28] was based on an average of poverty lines in a sample of low-income countries. This is converted to local currencies using purchasing power parities, and then applied to country household survey data. The

---

[25] For an application to Latin America, see Bérgolo *et al.* (2010).

[26] See Bossert, Chakravarty and D'Ambrosio (2008), Dutta, Roope and Zank (2010), Foster (2009), Hojman and Kast (2009) and Zheng (2007).

[27] It would be hard to disentangle the impact of the European Union's support for European farmers on particular countries and communities in the South, for example.

[28] This was updated to US$1.25 in 2004.

country-level poverty estimates are then aggregated to generate a measure of global poverty. The adoption of measures of US$1 and US$2 a day enables estimation of the global population in poverty. There is some agreement that measures of global poverty based on the US$1- and US$2-a-day levels have been influential in international poverty policy discussions, and have an immediacy that makes them effective as an advocacy tool (Hulme, 2010). They are also controversial, in terms of both their underlying cosmopolitanism and the inherent technical difficulties in measurement across countries (Deaton, 2001; Srinivasan, 2001).[29]

Conclusions

The main objective of this chapter was to familiarise readers with the basic poverty concepts and measures employed in the design, implementation and evaluation of social assistance programmes. Of necessity, coverage of these concepts and measures was selective. The materials in the chapter were organised around two main questions: what is poverty, and how should it be measured?

Poverty describes significant deficits in well-being considered unacceptable in a particular society. Poverty is firmly grounded in well-being, but there are different perspectives on what constitutes the informational basis of well-being. Theories are strongly evaluative. For some, well-being can be evaluated on the basis of the resources at the command of individuals, households or communities; for others, well-being is evaluated in terms of utility, primary goods or capability. This chapter noted these different perspectives, but worked on the assumption that it is feasible to translate across informational bases. For the most part, social assistance programmes work with income or consumption as the preferred informational basis.

Poverty analysis employs well-being indicators and particular thresholds to identify households in poverty. Poverty measures or indexes are then employed to aggregate poverty for particular groups or communities. In this chapter, single-dimension and multidimensional poverty indexes were introduced. A discussion on axioms and dominance tests

---

[29] Global poverty measures have marginal influence on social assistance programmes because they are, by and large, national initiatives. To date, there is no evidence to show that they influence aid allocations supporting transfer programmes in developing countries.

provided insights into the way that poverty analysis addresses two important areas of uncertainty: over poverty lines and over poverty measures. Poverty analysis combines poverty concepts and poverty measures to answer the question: how much poverty is in a particular household, community or country? Poverty analysis is essential to the design of anti-poverty programmes and to the assessment of their effectiveness. The materials in this chapter are an important building block for the rest of the book.

Three important findings from the discussion in the chapter need underlining. First, the discussion demonstrated (it is hoped) the fundamental role of ethical judgements in poverty analysis. Evaluative concerns are at the centre of theories of well-being underlying poverty. Poverty concepts and measures embed much of the ethics of assistance discussed in the previous chapter, especially the notions of priority and sufficiency. Second, well-being thresholds and poverty lines were conspicuous throughout the chapter, but their role is surprisingly limited. They are useful reference points at best, which acknowledges their discretionary character and tallies with the conclusions from the previous chapter. Increasingly, the identification of beneficiaries from anti-poverty programmes relies on ranking households in poverty, as opposed to binary 'poverty'/'not in poverty' identification criteria. Third, advances in poverty analysis provide a strong foundation for social assistance. On the one hand, they throw a strong beam of light on the ethical assumptions embedded in anti-poverty programmes and enabling informed public scrutiny. On the other, they inform policies to reduce and eradicate poverty. The next chapter follows on by examining how programmes providing direct transfers to households in poverty can be designed to maximise poverty reduction.

ADDITIONAL NOTES A3

A3.1 Equivalence scales

Equivalence scales provide a means of attributing household measured well-being to each household member in a way that accounts for economies in household size and differences in household composition. Focusing on income for short, adult equivalent household income is obtained by dividing household income by the number of adult equivalents in household i, AE, computed as

$$AE = 1 + (N_a + \alpha N_c)^\theta, 0 \leq \alpha, \theta \leq 1 \qquad (3.A1.1)$$

Where the first adult in the household is counted as 1, N_a stands for the number of additional adults in the households, N_c is the number of children, α is a child weight capturing the 'costs' of children relative to an adult and θ captures economies of scale. In the commonly used 'OECD scale', $\theta = 0.7$ and $\alpha = 0.5$, implying that public goods account for 0.3 of expenditure and children's 'costs' are 0.5 of an adult (Deaton, 1997; Lanjouw and Ravallion, 1995). Increasingly, studies use the square root of the number of household members as the adjustment factor.

A3.2 Poverty functions

For a population consisting of N units (individuals or households, but hereafter individuals for convenience) named i (i = 1,2,3,4,. . .,N), y_i describes a well-being indicator for household i (say income or consumption of the ith household). With a poverty line z, a household is in poverty if $y_i \leq z$.

Ranking individuals from poorest to richest yields an array:

$$y_1 < y_2 < y_3 < y_4 < ... < y_q \leq z < y_{q+1} < .... < yN \qquad (3.A2.1)$$

The set of individuals in poverty is Q ≡ [i | $y_i \leq z$], and q is the cardinality of Q.

A poverty function is a mapping P: Y x T → S such that, for every regime (y ; z) of a distribution of well-being indicators, P assigns each individual a real number intended to signify the extent of poverty in a regime (y ; z). For example, if S stands for the binary identification of whether individuals are in poverty or not, then P maps from the individual's well-being indicator y_i and the poverty line z to an indicator variable in such a way that $p(y_i; z) = 1$ if the individual i is in poverty and $p(y_i; z) = 0$ if the individual i is not in poverty.

For the multidimensional case, let $d \geq 2$ represent the number of dimensions. Let Y = [y_{ij}] denote the N x d matrix of indicators of achievements, where the typical cell $y_{ij} \geq 0$ is the achievement of individual i = 1,2,. . .,N in dimension j = 1,2,. . .,d. Each row vector y_i. lists individual i's achievements and each column vector y_j gives the distribution of the dimension j achievements across individuals. As with the single indicator, let z_j denote the threshold below which an individual is considered deprived in dimension j; and z is the row vector of thresholds for all $j \in d$.

In the multidimensional case, the poverty function maps from individual i's achievements y_i and the threshold vector z to an indicator variable in such a way that $p(y_{ij}; z) = 1$ if individual i suffers from deprivation and $p(y_{ij}; z) = 0$ if not. This yields a matrix $\mathbf{g} = [g_{ij}]$ denoting the 0–1 matrix of deprivations associated with Y, whose typical element g_{ij} is defined as $g_{ij} = 1$ if $y_{ij} \leq z$ and as $g_{ij} = 0$ if $y_{ij} > z$. It will be useful to define a column vector $\mathbf{c}$ of deprivation counts whose ith entry $c_i = | g_i|$ represents the number of deprivations observed for individual i. The set Z $[1,\ldots,N]$ represents individuals who are deprived in a given dimension j. The multidimensional analysis is meant to consider across the different dimensions, rather than just a single one, so a second threshold is needed to identify individuals in poverty. For a set of dimensions d, the union approach defines as being in poverty any individual who has at least one deprivation – that is, $p(y_i; z) = 1$ if and only if $c_i > 1$. The intersection approach identifies as being in poverty an individual who is deprived in all dimensions – that is, $p(y_i; z) = 1$ if and only if $c_i = d$. An alternative is to use an intermediate threshold level for c_i that lies somewhere between the union and the intersection approaches. For $k = 1,\ldots,$ d, let $p_k(y_i ; z) = 1$ whenever $c_i \geq k$ and $p_k(y_i ; z) = 0$ whenever $c_i < k$.

Alkire and Foster (2011) note that the dual threshold of the multidimensional poverty function is 'poverty focused', insofar as an improvement in an achievement level of an individual not in poverty leaves the value of the function unchanged. It is also 'deprivation focused', in that an improvement in any non-deprived achievement leaves the value of the function unchanged.

A3.3 Relational poverty measures

A more detailed discussion of relational poverty measures is included here to extend the discussion on the priority view in Chapter 2. Sen (1976a) proposes the following poverty index:

$$P_{Sen}(y; z) = \frac{2}{(q + 1)Nz} \sum_{i=1}^{q} g_i r_i(y_i; z) \qquad (3.A3.1)$$

Here, the first term on the right-hand side normalises the second term. In the second term, we have the poverty gap of individual i as g_i. To take account of the intensity of poverty felt by those with larger poverty gaps, the latter are weighted by $r_i(.)$. In Sen's poverty index, $r_i(.)$

represents the ranking of an individual, among all those in poverty, associated with regime $(y ; z)$. The ranking of the individual r is defined as a one-to-one function $r{:}Q \rightarrow [1,2,\ldots,q]$, which satisfies $r(i) > r(j)$ whenever $g_i(y ; z) > g_j(y ; z)$ (Foster, 1984). In the ranking, the poorest of the poor has a rank q and the richest of the poor (nearest the poverty line) has a rank of 1. Where two individuals have identical income, one is arbitrarily ranked below the other. P_{Sen} is therefore a normalised weighted sum of poverty gaps, the weights being the ranking of individuals in poverty.

The interesting point for our purposes is that, in the Sen measure, poverty in an individual is influenced by his or her relation to other people in poverty, as the ranking attached to the individual is the weight attached to his or her poverty gap. This poverty measure reflects a relational approach to poverty. The amount of poverty experienced by a person depends on his or her relation or position vis-à-vis others in poverty.

Foster (1984) finds two separate justifications for the use of this weighting scheme by Sen. First, Sen suggests that, in the absence of convincing alternatives, the position of the individual, in the ranking of individuals in poverty, could be used to generate a numerical weighting reflecting relational dimensions of poverty. To construct this weighting scheme, it must be assumed that the distances between two contiguous rankings are identical – that the distance between an individual ranked 11 with respect to an individual ranked 10, say, is the same as that of an individual ranked 24 with respect to an individual ranked 25. The ranking of an individual represents the relative deprivation he or she experiences relative to the least poor person. This has the advantage of 'cardinalising' what is in effect an ordinal measure, following Borda's voting scheme (Sen, 1976a).

Second, Sen justifies this weighting by reference to Runciman's description of relative deprivation arising from promotion in the military. Relative deprivation is thought to depend on the relation of an individual to his or her reference group, so that, for someone who is not promoted, his or her perception of relative deprivation is dependent on the number of others in the reference group who are promoted (Runciman, 1966). Taking persons in poverty as a reference group, the number of other persons with higher incomes can be argued to be a proxy for relative deprivation.

These two justifications for using ranking as a weighting scheme are open to criticism (Foster, 1984; Zheng, 1997). Atkinson has argued that 'the arguments about relative position and ranking are more persuasive for inequality measurement than for poverty measurement' (Atkinson, 1987: 755). It also seems wasteful to use rankings as a proxy of relative deprivation when information on income and poverty gaps is available. Furthermore, restricting the reference groups to poor households alone misses significant demonstration effects from the consumption and behaviour of the better off.

Subsequent work on Sen's index sought to address perceived weaknesses with this measure, in particular the fact that the Sen index does not satisfy the transfer axiom. This is the requirement that a transfer from some individual in poverty to a less poor person, and leading to the latter exiting poverty, should, other things being equal, be reflected in a rise in the poverty measure. However, Sen's measure may show a reduction in aggregate poverty. Kakwani (1980) has suggested that this could be resolved by raising each weight to a power k, as in

$$P_K(y;z) = \frac{q}{\phi_k(q)N_z} \sum_{i=1}^{q} g_i r_i(y_i;z)^k \qquad (3.A3.2)$$

where $\phi_k = \sum_{i=1}^{q} i^k$. This replaces Sen's ranking as the weight of the poverty gaps with a more flexible formulation. Kakwani suggests that it will always be possible to find a k large enough to ensure that transfers of this type produce a rise in the poverty measure. Thon (1979) has suggested instead replacing the normalisation in Sen by

$$P_T(y;z) = \frac{2}{N(N+1)z} \sum_{i=1}^{q} g_i(r_i(y_i;z) + N - q) \qquad (3.A3.3)$$

which now satisfies the requirement that transfers from poor to less poor persons that take the latter above the poverty line are reflected in a rise in poverty. The Thon measure can achieve this by including the non-poor in the ranking of individuals, so that the ranking of an individual in poverty is not now his or her ranking among those in poverty, but his or her ranking in the population as a whole. This ensures that, if a poor person crosses the poverty line, the denominator remains constant. Takayama has suggested instead replacing the truncated income variable used in the calculation of $P_{Sen}(y;z)$ with a complete but censored income variable. This takes care of the discontinuity in the income variable used in P_{Sen}, and precludes any distorting effect on the index from poor persons crossing the poverty line. The income variable truncated for the non-poor is replaced with a censored variable in which incomes above the poverty line are replaced by the poverty line itself, while leaving all other incomes unchanged (Takayama, 1979). For a vector of income **y**, a continuous version of the poverty function P is P^* (Foster and Sen, 1997). That is, $P^*(\mathbf{y}, z) = P(\mathbf{y}^*, z)$, where $\mathbf{y}^*$ is a censored distribution, as explained above. Shorrocks' (1995) version is:

$$P_{SST}(y; z) = \frac{1}{N^2} \sum_{i=1}^{q} g_i(2N - 2i + 1) \qquad (3.A3.4)$$

A3.4 Dominance

For additive poverty measures, such as the Foster–Greer–Thorbecke and the Watts measures, of the form $P(y;z) = \Sigma_N p(y_i;z)/N$ and where $p(y_i;z) = 0$ if $y_i > z$, and $p(y_i;z) > 0$ if $y_i \leq z$, first-order dominance applies if the cumulative density function for a distribution $F_Y^{-1}(p)$, where p is the share of the population with incomes less than a given income level, is at least as high as that of a cumulative density function $F_{Y'}^{-1}(p)$ for all $z\min < z < z\max$. Second order dominance focuses on the areas under $F_Y^{-1}(p)$ and $F_{Y'}^{-1}(p)$, the poverty gaps. $F_Y^{-1}(p)$ second-order dominates $F_{Y'}^{-1}(p)$ if its poverty gap curve is somewhere above, but never below, the poverty gap curve for $F_{Y'}^{-1}(p)$. Third-order dominance is defined in the same way as second-order dominance, but with the poverty gap squared as the basic ingredient.

A3.5 Selected poverty measure axioms

Focus axiom: for a poverty measure $P(y;z)$, $P(y';z) = P(y;z)$ whenever $y'\ldots Y$ is obtained from $y\ldots Y$ by an increment to a non-poor unit.

Weak transfer sensitivity axiom: $P(y;z) > P(y';z)$ whenever y and $y'\ldots Y$ are obtained from $y\ldots Y$ by transferring income $\delta(>0)$ from poor incomes y_i to y_j and from poor incomes y_k to y_l, with $y_j-y_i = y_l-y_k > \delta$, $y_k > y_i$, with none crossing the poverty line after transfers.

A3.6 Duration poverty measures

In the shortfall approach, persistent or chronic poverty is defined by $\hat{y}_i \leq z$, where $\hat{y}_i = [(\sum_{t=1}^{T} y_{it})/T]$ – that is, $\hat{y}_i$ is time-mean and T is time periods.

In the duration approach, persistent or chronic poverty is defined by $\max(y_{it}, y_{it+1}, \ldots, y_{iT}) \leq z$, where t indexes observation points $t = 1,2,3,\ldots,T$. Here z can be defined as equivalent to all observations or a fraction of them.

In the predicted consumption approach, chronic or persistent poverty is defined by $(y_{it}, E_t[y_{it+1}|v_{it} > n]) \leq z$, where v_{it} is a measure of vulnerability to future poverty and n is a threshold.

4 | Optimal anti-poverty transfers

This chapter provides an introduction to the analysis of anti-poverty transfer programmes and looks at the type of design features that can maximise their poverty reduction effectiveness: transfers are optimal if they minimise poverty. The focus of the chapter is not on specific types of programmes but, rather, on anti-poverty transfers in general. The aim is to gain an insight into the core elements of anti-poverty programmes in order to be able to develop a framework capable of organising the study of existing anti-poverty transfer programmes in developing countries, which will come in the next chapter.

The interest is in finding out the conditions or requirements that anti-poverty programmes need to satisfy in order to minimise poverty. In this chapter, these conditions or requirements are referred to as parameters. In modelling, parameters describe the factors that help define a model or system and set the conditions for its operation. Knowledge of the parameters is essential to finding a solution to the problem addressed by the model or system. They dominate research and policy discussions of transfer programmes in developing countries, such as the need for transfer programmes to be effective, to enjoy a measure of political support, to be financially sustainable, to preserve incentives – and so on. I examine the shape of optimal anti-poverty transfer programmes starting from the most basic parameter, effectiveness, then gradually incorporating additional parameters. This involves reviewing and synthesising materials from a scarce, but important, public economics literature. The findings from this literature are essential to a well-grounded understanding of existing social assistance programmes in developing countries.

The materials covered in the chapter are organised around three main questions: how best to allocate an anti-poverty budget? What is the optimal shape of anti-poverty transfer programmes in the presence of information and incentive issues? What should the size of an anti-poverty budget be? A brief justification for their selection acts as an introduction to, and description of, this chapter.

Let us take it for granted that political processes, perhaps informed by priority concerns of the kind examined in Chapter 2, lead policymakers to agree to address poverty through direct transfers to households in poverty. Poverty analysis, along the lines discussed in Chapter 3, should enable policymakers to identify accurately how much poverty there is in the population. A budget is set aside for the transfers. It is helpful to assume for the time being that it is a windfall budget, in the sense that it is unexpected and therefore unallocated. The anti-poverty budget is insufficient to lift every household in poverty out of poverty. How best to allocate this budget? The main parameter here is that transfers should minimise poverty, that they should be as effective as possible. The issue in this case is to identify the basis on which policymakers will decide whom to assist and by how much. This is the simplest case. The windfall nature of the budget obviates financing issues, and the population in poverty can be identified directly.

Addressing this first question provides valuable insights, but it is important to check whether these insights apply in more complex situations. In practice, the identification of households in poverty is not costless. In the presence of recurrent transfers, care needs to be taken to preserve incentives for self-sufficiency among beneficiaries. This leads directly to the second question: what is the optimal shape of effective anti-poverty transfer programmes in the presence of identification and incentive issues? Incentive and information issues impose additional parameters on transfer programmes. For a given level of poverty reduction, anti-poverty transfer programmes should be designed so that the information and incentive costs of anti-poverty transfers are minimised. Policymakers will need to ensure that transfers preserve incentives to overcome poverty, including incentives to work and invest in productive capacity. They will also need to consider carefully the costs and gains from alternative strategies for selecting potential beneficiaries and excluding others.

The third question is no less important. What should the size of an anti-poverty budget be? In the two situations considered above, the anti-poverty budget is assumed to be fixed. In fact, its size is, in most plausible situations, the outcome of policymakers balancing poverty reduction objectives with taxpayers' preferences. The requirement of sustainability and need for political support for anti-poverty programmes impose additional parameters on the design and implementation of optimal programmes. This implies considering transfers and taxes together, and the need to minimise the costs of the funds collected by the government for the purpose of financing anti-poverty transfer programmes.

These are the three main questions this chapter addresses. The answers will help in developing a framework for studying the design and implementation of existing anti-poverty transfer programmes in developing countries. They will throw light on the implications of alternative configurations of these parameters for the design of transfer programmes capable of ensuring that households achieve a satisfactory level of consumption, income or capability, at minimum cost to society.[1] The discussion that follows is divided neatly into three sections, each addressing in turn the main questions identified above.[2]

Optimal allocation of a limited anti-poverty budget

Suppose you are entrusted with the allocation of a fixed – but insufficient – budget to reduce poverty.[3] The budget is to be allocated as income transfers for households in poverty, in ways that minimise overall poverty. What guidance can theory provide? What are the main parameters guiding your decision?

This is the most basic model for identifying optimal transfer programmes. This way of formulating the problem simplifies the parameters needed to identify a solution. There is no need to address the issues associated with financing the poverty budget and its size;[4] they are assumed away by the 'windfall' nature of the budget. The model also abstracts from potential incentive effects, as the problem is formulated in purely static form, as a one-off redistribution. The budget is assumed to be insufficient to eradicate poverty, which implies the need to make choices in the allocation of the budget. Despite the simplicity in the formulation of the problem, key insights can be gained from the exercise.

---

[1] The parameters of specific transfer programmes have been discussed in the literature; see Coady (2004). Here, the focus is on developing a basic framework applicable to all transfer programmes addressing poverty.

[2] The discussion aims to provide an accessible account. The reader interested in a more technical approach would benefit from following up on the references included in the text, especially Besley (1997), Besley and Coate (1992; 1995) and Kaplow (2007).

[3] A substantial literature on this approach informs this section. See Bourguignon and Fields (1990; 1997), Gangopadhyay and Subramanian (1992) and Subramanian (2004).

[4] The financing could be taken to come from international aid, or from taxes on the rich.

The programme agency can observe directly well-being levels among all individuals (or households) in the population, enabling a ranking of individuals from poorest to richest (this is described more formally in additional note A3.2). It is also assumed that there is an agreed poverty threshold z representing a minimum living standard. The objective of the transfers is to minimise poverty, but this needs to be stated more precisely. There are several possible poverty measures available, and one of them will need to be selected. We could select the Foster–Greer–Thorbecke class of poverty functions (Foster, Greer and Thorbecke, 1984), introduced in the previous chapter and referred hereafter as P_α. An advantage of P_α is that, by varying α, it is possible to reflect ethical preferences concerning poverty – the extent of society's 'aversion to poverty'. As noted in the previous chapter, when $\alpha = 0$ the poverty function yields the poverty headcount. When $\alpha = 1$ the poverty function yields the poverty gap, the difference existing between the mean well-being shortfall and the poverty thresholds standardised as a fraction of the poverty threshold. When $\alpha > 1$ the poverty function is increasingly sensitive to distribution of the standard of living among the population in poverty.

The problem is now defined as how to allocate a fixed, but insufficient, budget so as to minimise a P_α poverty index, assuming full information on well-being levels, referred to hereafter as income, for simplicity.[5] The fixed budget B is to be allocated among those in poverty through income transfers t. The problem can be represented formally as (Bourguignon and Fields, 1990)

$$Min\ P_\alpha(y_i + t_i; z, \alpha) = \frac{1}{N} \sum_{i=1}^{q} [(z - y_i + t_i)/z]^\alpha, \alpha \geq 0$$

subject to

$$\sum_{i=1}^{q} t_i \leq B$$

$$t_i \leq (z - y_i) \quad \forall i \in Q$$

$$t_i \geq 0 \qquad \forall i \in Q$$

(4.1)

---

[5] For a discussion of optimal budget distribution in the context of imperfect targeting, see Kanbur (1987).

The first line in the programme above states the aim of minimising the poverty index P_α defined by three main parameters: individual income including transfers; a poverty threshold; and a measure of society's aversion to poverty, which must be 0 or greater. There are three main constraints on the minimisation of this poverty index. The first can be interpreted as a feasibility constraint: total transfers cannot exceed the available budget. The second is an efficiency constraint, implying that a transfer to an individual must not exceed the individual's poverty gap. This is important so as to avoid wasting transfers on those not in poverty. Finally, the third constraint rules out negative transfers.[6]

Running this programme for different values of α produces the following optimal solutions.[7] Figure 4.1 provides a graphic representation of the solution to the problem, under the assumption that the distribution of income in the population is uniform. With $\alpha = 0$, the objective is to minimise the poverty headcount rate. It is optimal to allocate the budget to the richest of the poor – those who are closest to the poverty line. Following Bourguignon and Fields (1990), I shall describe this allocation as 'R' type. With $0 < \alpha < 1$, the optimal allocation is also 'R' type. With $\alpha = 1$, the objective is to minimise the average poverty gap, and in this case any allocation is optimal. As long as transfers go to households in poverty, any of them, and individual transfers do not exceed the recipient's poverty gap (the last two constraints in Equation 4.1), any equal-size transfer allocations will have the same effect on the average poverty gap. With $\alpha > 1$, the poverty function becomes increasingly sensitive to the poorest of the poor, and it is therefore optimal to allocate the budget to the poorest households. In this case, the solution to the programme is to begin from the poorest households and provide them with a transfer sufficient to take them to the level of the next poorest, and continue in the same fashion until the budget is exhausted. Following Bourguignon and Fields, I refer to this allocation as 'P' type.

This exercise yields some interesting insights into the design of an optimal transfer programme. The design of optimal income transfers depends on the specific objective chosen – the poverty function that is to

[6] Ruling out negative transfers precludes the possibility of an anti-poverty policy based on redistribution financing solely from households in poverty.

[7] Gangopadhyay and Subramanian detail the formal solution to the programme; see Gangopadhyay and Subramanian (1992).

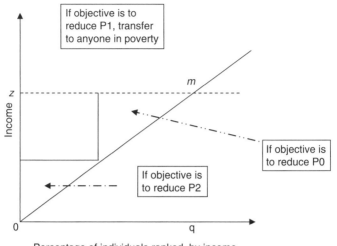

Figure 4.1 Poverty measures and the optimal allocation of a limited anti-poverty budget (individuals rank in ascending order by their income)
Notes: The figure assumes a uniform distribution of income. Individuals are ranked from poorest to richest; z is the poverty line and $zm0$ is the aggregate poverty gap. Policymakers aiming to minimise P0 will focus the limited budget on the richest of the poor. If they instead prioritise a reduction in the poverty gap squared (P2), they will focus resources on the poorest of the poor. If the objective of policy is to reduce the poverty gap (P1), transfers to any person in poverty will maximise poverty reduction, as long as they do not move above the poverty line.

be minimised. This requires replacing the rather loosely stated objective of 'minimising poverty' with the more specific one of 'minimising a particular poverty function'. When the objective is to minimise the poverty headcount, it makes sense to focus transfers on those individuals close to the poverty line. This way, more of them will reach the threshold. If the objective is to minimise the poverty gap squared, then transfers must be focus on the poorest of the poor. The specific poverty minimisation objective adopted is crucial to the design of the transfer programme.

Interestingly, and in light of the discussion in Chapters 1 and 2, the optimal shape of the transfer programmes – the solution to the budget allocation problem – reflects the ethical preferences embedded in α. The objectives of social assistance programmes reflect social preferences with regard to aversion to poverty, as defined in the understanding of poverty present in the minds of policymakers. Knowledge and processes of social preference formation and aggregation are essential to the design of an anti-poverty programme. Designing the allocation of an insufficient anti-poverty budget is as much an exercise in unveiling and assessing ethical preferences as it is one of technical programming.

Mixed or hybrid allocations are also feasible, whereby some of the budget goes to the poorest of the poor, and some to the richest of the poor.[8] With α = 1 – that is, opting to minimise the poverty gap – 'R', 'P' or, indeed, mixed strategies are equally optimal. As noted above, it makes no difference to whom the budget is distributed, as long as it reaches those in poverty and does not take them above the poverty threshold.

The exercise is revealing, despite the fact that it relies on several simplifying assumptions. In practice, more sophisticated models and approaches will be needed to define the optimal shape of anti-poverty transfer programmes in contexts in which beneficiary selection, information and incentives constitute additional parameters. The following section takes up these issues.

Income maintenance transfers

In this section, some of the restrictive assumptions made in the previous section are relaxed in order to explore further parameters guiding the design of social assistance transfers. In particular, the assumption that the programme agency has full information on the well-being of different individuals (or households) – their income, for short – is dropped, in order to enable consideration of beneficiary selection. Incentives issues are tackled directly by dropping the assumption that transfers constitute a one-off distribution. Discussion of the appropriate size of the transfer budget and its determinants is left for the next section. Instead of using the, admittedly unrealistic, device of a windfall budget to set the size of the budget, in the discussion in this section the budget is assumed to depend on the poverty gap, by assuming that the transfers to individuals in poverty will completely fill in their poverty gaps. Transfer

---

[8] Bourguignon and Fields (1990) show that a mixed strategy is optimal if the objective is to minimise the Sen poverty measure described in Chapter 3.

programmes of this type are usually referred to as 'income mainte-nance', used extensively in social assistance programmes in European countries (Atkinson, 1995). In such programmes, the objective is to ensure households with living standards below the poverty threshold receive a supplement that lifts them to the poverty line. Focusing on income maintenance programmes is useful to consider a more realistic way of fixing the budget.

Taxpayers' preferences and government anti-poverty policy

Following Besley (1997), it is helpful to simplify the policy process by which transfer programmes are designed by assuming that the govern-ment will act simply as an executive agency implementing taxpayers' preferences. The government collects taxes from taxpayers and redis-tributes to households in poverty.[9] Assuming a polarised society with population N, partitioned into k homogeneous groups, $k \in \{r, p\}$ (Besley, 1997; Zeckhauser, 1971), nr is the population not in poverty, loosely referred to as 'rich' or taxpayers in what follows, and np is the population in poverty, and $N = nr + np$. Income yi derives from labour earnings dependent on hours worked lp and a wage rate wp reflecting ability. Utility u for each k group is defined as

$$up = cp - h(lp)$$
$$ur = cr - \theta(cp, \delta r) \tag{4.2}$$

where c captures consumption and $h(.)$ represents disutility from work, which is increasing and strictly concave in hours of work. The rich do not work. They care about their own consumption, but also about the consumption of the group in poverty, with δ reflecting the strength of the motivation felt to redistribute income to the groups in poverty. This motivation could come from the impact of poverty on crime or social conflict, for example. It can be informed by knowledge of the effective-ness of anti-poverty transfers. θ is a parameter, with $0 > \theta > 1$.[10] In the

---

[9] Chapter 6 examines the critical role of government agencies.

[10] The parameter θ weighs the rich's interest in poverty. The parameter is eloquently described by Atkinson (2009), citing from Francis Edgeworth's *Mathematical Psychic* (1881): '[B]etween the frozen pole of egoism and the tropical expanse of utilitarianism [there is] the position of one for whom in a calm moment his neighbour's utility compared with his own neither counts for nothing, nor "counts for one", but counts for a fraction.'

formulation above, the rich care about the consumption of the poor, not their utility; they ignore the disutility of work experienced by the group in poverty.

The government is charged with collecting taxes from the rich and providing income maintenance transfers to the group in poverty. It responds to rich people's concerns with poverty eradication, and designs and implements a social assistance programme providing a direct transfer t to those in poverty. This is in fact a package $\{b, m\}$, where b captures the transfer itself and m captures the costs to beneficiaries of accessing and participating in the programme. These costs could effectively deter potential beneficiaries, if they exceed the benefits of participation.

Participation in the programme is voluntary, so that, for those participating, the following condition applies:

$$\text{Max}_{lp}\{yp + t - h(lp^*)\} \geq \text{Max}_{lp}\{yp - h(lp^*)\} \equiv up \quad (4.3)$$

where lp^* is the labour supply consistent with the group in poverty taking full advantage of available economic opportunities.

Because it is assumed that the government is captured by the rich – that is, taxpayers – the problem to be solved by the government is equivalent to maximising the income of the rich consistent with their preferences and motivation for redistribution. This yields the following:

$$\underset{cp, yp}{\text{Max }} yr - \left(\frac{np}{nr}\right)(cp - yp) - \theta(cp, \delta r)$$
$$\text{s.t. } cp - h(lp^*) \geq up \quad (4.4)$$

In this expression, the government's problem is to maximise yr minus the cost of the income maintenance transfer programme $np(cp - yp)$ shared equally by the rich nr, and taking account of the preferences of the rich for redistribution captured in the last term of the maximand. This is subject to the voluntary participation of the group in poverty.

A basic income maintenance programme

Following Besley (1997), the problem of designing an optimal income maintenance transfer programme can be broken down into two stages: a first stage concerned with programme design, aimed at minimising the cost of the programme (Dye and Antle, 1986), and a second in which the generosity of the transfers is determined by setting a specific poverty threshold. The first stage finds the cost-minimising programme design as

$$\text{Min}_{cp}\ np(cp - yp) \qquad subject\ to$$

$$cp \geq z \tag{4.5}$$

$$cp - h(lp*) \geq up$$

This part of the programme minimises the poverty gaps experienced by those in poverty, subject to two constraints. The first is that the consumption of the poor should meet at least a minimum level z, the poverty threshold. The second is that participation in the programme must be voluntary.

At the second stage, the generosity of the transfer is determined by setting the poverty threshold z. This can be written as

$$\text{Max}_z \left\{ yr - \frac{C(z)}{nr} - \theta(z, \delta r) \right\} \tag{4.6}$$

where $C(z)$ represents the solution to the cost minimisation programme design in the first stage.

The benefit t is set by the following schedule:

$$t \left\{ \begin{array}{c} (cp - yp), m\ if\ y_i = yp \\ 0 \quad otherwise \end{array} \right. \tag{4.7}$$

This is financed through a head tax on the rich, as in Equation 4.4 above; this is because the rich group is assumed to be homogeneous.

Note that, in the transfer programme described above, the poverty threshold is not exogenous, but determined by taxpayers' incomes and preferences. This fits in with the discussion in Chapters 2 and 3 concerning the limits of the sufficiency approach, and the marginal role of poverty lines in social assistance. It is also interesting to note that the preferences for redistribution among taxpayers – the rich – could easily be specified in terms of ensuring that the 'strains of commitment' among the groups in poverty do not become excessive, as discussed in Chapter 2. The next three subsections tackle key areas of transfer programme design associated with cost minimisation: classification, productive capacity and incentives.

Classification

Relaxing the assumption that the programme agency has full information on the distribution of the well-being of groups in poverty raises the issue of beneficiary selection. This is an important issue, which has often dominated accounts of transfer programme design.[11] The core issue here is the classification of the population into eligible and non-eligible groups. Cost minimisation requires an accurate classification of these groups. There are several channels through which classification problems raise the costs of transfer programmes. First, an accurate classification makes large demands on information gathering and analysis, with associated costs. Second, transfers to groups not in poverty misclassified as in poverty will generate deadweight losses for the programme. Third, the misclassification of households in poverty as non-eligible will reduce the poverty reduction effectiveness of the programme and therefore raise the costs of an anti-poverty programme. Several strategies to address classification problems are available to programme agencies (Coady, Grosh and Hoddinott, 2004).

Direct strategies refer to administrative selection methods implemented by programme agencies to identify eligible households. They include geographic selection, community selection, means tests, proxy means tests and categorical selection. Geographic selection involves identifying eligible households by selecting areas with a high concentration of households in poverty. Community selection decentralises the identification of eligible households, in the hope of exploiting local information on living standards. Means tests collect information on the income, consumption and/or assets of households, whereas proxy means tests use information from secondary variables, enabling an assessment of the distribution of well-being. Akerlof (1978) makes a case for using observable categories of people with a high incidence of poverty – age and disability, for example – to overcome information deficits. Provided that they are closely correlated with poverty, they could be used as a way of determining eligibility, which is described as 'tagging'.

The direct identification of beneficiaries generates costs for the programme agencies and sometimes for the eligible households (raising m

---

[11] See, among others, Besley and Kanbur (1990), Coady, Grosh and Hoddinott (2004), Cornia and Stewart (1995) and Ravallion (2007).

in the benefit package above). In terms of categorical selection, additional costs arise from the extent of noise in the signal provided by the specific categories. It could well be the case that some members of a particular group with a high poverty incidence might not be in poverty. At the same time, households in poverty without a member of that categorical group will be missed out from eligibility. To be effective as a classification method, membership of the particular category must be exogenous – a requirement that is sometimes difficult to fulfil in practice. Assistance to large families with children might generate adverse fertility effects, for example. Administrative selection will also involve costs for eligible households (Currie, 2004).

The cost minimisation condition requires that, *for a specific level of poverty reduction effectiveness*, programme agencies adopt the least-cost strategy or combination of strategies.

Indirect strategies exploit programme design features to provide incentives for potential beneficiaries to reveal the information required to assess their eligibility. One group of strategies focuses on the benefit component of the benefit package; another focuses on the cost side of the benefit package. It is helpful to work on the basis that the population of potential beneficiaries can be grouped into two categories: those who have no, or very little, productive capacity (to simplify matters, this group is assumed to be in extreme poverty, indexed as *ep*); and a second group with productive capacity that is sufficient under normal circumstances to generate an income equivalent to, or in excess of, the poverty threshold (to simplify matters, this group is assumed to be in moderate poverty, and is indexed *mp*). If a single transfer is offered, then some of those in the latter group will have incentives to claim the benefit. The problem then is to design transfer programmes to encourage self-selection among potential beneficiaries into these two groups.

A two-tiered benefit could be designed in a way that encourages the group with productive capacity to claim the benefit appropriate to them, as opposed to the benefit appropriate to the group with very little productive capacity. The two-tiered benefit schedule achieves a separating equilibrium. Its main requirement is described by Besley (1997) as

$$bmp + ymp - h\left(\frac{ymp}{lmp}\right) \geq bep + yep - h\left(\frac{yep}{lmp}\right) \qquad (4.8)$$

The package offered to the group in moderate poverty must be more attractive than the package offered to the group in extreme poverty, even if the work offered is consistent with the preferences of the group in moderate poverty. In this case, the government would offer a benefit *bmp** to the group in moderate poverty.

An alternative approach is to provide a benefit that consists of a mix of cash and in-kind transfers, such that the in-kind transfers are valuable only to the group in extreme poverty. In this case, in-kind transfers act as a restriction on the benefit schedule and encourage self-selection among recipients (Currie and Gahvari, 2007; Gahvari and Mattos, 2007; Nichols and Zeckhauser, 1982).[12] A special case is the provision of in-kind transfers only (Bibi, 2002; Tabor, 2002).[13]

A different set of strategies focuses on modifications to the cost component within the benefit package. Assuming these costs vary across potential programme beneficiaries, they can be used to encourage self-selection among them. Nichols and Zeckhauser (1982) discuss the role of work requirements, in-kind transfers and ordeals in this context. In their model, these design features would have the effect of raising the take-up costs for moderately poor households, persuading them to exclude themselves voluntarily from participating in the programme. Besley and Coate (1992; 1995) propose a screening model in which work requirements generate self-selection. In conditions in which the programme agency cannot observe income-generating ability, a work requirement to be carried out in the public sector will generate an additional cost to potential beneficiaries with potential private sector earnings above potential public sector earnings. In this situation, higher-ability individuals will decide not to participate in the programme. Work requirements will prove more efficient than unconditional income maintenance transfers in circumstances in which groups in extreme poverty are a fraction of the population targeted for the

---

[12] Pinto discusses the potential advantages of providing cash transfers in combination with services that are correlated with geographic concentrations of households in poverty – primary health care services, for example. See Pinto (2004).

[13] There is a large literature examining the conditions determining the mix of cash and in-kind transfers. The presumption is that transfers in cash are preferable, because they provide fewer restrictions on its deployment by households. See, among others, Blackorby and Donaldson (1988), Dye and Antle (1986), Rosenthal (1983), Ross (1991) and Thurow (1974).

programme, and when potential private sector earnings for this group are low.[14] Reworking Equation 4.8 to include disutility from the work requirement, the constraint can be written as

$$bmp + ymp - h\left(\frac{ymp}{lmp} + mmp\right) \geq bep + yep - h\left(\frac{yep}{lmp} + mep\right)$$
$$(4.9)$$

Here, the potential benefits for the groups in moderate poverty from masquerading as if they were in extreme poverty are equal to or less than the benefits from private sector employment.

Productive capacity

The extent to which social assistance transfers influence household decisions relating to their productive capacity is also of some importance. Cost minimisation includes a self-sufficiency requirement that households (or individuals) in poverty rely to the greatest possible extent on their own resources. Enhancing the productive capacity of households is an important parameter guiding the design of social assistance programmes.

Besley and Coate (1992) consider the possibility that a standard income maintenance programme might have adverse effects on beneficiary households' incentives to enhance their productive capacity, with the implication that they could become dependent on social assistance transfers. They set out a simple extension of the work requirement model discussed above, which relaxes the assumption that ability is exogenous. To the extent that households can invest in the ability or productive capacity of their members, then ability becomes partly endogenous. The probability of becoming a high-ability household M is assumed to depend on effort e, so that $M(e)$, with $M' > 0$. Effort is measured in units of disutility and is not directly observable by the programme agency. $M(.)$ is positively related to the returns to ability, measured as the difference in the unit wage of low- and high-ability households. The issue is that the income maintenance transfer reduces the gap in earnings between high- and low-income households, and could therefore blunt the incentives for low-income households to invest in their productive capacity. This proposition echoes commonly

---

[14] In practice, the non-wage costs of public works are substantial.

expressed concerns by policymakers that transfers to poor households may themselves contribute towards generating poverty traps, thus increasing the long-term costs of poverty programmes (Dilnot and Stark, 1989). Besley and Coate suggest that a work requirement could mitigate the adverse incentives of transfers on efforts to enhance the productive capacity of groups in poverty.

A work requirement attached to a transfer could in this case help achieve the objective of raising well-being among households in poverty while preserving incentives to invest in productive capacity. The work requirement has the effect of raising the disutility from work, by requiring participating households to provide work in excess of their preferred amount.[15] To be effective as a means to mitigate the adverse effects of transfers on investment in productive capacity, the work requirement must exceed the amount of work that households would have provided in the absence of the programme. Work requirements act as a 'deterrent' against disinvestment in productive capacity. It is the disutility from the additional work that mitigates the utility gains from the benefit.

Are there alternatives to work requirements? A new wave of transfer programmes in developing countries relies on conditions attached to transfers as a means of ensuring household investment in productive capacity (Das, Do and Özler, 2005; Skoufias, 2005). If the concern is that benefits may blunt the incentives for households in poverty to prevent poverty in the future, making the receipt of benefits conditional on the achievement of basic levels of investment in human development will mitigate potential disinvestment responses. In human-development-conditional transfer programmes, income transfers are made conditional on basic service utilisation – such as schooling, primary health care or nutrition training – that could enhance productive capacity.[16] In the context of human development conditions, the benefit package is now $t = [Ib, m]$, where I is an indicator variable taking the value of 1 if household investment in productive capacity d meets the

---

[15] Work requirements do not make sense in a welfare-maximising context. They make sense only in a non-welfarist context in which the programme agency is concerned with the income level reached by households, not their utility. See Kaplow (2007).

[16] Note that, in this context, conditions are a means to synergise investment in human capital and serve as a 'deterrent' against disinvestment. Conditions could also be used as a selection device, in the spirit of 'ordeals', as described by Nichols and Zeckhauser (1982).

requirement that $d^* = d > dmin$, and 0 otherwise. Here d denotes a required level of basic services utilisation. The benefit schedule is now

$$t \begin{cases} I(cp - yp), \ m \ \ if \ \ y_i = yp, I = 1 | d* = d > dmin \\ \quad\quad\quad 0 \quad otherwise \end{cases}$$ (4.10)

The voluntary participation constraint requires that the utility to households in poverty from participation exceeds the utility from staying out of the programme. Because the levels of basic resource utilisation will vary across households in poverty, the condition $d^* = d > dmin$ will bind on some households, but not on others that are already engaged with this level of investment.[17] This is illustrated in Figure 4.2.

For households in poverty, the line ab represents the quantities of schooling and all other goods available to them, given their income. An

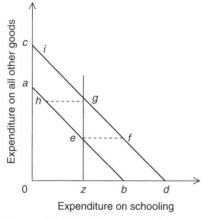

Figure 4.2 Conditions as a deterrent against disinvestment in productive capacity

Notes: The line ab is the budget constraint for households in poverty before any transfer. An unconditional transfer raises the budget line to cd. If policymakers set a minimum consumption of schooling z as a condition for receipt of the transfer, the budget line becomes $aegd$. A household at h needs to raise consumption of schooling to g to meet the eligibility condition.

[17] As Skoufias (2005) notes, for the households for which the condition binds, the transfer package involves both income and consumption effects, as the condition lowers the shadow price of service utilisation. For households for which the condition does not bind, the transfer package involves only an income effect.

unconditional cash transfer equivalent to *eg* makes it possible for the household to consume more schooling and all other goods, as their budget line is now *cd*. Suppose that in the absence of the cash transfer a household in poverty consumes *h*; then, with the cash transfer, household consumption will be in the range *ig* (at *i* the household consumes more of other goods, but no more schooling, and at *g* the household consumes more schooling, but no more of all the other goods; points in the range *ig* represent combinations of the two goods). A transfer programme designer concerned that households in poverty consume at least *oz* schooling could make the transfer conditional on achieving this minimum level of consumption of schooling. The transfer is now indicated by *aegd*. The household at point *h* before the transfer will now need to consume at *g* to secure entitlement to the transfer. A household consuming at point *e* before the transfer will now be able to consume in the range *gf*. For households for which the conditions bind, it is apparent from the description of the voluntary participation constraint that $bI(= 1)$ must exceed the costs of compliance *m*.

Work incentives

So far it has been assumed that participating households engage in paid work as much as economic opportunities allow. This might be an appropriate simplifying assumption in the static case, but it makes little sense in a more dynamic context. Here, transfers are likely to have an impact on incentives to work and save.[18] The standard income maintenance transfer raises concerns regarding work incentive effects. As the income maintenance transfer covers the difference between the earned income and the poverty threshold *z*, in a dynamic context beneficiaries will have only weak incentives to work. In practice, the income maintenance scheme implies a 100 per cent marginal tax rate on their earned income, as benefits are withdrawn in proportion to any additional income earned by the beneficiary household. High marginal rates of tax have strong implications for work incentives.

The impact of income maintenance transfers on work incentives has been studied extensively in the context of tax transfer schemes and in a

---

[18] Incentives to save are more significant in the context of social security than social assistance; see Hubbard, Skinner and Zeldez (1995).

welfarist context.[19] In the context of existing social assistance programmes in developing countries, the issue of work incentives is to date
a less pressing concern. This is in part because, in practice, fixed-level
transfers set well below a poverty threshold are the norm, and also
because few transfer beneficiaries are subject to personal income taxes.
Leaving a discussion of the empirical issues for later,[20] it is useful to
consider the extent to which a conceptual framework covering anti-
poverty transfers should cover work incentives in a non-welfarist context.

Work requirements were considered above as a design feature facilitating classification, and they also act as a deterrent against disinvestment in productive capacity. The question is whether work
requirements make sense as a means of enhancing work incentives. In
a non-welfarist context, work requirements can be justified as a means
of reducing potential deadweight losses from beneficiaries replacing
labour earnings with income transfers. This follows from the cost-
minimising requirement. As these losses are likely to be limited, for
the reasons given above, this particular role of work requirements is
also likely to be limited. Work incentives can be preserved in circumstances in which categorical information is available. They can be
deployed to classify households in poverty into two groups: households
in poverty with work capacity and households in poverty without work
capacity. A differentiated transfer schedule could provide a more generous transfer to the latter group and a less generous transfer to the
former group, sufficient to ensure work incentives (Akerlof, 1978;
Feldstein, 1987; Kanbur and Keen, 1989). Finally, Moffitt (2006)
explains the prevalence of work requirements in social assistance in
the United States by referring to paternalistic social preferences. Work
requirements make sense in a context in which taxpayers value both
poverty eradication and work, as two separate objectives.

Generosity

So far the focus has been on the need to minimise the cost of a transfer
programme. The second stage considers how to determine the

---

[19] Alternative tax transfer schemes have been considered in connection with the
expansion of social assistance in the United States and subsequent welfare reform
there and elsewhere, including negative income tax proposals and earnings
subsidies. For a comprehensive review, see Moffitt (2002).

[20] Chapter 6 considers the available evidence on this point.

generosity of transfers. This engages with political and political economy issues. Following Besley (1997), it is assumed that the government maximises the utility of the rich, as in Equation 4.6 above. The first-order condition of 4.6 with respect to z implies

$$\frac{1}{nr}\frac{\partial C(z)}{\partial z} = -\frac{\partial \theta(z, \delta r)}{\partial z} \qquad (4.11)$$

This equation provides interesting insights. With taxpayers assumed to have homogeneous preferences for poverty reduction – that is, $\theta(z, \delta r)$ and sharing equally the cost of the anti-poverty transfers – the policy-maker will set benefit levels consistent with equating the marginal cost of the transfer programme with its marginal benefits. The second term of the left-hand side in Equation 4.11 provides a measure of the marginal costs of transfers – that is, the change in $C(z)$ associated with a change in z. The marginal benefits, on the other hand, are given by the right-hand side of 4.11.[21] In this formulation, the level of the maximum benefit, or poverty threshold, is sensitive to the costs of the transfer programme and to changes in these costs, as well as to changes in the valuation of poverty reduction among the rich. The poverty line, or maximum benefit level in the case of income maintenance programmes, is a policy variable.

This section has focused on income maintenance transfers, which restrict the size of transfers to the poverty gap participant households' experience. In studies of anti-poverty transfers in developed countries, it makes sense to restrict the analysis to income maintenance transfers, as they are the norm. However, few developing countries have adopted income maintenance programmes;[22] instead, fixed-level transfers are the norm. The focus on income maintenance transfers in this chapter is useful as a device to restrict consideration of the level of transfers to a decision on poverty thresholds. Relaxing this assumption does not necessitate significant changes to the findings, especially as the poverty

---

[21] Besley (1997) considers the case when taxpayers differ in their valuation of poverty reduction, and the resulting benefit level is the outcome of a political process in which taxpayers participate.

[22] The Minimum Living Standard Schemes in China and South Korea are the exception, but their implementation introduces substantial modifications to the conventional European model. In particular, city-level poverty thresholds in China's *Dibao* introduce considerable flexibility into the scheme; see Chen and Barrientos (2006).

threshold is in fact a policy variable, but this underlines the importance of considering the social preferences of taxpayers in some detail.[23] This is done in the following chapter.

Welfarist approaches to optimal transfers

The approach to optimal transfers considered so far assumes that the rich do not work, or that if they do they have no disutility from work. The willingness of the rich to finance a transfer programme is driven solely by the strength of their preference for groups in poverty to achieve acceptable levels of well-being – acceptable to the rich, that is. In a non-welfarist approach to poverty eradication, the well-being of individuals and households not in poverty does not require close consideration. This flows from the focus axiom discussed in Chapter 3. Groups not in poverty are relevant to poverty eradication objectives primarily in their role as taxpayers. The assumption that the rich experience no disutility from work is helpful because it makes it possible to sidestep the issue of the impact of anti-poverty transfers on work incentives for the rich. Taking account of taxpayers' incentives requires a welfarist perspective, because of the need to incorporate into the design of anti-poverty transfer programmes consideration of the utility of the rich. Adverse work responses by the rich to taxes needed to support anti-poverty transfers might lead to lower anti-poverty budgets, even if the preferences of the rich for the well-being of those in poverty remain fixed. In order to identify the size of the anti-poverty budget in conditions in which the rich experience disutility from work, a welfarist approach to optimal transfers is required. This is presented below in brief and in a very simplified way. Kaplow (2007) provides a more detailed account.

In public economics, especially when focused on developed countries, the analysis of transfer programmes belongs within the study of tax transfer schemes (Kaplow, 2006; Mirrlees, 1971). The broad features of this approach are noted briefly here. In a developed economy with a population showing heterogeneous productive capacity, a social planner committed to maximising a utilitarian social welfare function could

---

[23] 'In my judgement the drawing of a single poverty line can often confuse rather than clarify the analysis of income distribution and transfers. [I]t diverts our attention from the central points which concern standards of living and redistribution between people at different levels of real income' (Stern, 1987: 139).

rely on a single instrument, the tax code, to redistribute income from the better off to the worse off. The justification for redistribution flows from the specific welfarist approach adopted. Diminishing marginal utility entails a representative individual drawing diminishing utility from increasing consumption. It follows that a transfer of income from the better off to the worse off raises aggregate social welfare. This provides a justification for progressive transfers. The extent of redistribution will depend on social preferences and on the efficiency of the tax code. Social preferences can reveal themselves through democratic processes generating specific mandates for elected representatives. The efficiency of the tax code depends on maintaining incentives, first among taxpayers to ensure that they are willing to finance redistribution, and second among transfer beneficiaries to ensure that they rely, as far as possible, on their own resources. A revenue agency collects taxes from the better off and pays benefits to worse-off groups at short intervals.[24] The optimal tax framework thus described provides a unified approach to transfers and their financing, ensuring an optimal trade-off between efficiency and equity objectives.

The optimal non-linear taxation literature developed from the seminal contributions of Mirrlees (1971) and Diamond (1967). They set out to provide a comprehensive account of taxes and transfers, taking account of incentives and information problems. Mirrlees and Diamond identify optimal tax transfers in situations in which individuals differ in their abilities – differences the government is unable to observe directly. In the absence of taxes and transfers, these differences in ability among the population will generate different levels of welfare. A concern with inequality and a concern for low-income households recommend that the social planner taxes the rich and provides transfers to households in poverty. The fact that the government is unable to observe ability levels directly means that the taxes required to implement redistribution to the worse off will necessarily affect incentives. A highly skilled individual might decide to go slow in order to masquerade as a low-skilled individual and reduce his or her tax liabilities. The issue is to minimise this distortion while maximising some social welfare function. This suggests a tax schedule, as in Figure 4.3. The tax schedule

---

[24] There are, of course, huge practical implications associated with the operationalisation of tax transfer schemes, even in the most advanced economies. For a discussion in the context of the United Kingdom, see Mirrlees *et al.* (2011).

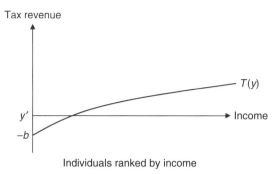

Figure 4.3 Optimal non-linear tax schedule

$T(y)$ involves a positive tax above a level of income y' but a negative tax $-b$ below this threshold. This tax schedule could be implemented through alternative and equivalent schemes. One possible scheme would involve a tax exemption below y' and a transfer $-b$ that phases out at this threshold. The approach thus provides a combined treatment of taxes and transfers.[25]

The optimal non-linear tax literature is hard to translate into practical guidance on the shape of tax and transfer schedules.[26] Bradbury (2004) identifies three main policy findings arising from this literature: (a) the marginal tax rate should be non-negative everywhere; (b) the marginal tax for the highest income individual should tend towards zero; and (c) it will generally be optimal to have at least some people choosing not to work. This is because their productivity is low and insufficient to compensate for the disutility associated with work.

What are the implications for the design of anti-poverty transfers?[27] The first finding from the optimal non-linear tax literature is consistent with the empirical finding that individuals in poverty often face high marginal tax rates. This is obvious in the context of income maintenance programmes, in which the phasing out of benefits amounts to a

---

[25] It is important to keep in mind that the focus here is not on particular transfer programmes, or particular taxes, but all taxes and transfers combined.

[26] As Kaplow observes, there 'is a natural reluctance to tether the study of transfer programmes to work on nonlinear income taxation. Explicit analysis is difficult to understand, much less perform; there are few general analytical results' (2007: 323). See also Diamond and Saez (2011) and Mankiw, Weinzierl and Yagan (2009).

[27] Kaplow notes 'a substantial gap between the existing literature on optimal nonlinear taxation and that on the design of transfer programs' (2007: 322)

marginal tax rate of 100 per cent.[28] In developing countries, on the other hand, transfers are fixed in level and often a fraction of the poverty gap, so the phasing out is in fact a cliff withdrawal. The fact that they are reviewed at fixed intervals, combined with widespread informality, means that work disincentives are weak. The second finding is not especially relevant or problematic, as it refers to the richest individual, not the richest group (Brewer, Saez and Shephard, 2010). The more interesting point on this finding is that simulations of the optimal non-linear taxation schedule suggest fairly flat tax schedules, as opposed to the rising marginal income tax schedules commonly associated with equity-oriented policy prescriptions, but with tax rates for high-income individuals at a much higher level than the current situation in developed and developing countries. The third finding is perhaps the most problematic from a poverty reduction perspective. It is consistent with persistent levels of unemployment among low-income groups.[29]

The framework required to study social assistance transfer programmes in developing countries will differ in important respects from the scheme described above (Kanbur, 1994). In the context of social assistance in developing countries, the primary focus of tax-financed transfer programmes is not utility maximisation but a non-welfarist objective:[30] to ensure that individuals and households reach a basic standard of living. Some parameters are shared across non-welfarist approaches to poverty eradication and welfarist approaches to redistribution, such as the need to address issues of information and incentives in the design of the programmes (Besley and Coate, 1995). Other parameters are unique to each approach.

---

[28] Studies covering developed countries find high phase-out rates, especially when the combined impact of separate social assistance programmes is considered. See Brewer, Saez and Shephard (2010).

[29] This is especially problematic in the context of proposals for 'global' redistributive schemes, such as those put forward by Pogge (2004), Mirrlees (2005) and Townsend (2009). A simulation of a 'global' optimal taxation approach finds that this would result in higher welfare in developing countries, but also significantly higher unemployment; see Kopczuk, Slemrod and Yitzhaki (2005).

[30] The dominant approach in poverty reduction is non-welfarist. Besley and Coate note that poverty 'seems universally to be measured without trying to gauge the value of any leisure enjoyed by the poor', a fact that they 'see as reflecting the attitudes of tax-payers who have to finance such programmes' (1995: 189). For a detailed justification of a non-welfarist approach in the context of anti-poverty transfers, see, among others, Besley and Coate (1995) and Kanbur (1994).

Kaplow's analysis of transfers in an optimal non-linear taxation setting generates some results that are in line with the findings from non-welfarist approaches discussed in the previous subsection. The optimal non-linear taxation approach is built on the assumption that ability levels are not directly observable. To the extent that some classification is feasible, the results from this approach will be different. In this new context, more generous transfers to groups with little or no ability would be optimal, and would be unlikely to affect work incentives. Kaplow (2007) notes that transfers based on age or disability in the United States are more generous than transfers to working-age groups. As regards transfers with work inducements, he concludes that these are optimal only in a context in which the externalities from work among lower-income groups are large – as, for example, when work raises human capital through work experience. Aside from this particular case, transfers with work requirements are suboptimal in a welfarist setting.

Some studies have considered the implications of reformulating the optimal non-linear tax approach within a non-welfarist setting. Bradbury (2004) argues that switching to a non-welfarist poverty eradication objective would naturally lead to a stronger focus on those at the bottom of the income distribution, perhaps drawing attention to the need to reduce marginal tax rates in order to provide stronger work incentives for this group. Bradbury points out, perhaps most importantly, that 'since there is no social benefit from the leisure of the poor, the need for income transfers to them is greater' (315). Kanbur (1994) provides a more rigorous analysis on the implications of switching to a non-welfarist poverty reduction objective. He concludes that the switch does not lead to results significantly different from those highlighted above, especially regarding the optimality of high marginal rates of taxation at the bottom of the income distribution. He does find that, if the employment of low-income groups constitutes an additional objective, then lower marginal tax rates at the bottom of the distribution, or earnings subsidies, are consistent with optimal tax transfer schemes.[31]

---

[31] In the context of developed countries, Diamond and Saez (2011) argue that, because work responses are most significant along the extensive margin, whether low-income individuals work or not, subsidies to low-income individuals in work can be optimal.

This result also emerges in circumstances in which categorical selection can provide information on ability levels (Immonen *et al.*, 1998).

Conclusions

This chapter has focused on identifying the key parameters guiding the design and implementation of optimal social assistance transfers. It is time to summarise the main conclusions.

How is it best to allocate an insufficient budget to an anti-poverty programme? Asking the question in a context in which information and incentives constraints are assumed to be unproblematic reveals that the design of an optimal anti-poverty transfer programme depends on its objectives, and particularly on the poverty index selected. Given that poverty indexes lay bare the embedded ethical judgements, selecting a poverty index to be minimised is as much an exercise in ethics as in programming. Policymakers seeking to minimise the poverty headcount will focus on those closer to the poverty line (Keen, 1992). Alternatively, minimising the severity of poverty, the poverty gap squared, recommends focusing resources on the poorest households.

What parameters need to be considered in the design of effective transfer programmes in the presence of identification and incentives constraints? The focus on optimal income maintenance transfers recommends separating out a first stage, identifying the main parameters of a cost-minimising transfer programme; and a second stage, specifying the poverty threshold. Minimising the costs for a particular level for poverty reduction requires paying attention to classifying the target population through direct and/or indirect strategies. Indirect strategies involve using programme design features, especially the benefit package, to facilitate screening and self-selection. Ensuring that beneficiaries rely as far as possible on their own resources suggests a need to pay attention to maximising investment in their productive capacity. Work requirements and service utilisation conditions were discussed as a means to provide a deterrent against disinvestment in productive capacity. Finally, design features to preserve work incentives were discussed briefly.

What should the size of an anti-poverty budget be? In an income maintenance transfer setting, the anti-poverty budget is dependent on the programme costs associated with given levels of poverty reduction and the poverty reduction preferences of taxpayers. Social preferences for poverty reduction largely determine the generosity of anti-poverty transfers through the determination of a target poverty threshold. Taking into account the potential effects of anti-poverty transfers on the work incentives of taxpayers requires a welfarist perspective. Applying a welfarist perspective to the design and implementation of anti-poverty transfers means that the size of the anti-poverty budget is determined by optimal non-linear taxation.

There are few policy prescriptions emerging from this literature, and they are contested. The literature focused on the intensive margin concurs on the need for positive high marginal rates of taxation for low-skilled workers, and therefore significant levels of unemployment for those at the bottom of the distribution. Paying attention to the extensive margin instead, or shifting to a non-welfarist approach, suggests that subsidies to low-skilled groups in work are consistent with optimal non-linear taxation. In-work subsidies can enhance the anti-poverty budget.

PART III

Practice

5 | *Anti-poverty transfers in practice*

This chapter provides an introduction to the main types of anti-poverty transfer programmes in developing countries, their objectives and their main features. The political and economic conditions within which social assistance has taken root in developing countries have ensured a focus on self-standing flagship programmes, as opposed to institutions. The reasons behind a programme approach to social assistance are complex and often country-specific. They include fiscal constraints, political opposition, knowledge gaps and uncertainty, the time window of aid and the hubris of 'silver bullets' in international development policy. As a consequence, the focus of attention in this chapter is on programmes. In the pioneer countries, a shift in policy and practice from flagship programmes to institutions that are stable and, more or less, permanent is under way. The shift towards further institutionalisation of social assistance will determine the future shape of social protection in the South.

The Introduction noted the astonishing growth of social assistance in developing countries since the middle of the 1990s. The *Dibao* scheme in China, for example, expanded from just over 2 million beneficiaries in 1999 to over 22 million in 2002, in response to rising unemployment; the child support grant in South Africa, introduced in 1998, managed to reach over 9 million children by 2007; and the Mahatma Gandhi National Rural Employment Guarantee scheme in India, which began in 2005, reached 49 million households by 2009. It is estimated that social assistance programmes in developing countries reached well over three-quarters of a billion people by 2010. The reach of anti-poverty transfer programmes in developing countries underlines their contribution to global poverty reduction, and signals their emergence as a key component of development strategies in the South.

There is significant diversity in programme design and objectives. This is a reflection of domestic political processes, as well as country experience and learning from past implementation of anti-poverty policies. Learning what does or does not deliver poverty reduction at the country and regional levels has informed innovation and adaptation in the design of social assistance programmes. The Mahatma Gandhi National Rural Employment Guarantee scheme in India developed out of the lessons from earlier public works programmes in rural India. Brazil's *Bolsa Família* reflects over a decade of learning and experimentation, leading first to the adoption of *Bolsa Escola* on a national scale and later to its integration into other anti-poverty transfer programmes. Despite the best efforts of multilateral organisations to claim credit for the expansion of social assistance, this is to a large extent a Southern initiative and a national response to policy challenges. The diversity in programme design across developing countries and regions reflects this.

The chapter begins by setting out a classification of anti-poverty transfer programmes in developing countries, based on the approach to poverty underlying their design. The taxonomic premise is that the programme design reflects an understanding of the nature of local poverty, and its remedies. Applying this approach generates a small number of programme types ('ideal types') and facilitates an understanding of key design features and expected effects. It also provides a means of comparing and assessing transfer programmes. Table 5.1 presents summary information on examples of programmes for each of these ideal types. The chapter then examines five key areas of programme design: programme objectives; strategies for beneficiary selection; transfer modalities; co-responsibilities and conditions; and duration and exit. These areas of programme design provide empirical counterparts and applications of the theoretical parameters of transfer programmes identified and examined in Chapter 4. Throughout, the chapter adopts a 'positive' approach in seeking to generalise from the information extracted from the specific design of existing programmes.

Social assistance in developed and developing countries

The anti-poverty transfer programmes emerging in developing countries stand in sharp contrast to the long-standing social assistance institutions in developed countries, distinguished from them by their function, scope and scale. In developed countries, social assistance is largely a residual safety net charged with protecting a small minority of

Table 5.1 *Social assistance in developing countries: summary information on selected programmes, most recent information*

Main type	Programme family	Title (start, scale-up)	Objective(s)	Selection	Transfers	Co-responsibility	Duration and exit
Pure income transfer	*Income transfers targeted at poorest*	Kalomo Pilot Social Transfer scheme, Zambia (2004). 10,000 households.	Reduce poverty and vulnerability among poorest households with children and no work capacity.	Proxy means test (assets, income sources, household demographics) implemented by village committees produces a ranking, checked by district committees. Selects 10% poorest households in village.	Household monthly transfer US$10–14 depending on number of children.	None.	Indefinite with regular review of eligibility.
	Categorical income transfer	Old Persons Grant, South Africa (1928, 1996). 2.4 million beneficiaries.	Reduce poverty and vulnerability among older people and their households.	Categorical: age 60 and over. Means test on income and assets of beneficiary and spouse only.	Monthly transfers. Maximum is US $118.	None.	Indefinite with regular review of eligibility.
		Child Support Grant, South Africa (1998). 9 million beneficiaries.	Reduce child malnutrition and poverty and facilitate investment in schooling.	Categorical: children aged below 18. Means test on parent/ guardian whether income and assets<10 times benefit.	Monthly transfer per child is US$35.	None, but under consideration by government.	Up to age 17 with regular review of eligibility.
Income transfers combined with asset accumulation	*Public works, cash for work, employment guarantees*	Mahatma Gandhi National Rural Employment Guarantee scheme, India (2007). 52 million households in 2010/2011.	Smooth seasonal employment and income fluctuations.	Categorical: unemployed heads of household. Geographic: rural areas. Self-selection through wage level <= minimum wage.	Up to 100 days work at minimum agricultural wage.	Supply labour.	Indefinite with regular review of eligibility.

Table 5.1 (*cont.*)

Main type	Programme family	Title (start, scale-up)	Objective(s)	Selection	Transfers	Co-responsibility	Duration and exit
		Productive Safety Net Programme, Ethiopia (2006). 1.7 million households.	Protect food insecurity households from seasonal variations in employment and prevent asset depletion.	Geographic: food insecure areas. Categorical: households with 3 years continued entitlement to food protection relief	January–June; 5 days work per month at US$1 a day.	Supply labour, not required for households receiving direct support.	Expected 5-year cycle before graduation.
	Human development targeted conditional transfers	*Bolsa Família*, Brazil (2001/2003). 12.7 million households in 2010.	Supplement income for poorest households to ensure improvements in consumption, investment in human capital; utilisation of basic services aiming to reduce current and intergenerational persistence of poverty.	Households in extreme poverty, per capita income below ¼ of minimum wage, or moderate poverty, per capita income between ¼ and ½ of the minimum wage.	Household monthly transfer is US$36 plus US$18 for each child aged up to 15 and US$20 for each child aged 16 or 17; moderately poor households receive child transfer only.	School attendance and health care utilisation.	Indefinite with regular review of eligibility.
		Oportunidades, Mexico (1997/2002). 5 million beneficiaries in 2009.	Supplement income for poorest households to ensure improvements in consumption, investment in human capital; utilisation of basic services aiming to reduce current and intergenerational persistence of poverty.	Initially geographic targeting, household proxy means test, plus community validation; now extended nationwide, therefore geographic targeting relaxed.	Household monthly transfer (US$18) and schooling transfers (average US$10 per child); old age (US $15). Preferential access to education and health providers; college transfer; microenterprise training.	School attendance and health care utilisation.	Initially for the duration of the programme, now indefinite with regular review of eligibility.
Integrated poverty reduction programmes	Integrated and sequential interventions	Challenging the Frontiers of Poverty Reduction – Targeting the Ultra	Stabilise consumption of poorest households and improve their human and	Geographic: districts with high incidence of ultra-poor. Participatory rural	Health services; asset transfers; microenterprise	Participation in health and microenterprise training.	3-year cycle, if successful leading to microcredit.

Programme type	Example	Objective	Selection/targeting	Instruments	Conditions	Duration
	Poor, Bangladesh (2002). 0.5 million households.	productive asset base to the point where conventional microfinance programmes could help asset accumulation.	appraisal to identify poorest villages. Proxy means test to identify ultra-poor households (no land, no male adult, no productive assets and children of school age in work).	training and support; income transfer.		
Broad-based social assistance	Dibao, China Minimum Living Standard scheme for urban population (1994, 2009). 24 million beneficiaries.	Compensate households in extreme poverty for poverty gap; ensure supportive services and active labour market instruments.	Means test to assess poverty gap.	Transfers vary by city, plus preferential access to services.	None.	Indefinite with regular review of eligibility.
Integrated poverty eradication programme	Chile Solidario, Chile (2004, replaced in 2012). 0.25 million beneficiaries.	Eradicate extreme poverty caused by social exclusion by supporting poorest households in achieving minimum thresholds across 7 main dimensions of well-being: income, employment, housing, health, education, registration and household dynamics.	Geographic: identified number of extreme poor and vulnerable in regions. Proxy-means test: ranks households applying for support – valid for 2 years.	Public subsidies. Preferential access to services. Intermediation and psychosocial support. Programme participation transfer.	Agreement on relevant activities and behaviour from household members aimed at meeting minimum thresholds.	2-year intervention phase plus 3-year monitoring phase. Households can go through the programme only one time.

Source: Barrientos, Niño-Zarazúa and Maitrot (2010).

individuals and households from the effects of poverty. Social assistance is residual because it kicks off only after all the other components of social protection – social insurance, basic services, labour market regulation – have proved unsuccessful.

Conditions in developing countries define a different role for social assistance. In most developing countries, social insurance covers at best a minority of the labour force, basic services are highly stratified and labour market regulations are thin and poorly enforced. Added to this, the incidence of absolute poverty and vulnerability in developing countries is significantly higher than in developed countries. As a consequence, social assistance is called to play an earlier and more comprehensive role than in developed countries (Barrientos, 2007; Leisering, 2010).

In developing countries, social assistance is far from residual. The incidence of absolute poverty and vulnerability in developing countries is high, especially in low-income countries.[1] The limited role of social insurance institutions, in part a reflection of the high incidence of informality, means that few have access to social protection. Social assistance is the only form of protection for a large section of the population. In addition to its protective role, social assistance in developing countries is called on to strengthen the productive capacity of households in poverty, whether through investment in human, financial or physical assets. It is also expected to improve access to basic services and therefore weaken social exclusion. In comparison with its essentially residual and compensatory role in developed countries, social assistance in developing countries is a key component of development strategies. It has a primary role within social protection; it is developmental in scope and increasingly large in scale.

In developed countries, the role of social assistance is being re-evaluated (Adema, 2006; Gough *et al.*, 1997).[2] The high and sustained unemployment experienced by Organisation for Economic Co-operation and Development countries in the 1980s led to social security reforms that focused on improving work incentives for beneficiaries of social assistance (OECD, 1994). They involved complementing income

---

[1] In low-income countries in sub-Saharan Africa, a majority of the population could plausibly be supported with social assistance.

[2] In developed countries, social assistance focuses on individuals, whereas, in developing countries, the focus is the household unit.

support with 'active' labour market policies: a combination of training, intermediation and subsidies focused on the unemployed. The recovery of employment levels in the 1990s further refocused active labour market policies on improving labour market participation among groups experiencing social exclusion (OECD, 1999). Social security reforms have transformed the role of social assistance in developed countries, widening it to include the prevention of extreme hardship, the promotion of social inclusion and cohesion, the integration of excluded groups into employment and the promotion of self-sufficiency. Adema notes that 'holistic' approaches in these countries combine financial assistance to achieve minimum standards of living, social support to deal with underlying deficits and 'employment supports to help households with their integration in the labour market thereby regaining their autonomy' (Adema, 2006: 14). Although these reforms suggest alignment in social assistance policies in the North and South, key differences remain.

In developing countries, the focus of social assistance remains the reduction of absolute, and often extreme, poverty. The leading role of social assistance in many developing countries calls for fresh approaches and models. Three innovations are especially important in understanding emerging social assistance programmes in developing countries: the role of incentives; the integration of related and complementary interventions; and the focus on asset accumulation. These three innovations are often combined in existing programmes.

At the core of most social assistance programmes in developing countries are direct transfers to households in poverty. These transfers are not expected, by themselves, to lift beneficiary households to the poverty line threshold. Even among the handful of programmes transferring benefits equivalent to the poverty line – such as social pensions in Brazil, which are pegged to the level of the minimum wage – widespread sharing of the transfer within extended households undermines any income maintenance objective. In most programmes, direct transfers to households in poverty amount to a fraction of the poverty threshold. Transfers are, effectively, a supplement to household income or consumption, which means incentive effects are particularly significant. Whereas income maintenance programmes are able to rely on the income effect of transfers to lift households out of poverty, in developing countries incentive effects are crucial to the poverty reduction effectiveness of social assistance programmes.

Direct income transfers to beneficiary households are increasingly combined with other interventions facilitating human, physical or financial asset accumulation.[3] Among households in poverty, human assets are the most significant. In Latin America, programmes combining income transfers with conditions relating to children's schooling and primary health care utilisation have attracted considerable attention. Transfers are guaranteed for a period of time on the condition that beneficiary households ensure that children attend school regularly and that all household members, especially expectant mothers and infants, attend health care units for regular check-ups. Chile's *Chile Solidario* takes this approach a step further, by combining income transfers with interventions on seven dimensions of well-being: housing, health, income, education, registration, employment and intra-household dynamics. The actual transfer is very small and mainly has the objective of ensuring that households remain in the programme. The core of the programme is focused on facilitating access to the whole gamut of public programmes and subsidies. While income transfers have a central and leading role in most social assistance programmes in developing countries, complementary interventions to ensure preferential access to services are important components too.

Social assistance programmes in developing countries have innovated in placing greater weight on the incentive effects of social assistance, but also in packaging related interventions, and in focusing attention on asset accumulation, broadly understood. These three innovations figure prominently in the design of programmes.

Typology of anti-poverty transfer programmes in developing countries

The diversity of programme design across developing countries makes it useful to identify 'ideal types'. A classification of transfer programmes will facilitate an understanding of the main features of these programmes.

---

[3] In international development, assets are commonly understood as physical productive assets, such as tools, seeds or tractors. In this book, the term 'assets' is used more broadly, to describe the productive potential of households, including human, physical and financial assets.

Before developing this classification, clarification is needed on the range of programmes included under social assistance. This makes it necessary to distinguish social assistance within the broader category of policies and programmes addressing poverty. The World Bank, and other Washington-based multilaterals, use the term 'safety net' in connection with all programmes and interventions focused on poverty reduction in developing countries (Grosh *et al.*, 2008; Weigand and Grosh, 2008).[4] For our purposes, it is important to make a distinction between emergency and humanitarian programmes, on the one hand, and social assistance programmes, on the other. The former include short-term assistance in response to crises, whereas the latter refer to long-term institutions focused on reducing and preventing poverty.[5]

The classification below focuses on the latter programmes, and excludes emergency and humanitarian assistance. Some low-income countries have programmes providing one-off transfers of assets (cash or agricultural inputs) aimed at supporting small-scale subsistence agriculture. These programmes are excluded from the classification below, which focuses instead on programmes providing regular transfers to households in poverty. In other countries, the reduction or elimination of user fees to access basic services has important implications for poverty reduction – such as Uganda's free primary education policy, Universal Primary Education. However, these interventions are also left out of the discussion below because they are not focused specifically on households in poverty. The same applies to voucher schemes when these are not focused on households in poverty. Our concern here is with tax-financed programmes providing regular transfers, in cash or in kind, to households in poverty.[6]

Analytically, it is useful to classify social assistance programmes into three main categories: pure income transfers; income transfers combined with asset accumulation; and integrated poverty reduction programmes.

---

[4] Safety nets are defined as 'non-contributory transfers targeted in some manner to the poor and vulnerable' (Weigand and Grosh, 2008: 2).

[5] Many linkages exist between emergency and humanitarian assistance and social assistance. Transfers in cash are increasingly common in emergency or humanitarian assistance, and there is also a great deal of interest in linking up short-term emergency assistance with longer-term institutions. See Harvey (2005).

[6] Programmes wholly or partially financed from official international assistance are also tax-financed, although taxes are collected in a different jurisdiction.

Pure income transfers include transfers in cash targeted specifically at households in poverty and also categorical transfers targeted at groups considered particularly vulnerable. Some pure income transfers are focused on households in (extreme) poverty. For example, the Kalomo Pilot Social Transfer scheme in Zambia provides direct transfers to the poorest 10 per cent of households in designated districts. Other programmes – such as child or family allowances or social pensions – are focused on specific groups in the population thought to be especially vulnerable. South Africa's social assistance is organised in the main through means-tested categorical grants focused on older people, people with disabilities, and children.

Income transfers combined with asset accumulation include programmes providing transfers in cash or kind, which are combined with, and facilitate, the accumulation of productive assets. The term 'asset' is used here in its broadest sense, to include human, physical and financial assets. Linking direct transfers with interventions aimed at asset accumulation underlines the fact that programmes of this type aim to strengthen the productive capacity of households in poverty.

This category includes two families of programmes now common in developing countries. The first group includes programmes that combine direct transfers with interventions facilitating household investment in human development, especially education and health. Mexico's *Oportunidades* and Brazil's *Bolsa Família* are well-known examples of this family of programmes. The second group includes programmes that combine direct transfers with interventions facilitating physical asset protection and accumulation. Examples of this type of programme include India's Mahatma Gandhi National Rural Employment Guarantee scheme (infrastructure or community assets) and Ethiopia's Productive Safety Net Programme (household and community assets). The latter combines transfers in cash or in kind with agricultural extension activities for households with work capacity, and direct support to households without work capacity. These programmes require beneficiaries to supply work to create or protect household or community assets. They can also be described as public works, cash/food for work or guaranteed employment programmes.[7]

---

[7] This family of programmes can also accommodate climate change adaptation and environmental protection programmes. The Chars Livelihood Programme in Bangladesh is an early prototype.

Integrated poverty reduction programmes are an important innovation in social assistance, combining a range of interventions focused on the poorest. Bangladesh's Challenging the Frontiers of Poverty Reduction – Targeting the Ultra Poor provides an integrated and sequential set of interventions strengthening the nutrition and health status of the poorest households, as well as training in preparation for the transfer of productive assets. Chile's *Chile Solidario* (like China's *Dibao* and South Korea's Minimum Living Standards scheme) is an additional example of only a handful of programmes providing an integrated set of interventions addressing a range of deficits responsible for keeping households in poverty.

Table 5.1 provides examples of these types of programme in developing countries, and summarises information on key dimensions.[8] These are discussed in the remainder of the chapter.

The conceptual basis for this classification is provided by the underlying understanding of poverty underpinning the programmes. Pure transfers rely on an understanding of poverty as largely to do with deficits in income or consumption. Transfers are expected to remedy these deficits and thus reduce poverty, and to that extent this type of programme borrows from social assistance in developed countries. Income transfers combined with asset accumulation share a broader understanding of poverty. They pay attention to deficits in income or consumption, but, important as these are, they also aim to address deficits in productive assets.[9] Programmes focused on human development, such as Mexico's *Oportunidades*, understand the persistence of poverty as arising from deficits in human capital. Ethiopia's Productive Safety Net Programme understands poverty and its persistence as arising from asset depletion and destruction affecting food-insecure households faced with droughts or other shocks. Programmes included in this group adopt a multidimensional understanding of poverty, but focus on a few dimensions. Integrated poverty reduction programmes also share a multidimensional understanding of poverty, but are distinguished both by a wider set of dimensions covered and by the fact that direct

---

[8] The table is extracted from the 'Social assistance in developing countries' database, which can be accessed at http://papers.ssrn.com/sol3/papers.cfm?abstract_id=1672090, where information on specific programmes mentioned in the chapter can be found.

[9] Asset deficits are usually described as deprivation in the developed country literature.

income transfers play only a marginal role in the overall support provided to households in poverty.[10] These programmes pay particular
attention to social exclusion as an important factor explaining poverty
persistence.

Programme objectives

To understand the scope and design of social assistance programmes, it
is essential to start from their stated objectives. All social assistance
programmes aim to reduce poverty, but they are grounded in specific
understandings of the factors generating poverty and, in particular,
assessments of the feasibility and effectiveness of potential remedies.
These result in a distinctive set of objectives for each programme.
Mexico's *Progresa*, for example, aims to reduce the intergenerational
persistence of poverty in rural Mexico.[11] India's Mahatma Gandhi
National Rural Employment Guarantee aims to protect poor households from the impact of seasonal unemployment among rural households in India. South Africa's Child Support Grant initially had the
objective of reducing child malnutrition.[12] Beyond a generic concern
to address poverty and vulnerability, social assistance programmes are
shaped by very specific understandings of poverty, which in turn are
shaped by knowledge, interests and values.

There is a distinction to be made, with far-reaching implications for
programme design, with regard to the extent to which programmes aim
to reduce current and/or future poverty. All transfer programmes seek
to improve current consumption among households in poverty, and
therefore to have an impact on current poverty. Pure income transfers
are typically focused on supplementing the current consumption of
households. Income transfer programmes combined with asset accumulation, and especially human development, aim to have an impact
not just on current poverty but also on future poverty, by facilitating
household investment in schooling and health care, for example.
Addressing poverty duration and persistence constitutes a core objective of these programmes. Co-responsibilities around children's

---

[10] The initial design of Chile's *Chile Solidario* was also distinguished by its focus on
capability; see Barrientos (2010a).

[11] For an account of the origins of the programme, see Levy (2006).

[12] An insider account of the origins of the programme is provided by Lund (2008).

schooling reflect directly on the objective of reducing future poverty, but other design features are relevant too. The design of the transfers also reflects on the objective of ensuring improvements in the productive capacity of the household over time and reducing future poverty. Such design feature examples include setting transfers per child of school age or raising the value of the transfer with the grade attended and achieved. These design features aim to reduce the likelihood of poverty in the future. Put in a different way, these programmes aim to generate outcomes over and above the improvement in current consumption supported by the transfer. An important factor in explaining programme design is the mix, and relative weight, of current/future poverty objectives in the design of the programmes.[13]

Programme objectives are underpinned by knowledge of the factors responsible for poverty. Increasingly, poverty analysis has converged on the view that poverty and poverty persistence in developing countries are a consequence of multiple deprivations, including limited economic opportunity, insufficient basic services and restricted voice and representation (Thorbecke, 2007). This multidimensional understanding of poverty, and especially poverty persistence, has influenced the design of anti-poverty transfer programmes in seeking to integrate a range of interventions relating to basic service access and utilisation. This is the perspective underpinning human development programmes in Latin America and elsewhere (Coady and Morley, 2003; Fiszbein and Schady, 2009).

More recently an understanding that social exclusion, and particularly economic exclusion, is a primary factor in explaining why people remain in poverty is beginning to influence programme design (Sen, 1999). The underlying perception is that economic growth and service provision often bypass the extremely poor, and that income supplements alone are insufficient to bridge this gap (Bourguignon, 2005). In many contexts, this reflects social exclusion of the poorest in its widest sense. Proactive engagement with households in extreme or persistent

---

[13] This point comes up in discussions on conditions and their feasibility in low-income country contexts (see Barrientos, 2011a). Some commentators argue that, for a variety of reasons, conditions are unnecessary and should be removed from human-development-focused transfer programmes. They often overlook the linkages existing between them and the objective of reducing future poverty. Removing conditions from transfer programmes may result in a change in the current/future poverty mix of the programme. This is taken up below.

poverty – including intermediation – through an integrated set of interventions is increasingly considered an effective means of strengthening their position. Chile's *Chile Solidario* is a good example of how programme design incorporates a multidimensional perspective on poverty, and of the need for proactive intermediation to overcome social exclusion (Ministerio de Planificación y Cooperación (MIDEPLAN), 2004).

Many programmes aim to tackle poverty and vulnerability. This is another way in which the current/future poverty mix of objectives emerges. Vulnerability is understood here as the likelihood that households will find themselves in poverty in the future (Dercon, 2006; Duclos, 2002). In the context of vulnerability, social assistance programmes aim to strengthen household resilience and contribute towards protecting consumption and assets in the event of shocks and crises. Ethiopia's Productive Safety Net Programme aims to protect household consumption and prevent asset depletion in food-insecure areas (Gilligan, Hoddinott and Seyoum Taffesse, 2008). The focus on vulnerability in programmes of this type constitutes a response to the seasonal nature of agricultural production and to the impact of environmental and weather shocks. At the same time, it is informed by an understanding that vulnerability is itself a factor leading to poverty persistence. High levels of vulnerability could in these contexts lead to short-term behavioural responses with long-term adverse consequences for the productive capacity of households.[14] The focus on vulnerability points to the need to incorporate into programme design an understanding of how households in poverty link current decisions to expectations about the future (de Janvry *et al.*, 2006).

Finally, the objectives of social assistance programmes increasingly include a 'productivist' dimension and a focus on strengthening the productive capacity of households (Barrientos, 2012). This is yet another area in which the current/future poverty objective mix is relevant. Permanent and sustainable exit from poverty in most cases involves engagement in economic activity by households in poverty, and productive capacity is crucial to achieving this. This has implications for the length of time that benefits are provided, for measures to

---

[14] There is a growing empirical literature lending support to this claim; see Dercon (2002), Elbers and Gunning (2003) and Imai and Gaiha (2004).

minimise adverse effects on employment incentives and for the integration of employment and microenterprise-oriented interventions.

To sum up, the study of emerging social assistance programmes in developing countries should begin by understanding programme objectives. All social assistance programmes aim to reduce poverty, but programme objectives reflect specific underlying perspectives on the main factors leading to poverty and assessments of appropriate and feasible interventions. In particular, the extent to which social assistance programmes mix current and future poverty reduction objectives strongly influences their design.

Beneficiary selection

Social assistance programmes employ a variety of strategies to select participants in line with programme objectives. This section introduces and assesses the main selection strategies.[15]

The overall effectiveness of social assistance programmes depends to an important extent on the effectiveness of selection processes.[16] The effectiveness of selection can be measured by the errors of inclusion (the extent to which selection wrongly includes non-poor households in a programme, or type II errors) and errors of exclusion (the extent to which selection wrongly excludes poor households from the programme, or type I errors) that different strategies generate. Political sensitivities around anti-poverty transfer programmes, relating to concerns over dependency, fairness and corruption, place further pressures and scrutiny on selection strategies. In many low-income developing countries, in which resources for poverty reduction are severely limited, it is often the case that only a fraction of households in poverty can be assisted, and selection is especially problematic.

I begin by distinguishing a set of programmes that rely on design features to induce the *self-selection* of beneficiaries (Besley and Coate, 1992; Ravallion and Datt, 1995). Typically, transfer programmes with work requirements can accommodate self-selection by making transfers

---

[15] Meta-studies of targeting strategies are available; see Castaneda and Lindert (2005) and Coady, Grosh and Hoddinott (2004).

[16] See Chapter 4 for a discussion of the role of selection in minimising the cost of programmes and Chapter 6 for a discussion on selection in the context of implementation issues. For a critical look at the focus of the literature on this issue, see Ravallion (2007).

conditional on the supply of labour, and setting programme transfers below the local market wage rate. The advantage of this approach is that people who are able to obtain employment at the market rate are unlikely to apply for transfers. The level of the transfer is crucial to ensuring an effective selection process. India's Mahatma Gandhi National Rural Employment Guarantee scheme sets transfers in line with the official minimum wage in agriculture, but a significant proportion of agricultural workers in India are paid well below the official minimum wage. This has led to concerns by private employers that the scheme may be restricting the pool of available workers and putting upward pressure on market wages. In circumstances in which the gender wage gap is large, the scheme could reinforce the segregation of women in subsidised work.

If self-selection is not feasible, programme designers must consider ways of selecting beneficiaries directly. *Categorical* selection based on easily identifiable demographic characteristics associated with high poverty incidence is one way forward (Akerlof, 1978). Selecting on the basis of the very young or the very old has the advantage that it fits with shared societal values, and assumptions, of life course variation in work capacity. This also applies, with modifications, to disability, orphanhood, single parenthood and widowhood. While it is true that shared perceptions leading to the identification of vulnerable groups are widely accepted and legitimised within most societies, it is often the case that only weak correlations exist between any of these characteristics and the incidence of poverty or extreme poverty.

A different approach to the selection of beneficiaries relies on some form of needs assessment. *Means tests* require potential beneficiaries to provide information on their income and assets, which programme managers use to determine eligibility. A disadvantage of means tests is that they provide incentives to beneficiaries at the margins of the entitlement thresholds to adjust their circumstances to meet the threshold. The old age grant in South Africa, for example, means-tests applicants on the basis of the income and assets of the applicant and his or her spouse, leaving aside the extended household. This is to prevent changes in household composition to meet the means test, which would result in elderly household members being unable to have the support of their families. In many contexts, the information that households provide is difficult, or costly, to verify. When budgetary constraints are binding, programme managers have incentives to use the test to manipulate the numbers of beneficiaries, for example by requiring costly documentation.

Proxy means tests use 'easy to observe – difficult to manipulate' household or individual variables to generate a welfare index, which is then used to decide on entitlement. Typically, the proxy means test is implemented through a visit by an enumerator to a household that is being considered for participation in a programme. The enumerator completes a short survey, capturing information such as the condition of the housing, the number of rooms or the number and age of household members. This information is processed and a score is generated for the household. The score is compared with a threshold level arrived at by examination of the scores of households on the poverty line in a relevant household survey.

There are several advantages associated with using proxy means tests. They produce a ranking of households, rather than the 'yes'/'no' assessment of means tests. They generate fewer incentives for households to manipulate their income or assets. They can be adapted to conditions in which large territorial differences prevail. Their main disadvantage is that the statistical models that generate the score are opaque to beneficiary households, and the scores generated could conflict with community assessments.[17] This lack of transparency can reduce support for the programme.

In low-income settings, means and proxy means tests might not be feasible or affordable. *Community selection* could be appropriate in this context. The advantage of community selection is that local information can be used to improve the effectiveness of the programme and enhance public support. However, community selection can be captured by local elites, and consistency in selection across communities can be difficult to achieve.[18] Several social assistance programmes in low-income countries in sub-Saharan Africa employ community selection. Social transfer programmes focusing on the poorest 10 per cent of the population in Zambia and Malawi select beneficiaries through village-level committees, which apply programme eligibility criteria and identify beneficiaries. The beneficiary lists are published at the village level and

---

[17] Programme managers have often sought to keep the formula used to generate the scores secret, in order to preclude manipulation – in the process exacerbating public concerns over selection. See Camacho and Conover (2009).

[18] The 10 per cent poorest in one village could be significantly better off than the 10 per cent poorest in another village.

scrutinised by committees at the district and regional levels (Schubert, 2008). Studies have found that the selection process works reasonably well, but the costs to the local communities are seldom accounted for.

In conditions in which poverty and vulnerability are concentrated spatially, *geographic selection* might prove effective. Territories can be ranked according to social and economic indicators, and programmes focused on the areas where poverty is concentrated. Techniques for generating poverty maps have been tested in different contexts and have proved effective as a means of identifying poorer areas (Bourguignon and Pereira da Silva, 2003).

All these strategies to select beneficiaries have been employed in developing countries, with varying degrees of success. The main findings from a meta-study in 2004 (Coady, Grosh and Hoddinott, 2004) are (a) that implementation is crucial to the effectiveness of selection and (b) that a combination of several selection strategies often works better than relying on a single strategy.

Mexico's *Oportunidades* employed a geographic ranking of communities to identify areas of operation. It then implemented a proxy means test to identify beneficiary households within selected communities, with the results later validated by local communities. This approach has been replicated in other human development income transfer programmes in Latin America, except for Honduras, where the incidence of poverty in marginalised communities was considered so high that it made more sense to 'select out' better-off households than to 'select in' households in poverty. In social assistance programmes in Brazil, the selection mix involves a comparison of per capita income with the national poverty line as well as categorical indicators, such as age or child labour.

Transfer modalities

In the recent literature on emerging social assistance, there is a strong emphasis on monetary transfers – cash as opposed to in-kind transfers. The cash versus in-kind option has special resonance in the context of low-income developing countries, in which international aid in the past focused on food transfer (Barrett and Maxwell, 2005). In Ethiopia's Productive Safety Net Programme, some beneficiaries are able to determine the mix of food and cash transfers they receive, which is helpful in the context of food supply and price volatility. Transfers in cash are the norm among emerging social assistance programmes in developing countries. However, a significant number of these programmes also include in-kind transfers, as well as preferential access to public programmes, as part of the transfer package.

Several factors influence the transfer package. From the perspective of economic theory, there is a presumption that transfers in cash dominate in-kind transfers when judged according to their impact on welfare (Besley and Kanbur, 1988; Thurow, 1974). In conditions in which markets operate reasonably effectively, in-kind transfers restrict the consumption of poor households in ways that could reduce the welfare gains from the transfer. Transfers in cash, on the other hand, leave beneficiary households free to allocate their consumption so as to maximise their welfare. With moderately developed financial institutions, transfers in cash are easier and cheaper to handle, and can be accounted for transparently.[19] In-kind transfers additionally involve procurement and distribution costs, and create incentives for monopolistic practices.[20]

Of course, there are several scenarios in which this presumption in favour of income transfers does not apply. Food price volatility, especially when a significant share of food consumed is imported, can undermine the poverty reduction effectiveness of cash transfers (Sabates-Wheeler and Devereux, 2010). Food transfers shift the impact of food price volatility onto programme agencies. In-kind transfers are employed in developing countries mainly to ensure that poor households actually consume certain goods and services; for example, taxpayers or programme managers may impose a particular form of consumption on programme beneficiaries, such as immunisations, vitamin A, nutrition supplements, primary health care utilisation, schooling, etc. *Bolsa Família* requires a minimum school attendance by children in beneficiary households. One can imagine circumstances in which in-kind transfers could be useful in facilitating self-selection among potential beneficiaries, such as when the transfer consists of goods or services that only poor households consume.[21] There are also situations in which a combination

---

[19] Transfers in cash through financial institutions can generate positive externalities. Beneficiaries of Brazil's social assistance programmes receive a magnetic card that signals to financial institutions that the bearer has a regular source of income, and has been observed to facilitate credit. See Delgado and Cardoso (2000).

[20] Food distribution is a case in point; see Tabor (2002).

[21] An example would be staple food of a lower quality than that consumed by better-off households. For a discussion of this approach and its limitations, see Bibi (2002).

of cash and in-kind transfers maximises the impact of a social assistance programme. For example, transfers to unemployed single parents are likely to be more effective if they are combined with preferential access to child care (Gahvari and Mattos, 2007).

An important feature of transfers is their regularity and duration. A key perspective informing the design of transfer programmes in developing countries is that facilitating exit from poverty requires support for extended periods of time that are sufficient to enable improved resilience and human development. Households in poverty are likely to use one-off transfers in different ways from regular and reliable transfers (Tabor, 2002). One-off income transfers are likely to be dissipated without observable medium-term effects, whereas regular and reliable transfers for a period of time could lead to a reallocation of household productive resources and/or investment in human development. Programme duration is discussed in more detail later in the chapter, but here it serves to emphasise the importance of regularity and reliability for transfers to achieve expected outcomes.

The level of transfers can be fixed or variable. Fixed transfers provide a given amount to a household (individual), independent of its needs or composition. With variable transfers, the level of the transfers is calculated on the basis of need or household characteristics. Fixed-level transfers are more common in low-income countries, given their limited financing and delivery capacity. These restrictions place a premium on simplicity in the design of the transfer. Fixed-level transfers help predict programme budgets with reasonable accuracy. Variable-level transfers are common in child-focused transfers, especially if attention is paid to the number and age of children in beneficiary households. They are also more common in middle-income countries with better administrative capacity. Few countries have needs-based income maintenance programmes, which dominate in developed countries. This is in part because of capacity constraints, but also follows from the different orientation of social assistance programmes. Categorical transfers are on the whole individually based, but in developing countries it is important to see them as a household transfer paid through a specified individual.[22]

---

[22] Studies have shown that categorical transfer beneficiaries share most of their transfer within the household; see Barrientos (2008a).

With regard to the value of the transfer, there is considerable variation across programmes and countries. Setting the level of the transfers often involves balancing programme objectives, available finance and delivery capacity. Programme objectives are the starting point. The level of the benefit should relate to the impact sought. Consider child-focused programmes, for example. If the objective of the programme is to reduce child labour, the level of the transfer should be sufficient to compensate households for the forgone earnings of children. If the objective of the programme is to facilitate school enrolment and attendance, the level of the transfer should be sufficient to compensate households for the monetary cost of children's schooling (fees, uniforms, transport, books, etc.).[23] Mexico's *Oportunidades* has a variable-level transfer, which includes a household consumption component plus additional amounts according to children's grade and sex, up to a ceiling. The child supplements are set to provide a larger incentive for girls to attend school, because their enrolment and attendance rates have been lower than those of boys; and are a step higher for secondary school grades, because enrolment and attendance rates dropped for secondary schools prior to the introduction of the programme. The value of the transfer should reflect the objectives of the programme.

In developing countries, resource availability often forces adjustment to the level of the benefit. In China's *Dibao*, benefit levels are supposed to cover the gap existing between the welfare of households in poverty and the city poverty line. It has been reported that the poverty line is set pragmatically at a level that reflects the available budget and the expected number of beneficiaries. India's Mahatma Gandhi National Rural Employment Guarantee scheme specifies 100 days' maximum entitlement per participant, but the actual average number of days worked varies significantly across estates. Interestingly, many governments, including those in Mexico, South Africa and Indonesia, responded to the global financial crisis in 2008/9 by raising the level of their social assistance programmes. As noted, in low-income countries delivery capacity is an important constraint on the design of transfers.[24]

---

[23] An appropriate benefit level in this case is equivalent to the measured private costs of education for households located on the poverty line. This benefit level would provide poor households with the same resources to spend on education as those available for households on the poverty line.

[24] It proved a great deal more difficult for low-income countries to respond in a similar fashion to the rise in food prices.

Looked at from the perspective of beneficiary households, the key measure of the value of transfers is the contribution of the transfer to household consumption. Even in the case of categorical benefits, which provide a transfer equivalent to the poverty line, sharing within households implies that the contribution to household consumption will be a fraction of the poverty line. Brazil's *Benefício de Prestação Continuada*, a non-contributory social pension, sets the benefit level at the official minimum wage; South Africa's old age grant has a very generous benefit of around US$75 per month. However, as a contribution to household consumption, these benefits are insufficient to lift poor households to the poverty line (Barrientos, 2008a). A rough and ready estimate of the median transfer level as a proportion of consumption in beneficiary households will be around 20 per cent. Although this is by no means a precise estimate, it underlines the fact that social assistance programmes in developing countries make a contribution to household income and expenditure, but are not sufficient to lift poor households to the poverty line. As a result, social assistance programmes contribute to reducing the poverty gap, but are unlikely to make a very significant contribution to reducing the poverty headcount. After two years of operation Mexico's *Oportunidades* managed to reduce the poverty gap among beneficiaries by 33 per cent, but the change in the poverty headcount was significantly lower (Skoufias, 2001).

It is therefore important to pay particular attention to the incentive effects of transfer programmes. Economists distinguish between income and substitution effects arising from additional household income. Take the hypothetical example of an income tax cut that leaves households with additional purchasing power. Households could consider raising their consumption evenly across the range of goods and services they purchase. This is the income effect of the tax cut. Now suppose that the government decides to cut value-added taxes collected on locally produced goods instead. This policy change is likely to lead to increased consumption by households across the goods and services they purchase (the income effect), but also a shift in consumption favouring locally produced goods. This is referred to as the substitution effect. In our context, transfers are equivalent to a tax cut, and transfers are likely to generate both income and substitution effects. Other programme design features, such as conditions, can reinforce a shift in the consumption of poor households. The incentive effects of transfers are particularly important here.

Co-responsibility and conditions

Many social assistance programmes make transfers conditional on participants investing in human capital or providing labour (Barrientos, 2011a; Barrientos and Santibañez, 2009a). Human development transfer programmes, such as Mexico's *Oportunidades*, require that children of school age in beneficiary households attend school, and that all household members attend primary health checks. The international literature describes these as conditions – that is, the requirements the programme imposes on beneficiaries are a condition of participation. In Latin American programmes, the term 'co-responsibility' is used to describe the conditions placed on beneficiaries and the responsibilities of programme agencies. In human development programmes, the main justification for the introduction of co-responsibilities is to achieve programme objectives relating to household investment in health and education. In programmes requiring beneficiary households to provide labour, the rationale for labour supply conditions is to do with facilitating the accumulation of assets, especially infrastructure.

There has been much critical discussion of conditions, focusing mainly on issues of effectiveness.[25] Critics of the use of conditions in anti-poverty programmes argue that conditions are ineffective, and unnecessary, as there is little hard evidence on their separate effect. Measuring the impact of human development programmes with and without conditions is extremely challenging in the absence of experimental data.[26] Given the ethical difficulties involved in such experiments, researchers have looked into programme implementation to identify whether 'natural experiments' could throw light on this issue.

The extension of the *Bono de Desarrollo Humano* in Ecuador, a human development transfer programme, is interesting. The programme was advertised to beneficiary households and the general public as including conditions on schooling and health, but in practice the government was not in a position to implement these. A study compared information on schooling responses from households that understood there was a relevant condition in the programme and households

---

[25] See the contributions to the August 2009 *Global Social Policy* forum (Yeates, 2009).

[26] Baird, McIntosh and Özler (2011) have tested the separate impact of unconditional and conditional transfers in Malawi.

reporting no knowledge of conditions. It found that the belief that conditions were part of the programme did positively influence their schooling decisions (Schady and Araujo, 2006). The initial introduction of Mexico's *Progresa* seems to provide another 'natural experiment'. Compliance with schooling conditions is monitored through a form that beneficiaries take to school to be filled in, but for administrative reasons a group of beneficiaries was not issued with the forms. A study compared the schooling responses of beneficiary households without forms or knowledge of conditions, and other groups of beneficiary households. Knowledge of conditions seems to have influenced schooling decisions at the secondary school level (de Brauw and Hoddinott, 2011).

These studies suggest that conditions may matter, but it is hard to generalise from these highly specific settings. At any rate, the effects are likely to be small. In Mexico, for example, school enrolment rates in primary education were above 90 per cent before the introduction of *Progresa*, so the effect of conditions could apply at best to the 10 per cent of children not enrolled in school. This is a point often missed in policy discussions. It is the marginal effect of conditions that measures their effectiveness (Barrientos and DeJong, 2006; Das, Do and Özler, 2005).

What justifications can be given for the inclusion of conditions in income transfer programmes? It can be argued that conditions are required to achieve programme objectives. In conditional transfer programmes aimed at securing an improvement in schooling or health status, the transfer can be made conditional on children attending school on a regular basis, or on regular access to primary health care by household members, in order to ensure that these objectives are achieved.

Conditions may be included for political economy justifications. To the extent that political, and therefore financial, support is predicated on taxpayers' perceptions of the objectives and effectiveness of anti-poverty programmes, conditions could help align programme objectives and priorities with taxpayers' priorities or preferences.[27] Alternative explanations for taxpayers' concerns are possible: paternalistic taxpayers may wish to impose their own values and priorities on beneficiaries; prudent taxpayers may be concerned to ensure that beneficiaries exit poverty, thereby limiting future liabilities; self-interested

---

[27] This explains, for example, the extent of work conditions in anti-poverty programmes in the United States; see Moffitt (2002). This, of course, does not imply that taxpayers' priorities are appropriate from a poverty reduction perspective.

taxpayers may be keen to prevent behaviour with adverse effects for themselves; for example, requiring children to be at school means they will be off the streets. Conditions could also be included to facilitate political support for income transfer programmes by signalling their focus on investment in human development and their strong commitment to delivering on programme objectives.

Although, in practice, conditions reflect a combination of the above, in Latin America the primary factor behind the adoption of co-responsibilities has been the need to achieve programme objectives (Cecchini and Martínez, 2011). These are deemed essential to help break the intergenerational cycle of poverty. Research has indicated that the utilisation of schooling and health care among those in poverty is low, even when these services are available. In the main, this occurs because those in poverty face high costs, relative to their resources, of accessing these services, and because of exclusion. Income transfers are supposed to help remove the cost barrier, while service providers are encouraged to reduce exclusion. Co-responsibilities are meant to ensure household investment in schooling and health care, and the co-responsibilities of service providers reduce exclusion and ensure a measure of coordination between programme managers and service providers. This is the theory; the practice can be more complicated.

There is considerable opposition to the inclusion of conditions in social assistance programmes. Some argue that conditions relating to health and education are unnecessary, because the majority of those in poverty would have sent their children to school, or attended primary health care, in the absence of conditions. They point to studies showing that social assistance programmes without conditions also show human development impacts. For example, studies of the impact of the old age grant in South Africa have concluded that school enrolments (Duflo, 2003) and health status (Case and Wilson, 2000) are higher in beneficiary households than in similar households without beneficiaries. This is fine up to a point, but we need to know more about the size of these effects, and why they appear to be strongly gendered in South Africa. The studies show that the school enrolment of girls, but not that of boys, rises when there is a female pensioner in the household. The studies also find no significant improvement in enrolment rates for boys and girls in households with male beneficiaries. By contrast, in Mexico's *Oportunidades*, enrolment rates of boys and girls show significant improvements, but especially among girls.[28]

Some make the point that conditions will not work where basic services are not available, especially in low-income countries in sub-Saharan Africa. Schooling conditions are unlikely to work when it is not possible to expand school places, but, if the objective of the programme is to increase enrolments and school attendance, unconditional income transfers will not work either. This point underlines the importance of co-responsibilities. The issue for low-income countries is to combine income transfers with improvements in basic service infrastructure.

Another argument against conditions focuses on the additional costs to the programme associated with their implementation. This is a programme-specific calculation, which should take account of benefits and costs. In rural Mexico, dropout rates at the start of secondary school, especially for girls, were unacceptably high. Estimates of the impact of *Oportunidades* suggest that, two years on from the start of the programme, enrolment rates had increased by as much as 9.3 percentage points (from a base of 67 per cent) for girls in secondary school (Skoufias, 2005). The calculation is whether the rise in enrolments is worth the 2 per cent of the programme budget absorbed by implementing conditions (Caldés, Coady and Maluccio, 2006).

A strong justification for not including conditions in social assistance programmes arises when these impose significant compliance costs on beneficiaries. To the extent that these costs are non-trivial, and are not accounted for in setting the level of the transfer, they are likely to compound the adverse situation of those in poverty.[29] As income transfer programmes seldom collect information on compliance costs, or attempt to account for these in setting benefits, this is an important concern.

A separate issue is whether developing countries should rely on 'soft' or 'hard' conditions (Bastagli, 2008). There is some evidence that it is the presence of conditions, and co-responsibilities, rather than their enforcement that encourages compliance among beneficiary

---

[28] Other factors are important too; the level of the Old Age Grant in South Africa is high, at US$75; and, in *Oportunidades*, the child-related transfers for girls are higher than for boys.

[29] Molyneux (2006) discusses the effects of compliance costs on mothers in *Oportunidades* and claims that these could contribute to reinforce gendered roles within the household.

households.[30] The suggestion here is that information and moral suasion might be doing most of the work in achieving programme objectives. Another lesson from the implementation of conditional transfer programmes is to 'economise' on the number of conditions included in the design of the programme. Jamaica's Programme of Advancement through Health and Education, a human development transfer programme, initially included nine conditions. These proved difficult to enforce, and were quickly reduced to three. Brazil's *Bolsa Família* uses cases of non-compliance as a signal that additional interventions might be required to support households in extreme poverty (Bastagli, 2008).

To conclude, many social assistance programmes require beneficiaries to invest in schooling, health care and nutrition. As with other design features of income transfers, conditions reflect programme objectives, social preferences and political factors, and have potential advantages and limitations. A particular concern with conditions is the extent to which they impose non-trivial compliance costs on beneficiaries that were not accounted for in setting benefit levels. Co-responsibilities can strengthen inter-agency coordination and priority setting, and as a consequence can strengthen the linkages between income transfers and basic services utilisation. Conditions are likely to be effective, if at all, at the margins.

Duration and exit

Another important, but less explored, dimension of social assistance in developing countries relates to the time window for interventions and for direct support to beneficiaries. In developed countries, the institutionalisation of social assistance is through more or less permanent institutions. In many developing countries, social assistance has been implemented as programmes or projects – that is, interventions with ad hoc administration and predefined time windows. Older programmes show a dynamic in their institutionalisation towards more stable and permanent institutions. Mexico's *Oportunidades* was introduced initially with a five-year window, and was later extended for a further five years. It is now difficult to imagine that it will be wound down; it is implemented through government agencies. Chile's *Chile Solidario* was

---

[30] See discussion on Ecuador's *Bono de Desarrollo Humano* and Mexico's *Oportunidades* above.

also introduced with a five-year time window, but it now has a permanent institutionalisation, with recognised legal status. Other programmes, such as Brazil's *Bolsa Família* and India's Mahatma Gandhi National Employment Guarantee scheme, have an open-ended time window and a permanent institutional structure. Among the programmes that did not survive long enough to secure institutionalisation is Nicaragua's *Red de Protección Social*.

There are several factors behind the shorter-term window of new social assistance programmes in developing countries. In some cases, funding fixes the time window. This applies especially to programmes that receive a significant share of aid donor funding. In other cases, changes in government undermine programme institutionalisation. This applies strongly to low-income countries (Barrientos, 2009a; Barrientos and Santibañez, 2009b).

Limited time windows sometimes reflect a concern of policymakers to avoid institutionalising dependency. It is a feature of new social assistance programmes that they identify some 'graduation' or exit process for beneficiary households. Most programmes include a regular review of eligibility, which can identify 'graduation' for some households.[31] Eligibility conditions can also provide demographic 'graduation', such as children growing beyond school age or the death of pension beneficiaries. Looking at the issue of 'graduation' purely from the perspective of the effectiveness of the programme, it should be questioned whether it constitutes a feasible objective. The evidence for developing countries suggests that there is significant mobility of poor households over time,[32] with the implication that aiming for 'graduation' is justified only if programmes cover all poor households. However, to the extent that programmes focus on the extremely or chronically poor, or when a large proportion of programme beneficiaries are in these two groups, 'graduation' is problematic.

This discussion points to a deeper issue: that of determining the optimal length of time for the support provided by social assistance. New forms of social assistance have a variety of objectives and

---

[31] In practice, reviews are far from being regular or strict; see Cecchini and Madariaga (2011).
[32] The *Chronic Poverty Report 2004–05* considers evidence emerging from a range of countries with longitudinal data sets, and suggests that, for countries with average conditions, around 40 per cent of the poor can be classified as 'chronically poor' (CPRC, 2005).

functions. Their main aim is to protect households in poverty from the harm done by persistent poverty, but they also aim to strengthen their productive capacity and their agency. The optimal length of time for assistance might well be different for each of these different objectives, and different again for different types of household. The protection role would be best performed by permanent institutions that come into play whenever households fall into poverty. The promotion role would be most effectively performed at specific points, such as school-age children or expectant mothers. It is hard to envisage a time window for empowerment, although in practice it would be carried out most effectively with a mix of time-specific interventions and entitlements (Yaqub, 2001).

The design of a programme's time window and the length of time for beneficiary participation should also take into account the nature, quality and coordination of the institutions charged with delivering public programmes. Graduation from a programme, in a context in which supplementary programmes ensure 'propulsion' away from poverty for beneficiary 'graduates', will be very different from graduation in a context in which the end of income transfer dumps beneficiary households straight back into precarious livelihoods. In the latter, graduation is problematic. It should be a matter for concern if programmes are designed with very limited timeframes and no structure of support after graduation. Without appropriate consideration being given to follow-up interventions to help graduating households avoid falling back into poverty, the effectiveness of social assistance programmes will be limited.

Conclusions

This chapter has provided an introduction to the main types of social assistance programmes in developing countries, and their core features. It began by pointing to the different role and scope of social assistance in developed and developing countries. In developed countries, social assistance has a residual role. It protects a small proportion of the population from poverty and vulnerability, after all the other components of social protection and the welfare state have failed to prevent poverty. In developing countries, by contrast, social assistance is a leading component of social protection, especially when social insurance and labour market regulation institutions are weak or absent. The leading role of social assistance in developing countries calls for fresh approaches and models. The rapid growth and wide diversity of social assistance programmes in the South reflect this.

The typology of social assistance programmes in developing countries yielded three main types: pure income transfers; income transfers plus asset accumulation; and integrated poverty reduction programmes. These 'ideal types' reflect distinct approaches to poverty and poverty reduction. Pure transfers see poverty largely as deficits in income or consumption. Income transfers combined with asset accumulation understand poverty, and poverty persistence, as resulting from deficits in consumption and productive capacity. Transfers are therefore combined with interventions facilitating human, physical or financial asset accumulation. Integrated poverty reduction programmes understand poverty as multidimensional, and combine interventions aimed at a range of dimensions of well-being or capabilities. The taxonomy leads to the core features of these programmes.

The discussion then turned to some key dimensions of social assistance programmes, with a view to extracting information on the rationale and role of design features. Programme objectives are the starting point for understanding the diversity in programme design. In particular, the balance of current/future poverty reduction objectives is central to explaining recent innovations in programme design. Next, the main strategies in use for the selection of participants were introduced and considered. The two main conclusions from this discussion were, first, that selection reflects programme objectives and, second, that most programmes in fact use a mix of strategies.

The main focus of the comparison of transfer modalities was on the level and nature of transfers. Developing country programmes show a mix of fixed- and variable-level transfers, aimed at maximising incentives. With few exceptions, the value of transfers in developing countries is such that they make a contribution to household consumption, and are insufficient to lift households to the poverty line. There has been much emphasis on the fact that, increasingly, transfers are in cash, but the cash/in-kind dichotomy has been overemphasised. A large number of programmes combine cash and in-kind transfers, especially through preferential access to services. Again, the mix of transfer modalities reflects the need to maximise incentives to achieve programme objectives.

Conditions and co-responsibility are discussed exhaustively in the literature. On paper, conditions can be motivated by a variety of concerns, including over-selection, political economy and programme incentives. In practice, conditions and co-responsibilities in human development programmes are motivated strongly by the need to achieve programme objectives. Work conditions, on the other hand, often reflect a mix of programme objectives relating to building community assets, political economy concerns and minimising the costs of selecting beneficiaries.

Existing social assistance programmes taken as a whole, but particularly those in low-income countries, show weak institutionalisation. They have tended to originate in programmes and projects, rather than policies. However, there is a dynamic for projects to become programmes, and programmes to become policies, but there is some way to go to achieve adequate levels of institutionalisation. Many programmes stress beneficiary exit, partly in order to avoid dependency; this can be problematic when programmes focus on households in extreme or persistent poverty. In practice, programmes have a variety of graduation gateways. Those focused on children and older people, for example, rely on demographic graduation. The norm is for programmes to rely on regular reviews of eligibility to identify exit conditions.

The chapter developed a systematic understanding of social assistance programmes in developing countries, through a discussion of 'ideal types' and key design dimensions. It is helpful to end by reiterating three main areas of programme design innovation in developing countries. First, social assistance programmes in developing countries pay a great deal of attention to incentives, rather than relying solely on income effects. This is in part because transfers amount to only a fraction of household consumption. Second, social assistance programmes increasingly aim to address multidimensional poverty by packaging a set of interventions around the transfer. Third, programmes show a growing awareness of the need to strengthen the productive capacity of households, especially through interventions aimed at asset accumulation, and especially human asset accumulation.

6 | *Incidence, implementation and impact*

This chapter focuses on three core processes that, combined, enable an assessment of the effectiveness of anti-poverty transfer programmes: incidence, implementation and impact (the 'three 'I's'). It signals a change in approach: Chapter 4 set out a framework for understanding the main parameters of anti-poverty transfers and Chapter 5 examined how these parameters influenced programme design in practice; this chapter facilitates an assessment of whether the parameters chosen proved appropriate and effective. The chapter examines the bases on which an evaluation of existing programmes can be performed, and the lessons emerging from this exercise.

The focus on the three 'I's requires a brief justification. Anti-poverty transfer programmes reach millions of households in the South – as many as 200 million of them on present calculations. This is impressive, taking into account the short time in which the majority of these programmes have emerged, but it is also important to ask whether they reach all households in poverty in the South. What is the incidence of social assistance programmes? Which households are reached? These are important questions, which can cast a powerful light on the programmes' orientation, their effectiveness and their likely impact on national and global poverty. To the extent that programmes addressing poverty through direct transfers to households fail to reach a majority of households in poverty, or that households not in poverty capture a significant proportion of the transfers, their effectiveness would need to be seriously questioned. Studies of programme incidence or 'targeting' have to date dominated assessments of the effectiveness of social assistance in developing countries. However, studies of targeting have focused primarily on measuring leakages to households not in poverty; much less attention has been paid to measuring how much anti-poverty transfers fail to reach all households in poverty. Efforts to rectify this bias have stimulated discussion as to whether measures of incidence currently applied to social assistance are appropriate.[1]

Few would dispute the view that programme implementation is crucial to effectiveness. However, the analytical and comparative literature on the implementation of social assistance is scarce – indeed, almost non-existent. What is available is often programme-specific and focused on minutiae. This knowledge gap is largely a reflection of the dominance of the 'project' or programme approach to social assistance in developing countries, as opposed to a more appropriate focus on institution building. What type of institutionalisation is required to enhance the effectiveness of anti-poverty transfer programmes? The discussion below attempts to draw some lessons from experience on this crucial question.

Precisely the reverse situation applies to impact: there is a large and fast-growing literature assessing the impact of social assistance programmes in developing countries. The standards applied to the impact evaluation of Southern anti-poverty transfer programmes are arguably higher than those applied to the much larger and more costly social assistance programmes in the North. This is to be welcomed. Knowledge of what works and what does not in anti-poverty policy is essential for global poverty eradication, but this varies significantly in scope and quality. There are glaring gaps in impact assessments in low-income countries, for example. Notwithstanding this, the information available on the impact of anti-poverty transfer programmes is sufficient to support a general assessment of their effectiveness. The discussion below provides answers to these questions.

Incidence

The incidence of anti-poverty transfer programmes – who receives transfers – is an important indicator of their effectiveness. In a developing country context, where high levels of poverty combined with budgetary constraints often make it necessary to focus on a subset of households in poverty, information on programme incidence is particularly valuable. In fact, a majority of existing programmes are aimed explicitly at groups in extreme and persistent poverty, and so require appropriate tools for classifying households in poverty. Chapters 3 and 4 examined the conceptual underpinning of these tools. The analysis of incidence provides

---

[1] See, in particular, Coady and Skoufias (2004) and Ravallion (2007; 2008).

information on whether social assistance programmes reach their target population. Across programmes, information on the incidence of transfer programmes helps assess their effectiveness, and prospectively helps assess what types of programme design are likely to work in which contexts.

At the same time there has been a tendency for studies in this area to privilege one aspect of incidence – namely the extent to which transfers leak out to households outside a programme's target group – almost to the exclusion of other relevant dimensions. 'Targeting', understood as the capacity of programmes to prevent leakages, has come to dominate discussion of incidence. The dangers of this narrow approach have long been understood and are well documented (Cornia and Stewart, 1995). The discussion in this chapter takes a different tack. The focus is on incidence and reach, rather than targeting. The chapter also focuses on lessons from experience. The comparative literature on the incidence of transfer programmes comes to the, perhaps unsurprising, conclusion that the relative advantages of alternative techniques for selecting beneficiaries tend in practice to be overwritten by differences in context and implementation (Coady, Grosh and Hoddinott, 2004).

It is essential to pay attention to process. Many discussions of targeting flatten out the different processes involved in selecting beneficiaries. It is helpful to introduce the main process involved. To begin with, the design of social assistance programmes defines a target population – say households in extreme poverty, orphans and vulnerable children, older persons without means of support, displaced communities, etc. Programme implementation identifies the eligible population in practice using a variety of possible techniques. Anti-poverty transfer programmes are voluntary, so the programme and its objectives need to be publicised adequately among the target population. The next stage is to register programme participants. After participants are registered, and able to access their entitlements, it is necessary to consider recertification processes that take account of beneficiary households' changing circumstances. The incidence of a programme is an outcome of the interaction of these different processes of identification, publicity, eligibility tests, registration and recertification.

Measuring errors in selection

The implementation of these processes normally produces errors in the selection of programme participants. Table 6.1 is a contingency table

Table 6.1 *Exclusion and inclusion errors of selection*

	Poor households	Non-poor households
Households receiving transfers	Correct inclusion	Type II 'inclusion' error
Households not receiving transfers	Type I 'exclusion' error	Correct exclusion

with all four possible outcomes. The cases in which households have been correctly included or excluded do not require further discussion. Type I errors apply to households that are eligible for the transfers but are not receiving them. This is also described as 'under-coverage'. Type II errors apply to households that are in receipt of transfers but are not eligible for participation in the programme. These are also described as 'leakages'. Indicators of efficiency in selection focus on measuring the size of type I and type II errors.

A variety of indicators are used in the literature.[2] Some focus on coverage rates – for example, the share of programme participants with standards of living below the poverty line in the absence of the programme. This indicator can be written as $Cp = N[D = 1; y_i < z] / N[D = 1]$. N is the total number of households; D is an indicator variable denoting participation status ($D = 1$ if participating, $D = 0$ if not participating); z is the poverty threshold; and y_i is the welfare indicator for individual i. Along similar lines, it is feasible to measure the share of the transfer budget going to individuals in poverty, which can be written as $Bp = tN[D = 1; y_i < z] / tN[D = 1]$. This assumes a 'uniform' or average transfer t. These two widely used indicators have a number of drawbacks. They are insensitive to the distribution of the transfers within the group in poverty. Transfers could be concentrated among those close to the poverty line or among those in extreme poverty, but this is not reflected in the level of the indicators. The coverage indicator does not take account of the size of the transfers or the size of the poverty reduction budget, and as a consequence it might not be very informative on the capacity of transfers to reduce poverty.

Indicators of selection effectiveness have an implicit benchmark against which they assess particular programmes. In the two indicators

[2] See additional note A6.1 for more detail.

above, the benchmark is a programme with 'perfect' selection. Coady, Grosh and Hoddinott (2004) propose a measure of effectiveness (hereafter referred to as CGH) that uses a more reasonable benchmark: the distribution of transfers that would have been generated by a uniform transfer programme. In a uniform transfer programme, all recipients receive the same transfer regardless of their poverty status. In the benchmark case, the transfer budget is simply allocated evenly to all individuals or households. The CGH measure normalises the share of the transfer budget going to households in poverty, Bp above, with the share of the population in poverty. The latter represents the share of the budget that households in poverty would have received with a uniform transfer programme. Define the share of the population in poverty as q, then the CGH measure is CGH = Bp/q. To illustrate with an example, suppose that 20 per cent of the population are in poverty and that the share of the programme budget going to the population in poverty, Bp, is also 20 per cent; then the CGH measure equals 1. Households in poverty receive a share of the transfers equal to what would have emerged from a uniform transfer.

This is a useful benchmark, because values for the CGH in excess of 1 reflect a progressive or pro-poor distribution of the budget. If in the example above households in poverty receive 40 per cent of the budget instead, the CGH is 2, implying that the selective transfer programme allocated them double the transfers they would have received under a uniform transfer programme. If, on the other hand, households in poverty receive only 10 per cent of the programme budget, with the share of the population in poverty remaining at 20 per cent, the CGH is now 0.5, with the implication that households in poverty would have been better off in a uniform programme. In this case, the selective programme is regressive. There are several drawbacks with the CGH measure. The disadvantages associated with the Bp measure noted above apply to the CGH measure too.[3]

Skoufias, Lindert and Shapiro (2010) examine the distributional impact of social insurance and social assistance programmes in Latin America and develop a measure of redistribution that can be deployed to consider the effectiveness of selection in social assistance

---

[3] Coady, Grosh and Hoddinott developed this measure to support a meta-study of anti-poverty programmes. It is an advantage of this measure that its raw materials are commonly reported in programme evaluations.

programmes.[4] Their measure, the distributional characteristics index, or DCI, adds the fraction of the budget going to each individual in the population multiplied by each individual's welfare weight. This is interpreted as the social welfare gain per unit of currency transferred.[5] This measure has several advantages. It considers the full distribution of welfare in the population, not just the welfare of groups in poverty, and it does not rely on a discretionary poverty line. It is appropriate to measure the effectiveness of redistributing income to low-income households.

Table 6.2 shows the values for these measures of selection effectiveness for a range of programmes in Latin America and the Caribbean estimated from household survey data (Lindert, Skoufias and Shapiro, 2006; Skoufias, Lindert and Shapiro, 2010).

The figures in Table 6.2 demonstrate the difficulties involved in achieving a satisfactory ordering of programmes according to the different measures of selection effectiveness. The ranking of programmes according to the DCI measure is not fully consistent with a ranking using the CGH scores, which in turn is not fully consistent with rankings using the Bp or Cp measures. All the measures provide some useful information on the potential effectiveness of the programmes, but none of them is unarguably superior to the others.

A large scale meta-study including all types of anti-poverty programmes relying on the CGH measure suggests that selection methods are at best a contributory factor in selection effectiveness (Coady, Grosh and Hoddinott, 2004). This study also concludes that selection methods that reach the household or individual level are more effective than those that remain at the community level; that interventions relying on means and proxy means tests tend to have better scores than categorical selection methods; and that self-selection based on work requirements tends to have better effectiveness scores than self-selection based on consumption. The main message emerging from the meta-study is that country conditions and implementation matter as much as, or perhaps even more than, selection techniques. Countries with better implementation capacity and greater differentiation among households in poverty show better selection scores than countries with low implementation capacity.

---

[4] Other relevant applications are by Coady and Skoufias (2004) and Skoufias and Coady (2007).
[5] See additional note A6.1 for a more formal definition.

Table 6.2 *Measures of programme incidence for selected anti-poverty transfer programmes in Latin America*

Country	Year	Programme	Mean transfer (US$ PPP)	Cp Q1 (%)	Bp Q1 (%)	CGH Q1	CGH Q1+2	DCI $\epsilon = 2$
Chile	2003	SUF	5.5	31	60	2.98	2.1	2.31
Brazil	2004	PETI	5.5	2	66	3.3	2.24	2.26
Chile	2003	*Chile Solidario*	6.2	3	56	2.81	2.02	2.1
Brazil	2003	Auxilio Gas	1.5	16	48	2.39	2.01	1.87
Argentina	2003	Heads of household	35.9	30	32	1.6	1.8	1.76
Mexico	2002	*Oportunidades*	6.8	32	35	1.73	1.58	1.67
Brazil	2003	*Bolsa Escola*	5.5	27	40	1.98	1.63	1.47
Chile	2003	Disability PASIS	31.3	7	35	1.74	1.66	1.28
Colombia	2003	FAMI	8.9	3	38	1.91	1.53	1.14
Chile	2003	Old age PASIS	38.6	6	26	1.32	1.47	0.94
Dominican Republic	2003	Gas subsidy	15.7	74	9	0.46	0.59	0.9
Chile	2003	Water subsidy	2.9	14	24	1.18	1.27	0.89
Chile	2003	Family allowance	4.6	28	24	1.19	1.3	0.79
Mexico	2002	PROCAMPO	6.7	11	12	0.6	0.6	0.53
Guatemala	2000	Nutrition pension	36.7	1	1	0.06	0.17	0.12

Source: Lindert, Skoufias and Shapiro (2006).

Notes: PPP stands for purchasing power parity. Cp Q1 (%) is the percentage share of programme participants in quintile 1. Bp is the share of the budget going to the population in quintile 1. CGH Q1 is the share of the budget going to quintile 1 normalised by the share of population in quintile 1. CGH Q1+2 is the share of the budget going to quintiles 1 and 2 normalised by the share of population in quintiles 1 and 2. DCI is the sum of the fraction of the budget going to individuals in the population multiplied by their welfare weight constructed as $\beta^i = (y^k/y^i)^\epsilon$, where k indexes a reference household and ϵ is assumed as $\epsilon = 2$.

A study of selection processes in China's *Dibao* led Ravallion to question the usefulness of narrow targeting studies as a means of assessing the effectiveness of anti-poverty programmes. He finds that ex ante indicators of poverty reduction for the *Dibao* programme, obtained by comparing poverty estimates from reported well-being and poverty estimates from reported well-being minus the transfer, across cities in China are not positively correlated with the *Bp* and CGH selection effectiveness scores (Ravallion, 2007).[6] According to him, too much weight has been placed on targeting approaches at the expense of attention to other factors responsible for programme effectiveness. These include the size and structure of programmes, the pattern of incentives that develop in response to the programme and issues of political support and cost-effectiveness. More importantly, the principal indicator of the effectiveness of a programme is the extent to which it reduces poverty.

A process approach

One of the main conclusions emerging from this discussion is the need to pay attention to implementation. A process approach to incidence involves going back to the components of selection strategies: identification, selection, registration and certification.

Micklewright, Couduel and Marnie (2004) provide an illuminating discussion of this approach in the context of a low-income country with low administrative capacity. Uzbekistan introduced a decentralised social assistance programme in 1994 to provide transfers to households in extreme poverty. The selection of beneficiaries and the setting of transfer levels were done by neighbourhood groups called *mahallas* (traditional community organisations). The government set out general guidelines for the eligibility criteria, which guided, but did not bind, *mahallas'* decisions on eligibility and transfer levels. Selection by community organisations is often advocated, on the grounds that local knowledge is better.

---

[6] Ravallion proposes a measure of coverage Cr, defined as $[N(D=1, yh<z)/N(Y<z)]$ $-[N(D=1, yh \geq z)/N(Y \geq z)]$ – the difference between the participation rate of households in poverty within the population in poverty minus the participation rate of non-poor households within the non-poor population. This measure is correlated with predicted poverty reduction outcomes and with measures of cost-effectiveness.

Survey data enabled researchers to distinguish between awareness of the scheme and application and award outcomes. The study found that awareness of the programme was high and inversely related to household income. Six out of every seven households in the bottom quintile reported that they were aware of the programme. Self-selection was strong at the application stage. Fewer households with higher incomes applied. Conditional on having made an application, the probabilities of receiving an award were similar for low- and high-income households. Finally, transfer levels did not vary significantly across households, and seemed to be unrelated to household income. Community selection appears to have maximised awareness of the programme, and to some extent reduced moral hazard among non-poor households, but it was less successful in differentiating benefit awards and levels by household socioeconomic status.[7]

Brazil's *Bolsa Família* provides an example of beneficiary selection processes in a middle-income country. There are three main stages in the process of selecting beneficiaries for *Bolsa Família*. First, the federal government allocates quotas of participants to municipalities, based on poverty incidence data generated from the analysis of household survey data. At the second stage, publicity about the programme leads to the registration of potential beneficiary households, which involves collecting self-reported socioeconomic information from households. Municipalities employ poverty maps and other sources of information to identify geographical areas with higher poverty incidence. The range of locations at which registration is performed demonstrates engagement with local organisations. Registration is carried out predominantly at schools, clinics, churches and community organisations; it takes place in government offices only for a minority of potential beneficiaries (Lindert *et al.*, 2007). At the third stage, household information is processed at the federal level and eligibility is established. This information is then sent back to municipalities.

A recent study has attempted to identify the impact on beneficiary selection of the different stages in the process (Barros *et al.*, 2008). The benchmark for the effectiveness of selection was random selection. The study used 2005 National Household Survey data. Households are eligible for participation in *Bolsa Família* if their per capita household

---

[7] The study also reports some evidence of social exclusion against Slavic minority groups.

income is less than one-half of the minimum wage. Random selection is able to identify only 19.8 per cent of eligible households. Applying federal government quotas for municipalities but randomising selection within them 'finds' 32 per cent of the eligible population – a 12 percentage point improvement in selection effectiveness. The next step is to consider only those registered households, those included in the Single Registry,[8] and randomising selection within the group; this exercise 'finds' 55 per cent of eligible households, a 23 percentage point improvement in selection with respect to the benchmark. Finally, using the information in the Single Registry on self-reported income adds 2.1 percentage points to raise the proportion of eligible households found to 57.1 per cent. Barros *et al.* conclude that the main contribution to programme selection comes at the point at which potential beneficiaries register. This implies that the assessment by municipalities of the locational distribution of households in poverty and the quality of engagement with civil society to facilitate their registration emerge as key factors in ensuring effective selection in *Bolsa Família*, with federal quotas the second most important factor.

Studies of selection outcomes in *Bolsa Família* indicate that a significant share of the eligible population is not selected, around 42.9 per cent (Soares, Ribas and Soares, 2009). What factors explain this high proportion of selection errors? It is common to find that administrative programme data and coverage data from household surveys provide diverging estimates of the eligible population. There are several reasons for this. The sampling of household survey data is subject to a higher probability of error at the two extremes of the distribution of income. Low- and high-income communities are notoriously difficult for field workers to reach. The income base in household surveys might be slightly different from the income base used by programme regulations to assess household resources. It is also likely that respondents' incentives for providing accurate responses vary according to the context in which the information is sought. Responses may turn out to be different in the context of a means test from those under a household survey. There is also the possibility of information manipulation by programme agencies and households.

---

[8] The Single Registry collects information on all households and individuals applying for government support.

Soares, Ribas and Soares argue that volatility in employment and income among low-income Brazilian households is large and provides an important explanation for the selection errors in *Bolsa Família*. This implies that households above the eligibility threshold in, say, June might well be found to fall below it by September, when National Household Survey data are collected. In September they would therefore show up as eligible, but not receiving transfers. At the same time, some households identified as eligible in June might well rise above the eligibility threshold by September and show up as leakages. On the basis of an estimate of vulnerability – the likelihood that households will be below the eligibility threshold in the future – they estimate that *Bolsa Família* would need 15 million participants to ensure that in any particular month 11 million people currently below the eligibility threshold are all covered. Eliminating type I errors in selection involves extending the scale of the programme to cover households that are just above the poverty line and might fall below it at some point. This suggests the presence of a 'scale effect' in selection, according to which large-scale programmes are better able to reduce type I errors than small-scale programmes.[9]

To recap, examining the incidence of anti-poverty transfer programmes provides important information on programme effectiveness. However, a concentration on type II errors in the 'targeting' literature has limited the usefulness of the information generated. Efforts to address this bias have stimulated research into broader incidence measures. The findings from studies comparing the advantages of alternative measures of incidence indicate that implementation issues are as important in determining programme effectiveness. A process approach to incidence pays attention to the influence of selection, publicity, eligibility determination, registration and recertification in assessing selection effectiveness. Two examples, one each from a low- and a middle-income country, illustrated the importance of the process approach.

---

[9] On the scale effect, see Ravallion (2007). Extending the scale of the programme also generates type II errors. For Brazil's *Bolsa Família*, the expansion of the programme in 2006 enabled measurement of the elasticity of type II errors relative to the size of the programme, estimated at 1.2. See Soares, Ribas and Soares (2009).

Implementation

Efficiency considerations require that programmes maximise the poverty impact of a given budget. Implementation is central to meeting this requirement. The implementation of anti-poverty transfer programmes raises a wide range of issues, but here the focus is on the extent of the institutionalisation of these programmes and the role of information. Perhaps the greatest challenge facing anti-poverty transfer programmes in developing countries is associated with their institutionalisation. Institutionalisation is the process by which anti-poverty programmes acquire legal and administrative status, transparent budgetary allocation rules and effective means of coordinating their activities with other public agencies and programmes. In most cases, anti-poverty transfer programmes began life as discretionary interventions with a limited time window, as projects. As they become established, many programmes developed stable and embedded institutional structures. Institutionalisation is a dominant factor in programme implementation.

Among the different functions and activities associated with the implementation of social assistance, information is central to their effective operation. Information is central to the selection of beneficiaries, the tracking of their progress and programme monitoring and evaluation. The latter are in turn a vital component for institutional learning and reform. The discussion below highlights the crucial role of information in social assistance.

Vertical and horizontal coordination

There are several examples of large-scale social transfer programmes with decentralised implementation. The scope and structure of decentralisation varies across countries. In India's Mahatma Gandhi National Rural Employment Guarantee scheme, central government part-finances programme budgets, with state governments and district-level authorities managing implementation. The core features of the scheme are fixed by national legislation, but states can supplement the programme by adding interventions or financing higher transfer levels. Heterogeneity in delivery capacity across districts generates variations in the quality of the service provided to beneficiaries.

The main implementation issues involved include (a) vertical coordination between the different levels of government to ensure effectiveness and fairness in implementation;[10] (b) horizontal coordination to ensure the cooperation of different ministries and that poverty reduction programmes at the local level are sufficiently well integrated and administration costs are minimised; and (c) the standardisation of provision and service for beneficiaries.

In Brazil's *Bolsa Família*, the issue of vertical coordination has been addressed through incentives and monitoring structures. The central government relates directly to municipalities in charge of delivery.[11] Central government negotiates cooperation agreements with municipalities for the delivery of the programme, monitors performance through an Index of Decentralised Management and ties the reimbursement of programme cost to the municipalities to their scores on this index (Lindert *et al.*, 2007). Standardisation in service provision is supported by a two-part cost reimbursement structure: a basic cost reimbursement amount, supplemented by top-up payments for municipalities with low levels of capacity. Cooperation agreements between the federal government and the municipalities fix standards of service, but these are complemented by financial incentives. In India, monitoring of the Mahatma Gandhi National Rural Employment Guarantee scheme is managed through community participation, through social audits at village assemblies (*gram sabha*) designed to assess effectiveness and fairness in implementation.

In decentralised programme implementation, horizontal coordination is an issue at both central government and local levels. At the central government level, inter-sectoral coordination is often hard to achieve, especially in programmes that bundle human development interventions.[12] Typically, the main agency responsible for programme implementation is a dedicated ministry, necessitating close coordination with ministries of education and health. There are few examples of anti-poverty transfer programmes developed within these ministries. This is in part because of the supply-side ethos of these ministries and in part

---

[10] Human rights perspectives emphasise a set of basic principles of direct relevance to issues of implementation. Anti-poverty transfer programmes are expected to adhere to the principles of equality and non-discrimination, accountability, transparency, access to information and participation. See Sepúlveda Carmona (2009).

[11] Interestingly, this is also the case for Mexico's *Progresa*, which effectively bypassed the state government level.

[12] For Latin American experiences on this issue, see Cecchini and Martínez (2011).

because they are often legally required to cover the whole population. An important lesson emerging from Latin American countries is the need to establish social protection networks across governmental and non-governmental agencies in order to orchestrate this coordination (MIDEPLAN, 2009). Horizontal coordination issues also emerge at the local level, related mainly to coordination with other programmes managed at this level. Typically, there are gains in effectiveness and cost minimisation if functions common to multiple programmes can be shared – registration and selection, for example.

Coordination is particularly difficult in low-income countries with low implementation capacity. In sub-Saharan Africa, social transfer programmes are often the responsibility of ministries of gender or social development, which have relatively limited capacity to formulate and implement social transfer programmes compared with ministries of health or education. The presence and influence of donors and a reliance on a mix of non-governmental and for-profit providers[13] adds greater complexity to implementation and places stronger demands on coordination functions. The scaling up of social transfer pilots in these countries will inevitably magnify issues of coordination. Concerns over the possibility of corruption and political capture are stronger in decentralised programmes in low-income countries (Pellissery, 2008).

Information

The crucial role of information and information systems in the effective implementation of social transfer schemes is often underestimated. Information flows enable a social transfer programme to identify beneficiaries with accuracy; ensure their registration; track their progress; support the deployment of transfers and services; coordinate the work of programme agencies; and provide the inputs needed to refine and reform transfer programmes.

---

[13] In low-income countries with limited implementation capacity, donors rely on international NGOs or for-profit providers. This is leading to pluralism in provision, with parallels in the provision of health care in developing countries. A key concern is that a 'project' approach to delivery could fail to develop capacity and leadership within public agencies, essential to the institutionalisation of social assistance. See Barrientos and Santibañez (2009b), C. Moore (2008) and Niño-Zarazúa *et al.* (2012).

Most social assistance transfer programmes in developing countries are oriented to a specific population: families in extreme poverty, orphans and vulnerable children, older people suffering from deprivation, etc. Information on their target population is a crucial input to the work of programme agencies. Household information is normally provided through a survey of socioeconomic conditions. The scope, quality and timeliness of the information influence the effectiveness of the programme. Beneficiary selection relies on information across a range of directly observable indicators, which are difficult to manipulate and relatively costless to collect. The selection of indicators needs to be in line with programme objectives.[14] Tried and tested processes to validate the information collected are needed to preclude manipulation of the data by potential beneficiaries and programme agencies.[15] Information relating to eligibility needs to be updated regularly, as household circumstances change over time. Regular updating is essential to enabling the transfer programme to address poverty as a dynamic process rather than a static one (Soares, Ribas and Soares, 2009). Latin American countries have made significant advances in setting up the information systems needed to ensure accurate and comprehensive information flows, in order to identify potential beneficiaries (Azevedo, Bouillon and Irarrázaval, 2011).

In programmes relying on self-selection, information flows to beneficiaries are essential to ensure programme effectiveness. Shankar, Gaiha and Jha (2011) studied information flows in India's Mahatma Gandhi National Rural Employment Guarantee scheme, and find that differences in access to information can explain the fact that a majority of participants do not come from groups in extreme poverty. Differential publicity of programme information to groups in extreme poverty and groups in moderate poverty is a factor in current reach. Information is useful to all participants, as in enabling them to avoid being short-changed by district officials, but it is used most effectively by groups in moderate poverty and groups not in poverty.

Structured information flows are also important to the horizontal and vertical coordination of the different agencies involved in the

---

[14] For a discussion on the role of programme orientation in determining the information flows required to determine eligibility, see Santibañez (2005).
[15] For a discussion of manipulation of eligibility information and the need for checks, see Camacho and Conover (2009).

implementation of the programme. The Index of Decentralised Management in Brazil's *Bolsa Família* enables an assessment of the effectiveness of municipalities, but it is also a tool for resource allocation and capacity development. In human-development-conditional transfer programmes, a measure of coordination between the ministry of health and the ministry of education and the programme agencies around the verification of conditions needs to be supported by adequate information flows (Cecchini and Madariaga, 2011). In fact, the absence of appropriate information flows has been identified as a barrier to effective coordination (Soares and Britto, 2007).

Information flows on the performance and evolution of social transfer programmes are a key input, not only for their operational effectiveness but also for their capacity to respond to changing conditions and new challenges. Monitoring and evaluation processes are essential for ensuring that programme effectiveness improves over time. The literature on social assistance in developing countries has focused on impact evaluation, largely around the role of randomised evaluation (Duflo and Kremer, 2003; Ravallion, 2005). The findings from impact evaluations inform debate on the desirability of interventions and throw light on the relative cost-effectiveness of alternative policies. They can generate crucial knowledge on behavioural and institutional responses to policy (Pritchett, 2002). The nature and scope of programme evaluation also has a role in protecting transfer programmes from day-to-day political volatility (Levy, 2006).

Impact

What is the impact of social assistance programmes? Surprisingly, perhaps, this is not an easy question to answer. Chapter 5 described the large diversity in programme design and objectives across developing countries. This chapter has considered the limitations of targeting indicators and emphasised the crucial role of implementation in programme effectiveness. In addition, laboratory conditions seldom apply in countries' poverty outcomes. Attribution is a challenge. It follows that this question can be answered intelligently only if it is properly contextualised.

There is a lively discussion on the role of impact evaluations on policy and research in development. Randomised evaluation techniques have been described and advocated as the 'gold standard' in the context of assessing development interventions (Duflo and Kremer, 2003). They have been implemented more widely in the context of transfer programmes than for any other group of development interventions. Perhaps because of their ubiquity, concerns have been raised about their dominant role, scope and cost-effectiveness (Barrett and Carter, 2010).

As discussed in Chapter 5, social assistance transfers share a core poverty reduction objective, but they vary considerably in the way this objective is articulated in the context of each programme. In most programmes, a set of intermediate or proximate objectives is identified, which is understood to help deliver the core poverty reduction objective. Intermediate objectives are programme- and context-specific. Human-development-conditional transfer programmes, for example, set household investment in human development, especially health care, schooling and nutrition, as intermediate objectives. The Productive Safety Net Programme in Ethiopia sets food security and asset protection as proximate objectives. Beyond core and intermediate objectives, researchers are often interested in the wider impacts of a transfer programme. Do programmes empower women? Do they strengthen or undermine community organisations? Do they strengthen governance and accountability? A growing literature has emerged, looking at the externalities of transfer programmes – their potentially unintended effects.

The impact evaluation literature on anti-poverty transfer programmes is vast and growing. It is therefore imperative to focus the discussion that follows. The first focus is on quantitative impact evaluation studies, as their methodology facilitates a comparative discussion across countries and programmes.[16] The second focus is on the impact of programmes on core and intermediate objectives. Monitoring and evaluation processes in existing programmes identify indicators by which to measure the extent to which programme objectives are met. As a result, evidence on these is more widely available. Then the discussion focuses on a few indicators: poverty, consumption and productive capacity. There is sufficient common ground in the primacy of these three indicators. Most, if not all, social assistance programmes aim primarily to reduce poverty and improve consumption among households in poverty. There is also an expectation that transfer programmes will facilitate improvements in the capacity of households to improve their consumption in the medium and longer term. The fourth focus is

---

[16] For an example of a qualitative impact evaluation, see Escobar Latapí and González de la Rocha (2009).

on benchmarking the impact of social assistance programmes. The objective is to assess the evidence emerging from a selective group of programmes with strong evaluation processes and to establish what impact can be expected from well-designed and well-implemented programmes. This provides a more secure footing than attempting to measure a poorly defined average across many programmes and countries, especially as a large proportion of anti-poverty transfer programmes in the South have not implemented reliable impact evaluations. The focus of the discussion below results inescapably in a bias towards middle-income countries, especially in Latin America, and towards well-established programmes.

Impact on poverty

Impact evaluations of Mexico's *Progresa/Oportunidades* provide the earliest and perhaps strongest estimates of the poverty reduction capacity of well-designed and well-implemented anti-poverty transfer programmes. Table 6.3 presents poverty estimates for a sample of *Progresa*-eligible beneficiaries spanning 1997, when the programme was about to be implemented, and 1999, when the programme had been extended to all eligible households. Because of administrative constraints, some locations were not incorporated into the programme until late 1999. This made possible a quasi-experimental approach to estimating difference-in-difference measures of poverty outcomes. Households incorporated into the programme in 1997 are described as the treatment group, and households incorporated in 1999 as a control group. The data in the table show the difference in poverty measure between 1997 and 1999 for the treatment and control groups, and also across the two groups.[17]

A comparison of poverty incidence estimates suggests that measured P0 increased for the control group between 1997 and 1999, and decreased for the treatment group. The reduction in poverty incidence within the treatment group was about 7.5 percentage points. The trend observed for the control group indicates what the situation would have been in the absence of the transfers: a rise in poverty incidence. The impact of *Progresa* on poverty incidence is more appropriately

---

[17] See additional note A6.3 for a more detailed explanation of difference-in-difference estimates.

Table 6.3 *Poverty estimates for a sample of* Progresa-*eligible beneficiaries, 1997–1999*

	October 1997	November 1999	Dif	Dif2	% change
P0					
Control	0.652	0.694	0.042		
Treatment	0.674	0.599	−0.075	0.117	17.36
P1					
Control	0.319	0.339	0.020		
Treatment	0.357	0.248	−0.109	0.129	36.13
P2					
Control	0.211	0.226	0.015		
Treatment	0.252	0.152	−0.100	0.115	45.63

Source: Skoufias (2005).

Notes: Poverty line is fiftieth percentile of per capita household consumption. 'Dif' stands for the difference in the values of the estimates, calculated as Pα99 – Pα97. 'Dif2' stands for the difference in difference and is calculated as

$$\text{Dif2} = [(p_{\alpha t1}d = 0) - (p_{\alpha t0}|d = 0)] - [(p_{\alpha t1}|d = 1) - (p_{\alpha t0}|d = 1)];,$$

where $t1$ = 1999, $t2$ = 1997, d = 1 if treatment group and d = 0 if control group. '% change' is calculated as $\text{Dif2}/(p_{\alpha t0}|d = 1)$.

measured by subtracting the change in the treatment group from the change in the control group. This is consistent with an 11.7 percentage point reduction, or a 17.3 per cent change from the baseline.

Along similar lines, it is possible to identify difference-in-difference estimates for the poverty gap and the poverty gap squared. The impact of *Progresa* on the poverty gap is larger, at 36.1 per cent. It is also stronger for the poorest, as the reduction on the poverty gap squared is 45.6 per cent. A focus on the change in the poverty gap or the poverty gap squared measures makes sense, because, as a rule, transfers in developing countries are a fraction of household consumption. Only those house-holds sufficiently close to the poverty line might be lifted above it by the transfer. The impact of transfer programmes on the poverty headcount is often small, especially for programmes focused on households in extreme poverty. The choice of consumption as an indicator of welfare is signifi-cant, because a large share of household consumption comes from own production and few beneficiaries are employed in formal jobs. Income indicators might not be appropriate in this context. At the time of the introduction of *Progresa*, economic conditions in rural Mexico showed a worsening trend in the medium term – a principal motivation behind the introduction of the programme. As noted with the difference-in-difference estimates above, estimates of the impact of an anti-poverty transfer programme on the treated, and without reference to a control group, would have failed to take account of worsening economic conditions and underestimated the impact of the programmes.[18] To isolate the impact of the programme on poverty, it was necessary to compare changes in the treatment and control groups.

As this example demonstrates, measuring the impact of anti-poverty programmes is demanding. The broader conclusion is that well-designed programmes have the potential to make a significant contribution to poverty reduction. The level and design of transfers in developing countries suggests that the impacts on the poverty gap and poverty gap squared are likely to be more important than the impact on the poverty headcount.

Impact on consumption

The most direct impact of transfers is on household consumption. With few exceptions, impact evaluation studies observe a rise in household consumption following the receipt of transfers by households in poverty. Table 6.4 is drawn from data presented by Fiszbein and Schady (2009) on several human-development-conditional transfer programmes. All programmes, except that in Ecuador, registered a rise in consumption among beneficiaries relative to a control group. Why was there no rise in consumption in Ecuador? The level of the transfer was relatively small compared with the programmes in other countries, but Schady and Araujo (2006) suggest that a contributory factor is the large effect of the programme in reducing child labour, so the transfer might have simply replaced the forgone earnings from children working. For the other programmes, the observed rise in consumption is in line with the size of the transfer relative to household consumption. This could be interpreted to mean that beneficiary households consumed the bulk of the transfer. It is interesting to speculate on households' use of the difference between the additional consumption and the level of the transfer. Several explanations are relevant, including private transfers

---

[18] In fact, anti-poverty transfers can be extremely effective in such contexts if they prevent poverty from rising.

Table 6.4 *Impact of transfers on consumption in selected human development transfer programmes*

		Median consumption daily per capita US$	Transfer daily per capita US$	Transfer as % of median household consumption	Change in consumption median household %
Colombia	*Familias en Acción* 2006–7	1.19	0.13	10.9	10.0
Ecuador	*Bono Desarrollo Humano* 2003–5	1.13	0.08	7.1	0
Honduras	PRAF II 2000–2	0.68	0.06	8.8	7.0
Mexico	*Oportunidades* 1998–9	0.59	0.13	22.0	8.3
Nicaragua	*Red de Protección Social* 2000–2	0.52	0.15	28.8	20.6

Source: Fiszbein and Schady (2009).

to relatives, neighbours or faith and community organisations, payments to officials, saving and investment, to name a few.

The impact of transfers on consumption reported in Table 6.4 reflects fairly accurately the findings from studies of other programmes and regions.[19]

Studies focusing on the distribution of consumption find a more than proportionate growth in food consumption (Rubalcava, Teruel and Thomas, 2002). Households receiving support from the *Bono de Desarrollo Humano* in Ecuador had a 25 per cent increase in food expenditure, which was linked to improvements in nutritional status (Ponce and

[19] Most studies find a positive correlation between transfers and a rise in household consumption. See Arroyo Ortiz *et al.* (2008a), Case and Deaton (1998; 2003), Gao, Zhai and Garfinkel (2009), Hoddinott and Skoufias (2004), Maluccio (2005) and Skoufias, Unar and González-Cossío (2008). However, studies on the extension of *Oportunidades* in urban areas did not find a positive impact on consumption. See Angelucci and Attanasio (2009).

Bedi, 2010). In Colombia, a substantial increase in the intake of protein-rich foods and vegetables was reported as a result of participation in *Familias en Acción* (Attanasio, 2003). Fiszbein and Schady suggest that transfers might have the potential to shift the share of food consumption in total consumption, the Engel curve, among beneficiaries.

Returning to the apparent absence of consumption effects in Ecuador, it is important to take account of factors that could counteract the transfers. Two factors are extremely important. The *Bono de Desarrollo Humano* case demonstrates that behavioural responses to the transfer may reduce its impact on consumption. The main focus of attention on this point is the labour supply responses of children and adults. The bulk of the evidence on labour supply responses to transfers in developing countries indicates that these are marginal.[20] A second important factor relates to the extent to which transfers lead to changes in private transfers. They could work both ways, for example through beneficiary households sharing their transfers with relatives and friends or through a reduction in private transfers from others in response to the new status of beneficiary households. On this point, again, the evidence suggests that private transfer responses are marginal.

Impact on productive capacity

In addition to improving household consumption in the short run, most transfer programmes aim to improve participants' productive capacity as a means to reduce the likelihood of poverty in the longer run (Barrientos, 2012). In the simplest case, improvements in current consumption are expected to have medium-term effects on human development, with implications for productivity. Addressing child nutrition, for example, is likely to improve child welfare, but also to facilitate learning. Increasingly, transfer programmes combine a concern to strengthen current consumption with a concern to facilitate investment in households' productive capacity. Asset-based programmes focus directly on enhancing the protection and accumulation of physical or financial assets. These, in turn, are expected to improve household productive capacity in the medium and longer run. The same applies to human-development-focused programmes, which aim to improve the health status of household members and the schooling of children. Improvements in households' productive capacity are essential to

---

[20] This is discussed in more detail below.

sustainable and permanent exit from poverty. To that extent, anti-poverty transfer programmes can have an impact on the probability of poverty in the future.

Nutrition can be measured with anthropometric data. Weight-for-age indicators provide insights into the short-term impact of improved nutrition, whereas height-for-age indicators provide information on the long-term effects of improved nutrition. Height for age is particularly informative with regard to the longer-term impact of transfers, including labour productivity and persistent deprivation (Case and Paxson, 2008). Studies have found that height deficits established early in life often persist into adulthood, causing adverse impacts on cognitive development (Hoddinott and Kinsey, 2001) and future earning capacity (Thomas and Strauss, 1997). Measures of the impact of anti-poverty transfers can provide information on improvements in productive capacity. A study of the Child Support Grant in South Africa finds that beneficiary children are predicted to be 3.5 cm taller as adults (Aguero, Carter and Woolard, 2007), with implications for future earnings and programme cost-effectiveness. The authors of this study simulate the present value of increased future earnings to be 60 to 130 per cent greater than the cost of the grant. Improvements in long-term nutrition have been observed among girls living in recipient households of South Africa's old age pension (Duflo, 2003). Evaluation studies of Mexico's *Progresa/Oportunidades* find that children exposed to the programme gained 1 cm in height for age compared with a control group, two years after the start of the programme. The gain was 0.65 cm six years after the start of the programme and four years after the control group had been co-opted (Neufeld *et al.*, 2005).

Some transfer programmes have the explicit objective of improving access to, and utilisation of, health services. An evaluation of Colombia's *Familias en Acción* reported a rise in the percentage of children under twenty-four months attending health care check-ups, from 17.2 per cent to 40 per cent. For children aged between twenty-four and forty-eight months the corresponding rise was from 33.6 per cent to 66.8 per cent (Attanasio *et al.*, 2005). Improved utilisation of health care facilities reduces morbidity rates. The proportion of children affected by diarrhoea declined from 32 per cent to 22 per cent among children under twenty-four months, and from 21.3 per cent to 10.4 per cent among older children. Similar improvements in health care utilisation have been reported for Chile, Mexico, Nicaragua and Peru. In

Mexico, the introduction of *Progresa/Oportunidades* is reported to have doubled health care visits in rural communities (Coady, 2003). In Peru, *Juntos* led to a 30 per cent increase in immunisations among children under the age of one, and a 61 per cent increase for children aged one to five years. In Nicaragua, *Red de Protección Social* is associated with an 18 per cent increase in immunisation amongst children aged between twelve and twenty-three months (Maluccio and Flores, 2004). Timely immunisations can play a significant role in reducing illness and premature deaths among toddlers.

A large proportion of anti-poverty transfer programmes directly target improvements in schooling among children in households in poverty. A study on *Chile Solidario* reports that school enrolment in primary education improved in the order of 7 to 9 per cent relative to non-participants (Galasso, 2006). In other middle-income countries, where enrolment in primary education is almost complete, the impact of anti-poverty transfers has been more significant on secondary education. In Colombia, for example, *Familias en Acción* did not affect school attendance rates among children aged eight to eleven, but the programme did report a 10 per cent improvement in schooling among children aged twelve to seventeen living in rural areas, and a 5.2 per cent improvement among children living in urban areas (Attanasio *et al.*, 2005). In Brazil, a study finds that school attendance among poor children rose by 4 per cent as a result of participation in *Bolsa Familia*. In Ecuador, a randomised study estimates that *Bono de Desarrollo Humano* increased school enrolment for children aged six to seventeen by about 10 percentage points (Cardoso and Portela Souza, 2003). In Mexico, participation in *Oportunidades* is associated with higher school enrolment, less grade repetition and better grade progression, lower dropout rates and higher school re-entry rates among dropouts. Dropout rates decreased by 24 per cent, with a corresponding rise in completion rates of 23 per cent for rural secondary schools (Skoufias and di Maro, 2008). These results predict an increase in children's future permanent earnings by about 8 per cent when they reach adulthood. Schooling improvements are not restricted to human development programmes in Latin America, as pure income transfers also report important impacts on children's schooling. School enrolment and attendance are necessary, but not sufficient, conditions to ensure that children in participating households reach the labour market with higher levels of human capital. The quality of schooling and the transition from school to work are also important (Fiszbein and Schady, 2009).

Some anti-poverty transfer programmes explicitly target the protection and/or accumulation of physical and financial assets. For credit-constrained households, investment decisions mean increasing savings and therefore reducing current consumption. This is particularly difficult to achieve for households in poverty or extreme poverty. Transfers can be aimed at easing this trade-off for poor and poorest households. The Targeting the Ultra Poor programme, run by BRAC (Building Resources across Communities), a development organisation, in Bangladesh, has been specifically designed to facilitate a process of productive asset accumulation as a foundation for successful participation in microcredit programmes at a later stage. This programme combines asset transfers, microenterprise training and support, health and nutrition interventions and a small transfer in cash to stabilise household consumption. Evaluations by BRAC have identified strong and sustainable asset accumulation among participant households, especially livestock (Ahmed *et al.*, 2009). Interestingly, no significant effects are observed on primary school enrolment among children in these households, suggesting a measure of 'specialisation' across human development and physical and financial asset anti-poverty programmes.[21] Regular and reliable transfers can facilitate access to credit. In Brazil's non-contributory pension scheme, *Prêvidencia Social Rural*, it was observed that beneficiaries are able to access formal credit by showing the magnetic card used to collect their pensions (Schwarzer, 2000).

It is very important to keep firmly in mind that current knowledge on the impact of anti-poverty programmes is far from systematic. The focus has been on benchmarking programme impact in well-designed and well-implemented programmes.

Long-term effects of transfers?

The expansion of social assistance transfer programmes in developing countries has been concentrated in the past decade, and existing programmes have a relatively short lifespan. As a consequence, knowledge on the long-term effects of anti-poverty transfer programmes is limited. Very few countries have a longitudinal data set suitable for the

---

[21] This was also observed across anti-poverty programmes in Mexico (Sadoulet, de Janvry and Davis, 2001).

analysis of medium-term effects, let alone longer-term effects. *Oportunidades*, launched in 1997 in rural areas of Mexico, provides the richest laboratory in which to research longer-term effects. There are significant methodological problems involved in this. The main challenge is to identify strategies able to ascertain future effects from information on current outcomes. As discussed above, several studies have used information on the impact of *Oportunidades* on schooling to generate insights on future labour market outcomes of children. Observed schooling outcomes are used to simulate the impact on future earnings from increased years of schooling for children participating in social transfer programmes (Bourguignon, Ferreira and Leite, 2003; Freije, Bando and Arce, 2006; Todd and Wolpin, 2006). Parker and Behrman (2008) examine the effects on school achievements and performance in mathematics and reading tests among long-term beneficiary children in order to explore whether potential gains in labour productivity are sufficient to cover the programme costs. They find that the cost of *Progresa/Oportunidades*, equivalent to about 0.3 per cent of GDP, is more than offset by gains in labour earnings in the future.

Very few studies attempt to observe longer-term effects directly. Arroyo Ortiz *et al.* (2008a) analyse the impacts of *Progresa/Oportunidades* on household consumption and investment over a ten-year span of data. They find that households with long-term exposure to treatment show higher food consumption than those with a shorter period of treatment. Nine-year participants have 14.3 per cent higher consumption of purchased food and 17.2 per cent higher consumption of own produce compared with three-year participants in the programme (see Figure 6.1). Furthermore, Arroyo Ortiz *et al.* find that households that joined the programme in 1998 showed gains in land, livestock and productive assets of around 4 per cent compared with households joining in 2003. As anti-poverty transfer programmes in developing countries extend in time, the opportunities for learning about their medium- and longer-term effects will expand. This is an important research agenda.

Labour supply effects

Standard economic models predict that income transfers will have adverse labour supply effects among beneficiary households, on

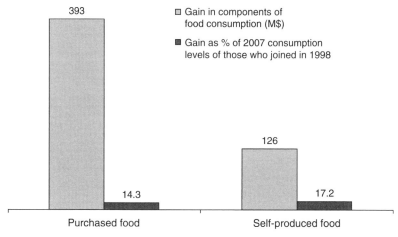

Figure 6.1 Longer-term impact of transfers on food consumption
Note: Figure depicts mean gain in food consumption for nine-year participants as compared with three-year participants.
Source: Arroyo Ortiz *et al.* (2008b).

participation and hours of work. A concern with minimising labour supply disincentives has dominated discussions on the optimal design of transfers in developed countries, and has informed policy discussions around welfare reform (Moffitt, 2002). In developing countries, this issue has been researched in some detail.[22]

In many anti-poverty transfer programmes, labour supply responses are a primary and explicit objective, as in programmes with a work condition or those aiming to reduce child labour or improve school attendance. Among programmes focused on human capital investment through schooling, reducing or eliminating child labour is an implicit objective. The success of these programmes in reducing child labour has been mixed. Given that children's time could be split into schooling, working and other activities, education subsidies providing incentives for schooling may not, by themselves, result in a proportionate

[22] There is a large literature on this issue. See, among others, Alzúa, Cruces and Ripani (2010), Ardington, Case and Hosegood (2009), Bertrand, Mullainathan and Miller (2003), de Carvalho (2008a; 2008b), Cortez Reis and Camargo (2007), Edmonds (2006), Ferro and Nicollela (2007), Foguel and Paes de Barros (2008), Freije, Bando and Arce (2006), Lam, Leibbrandt and Ranchhod (2004), Posel, Fairburn and Lund (2004), Skoufias and di Maro (2008) and Skoufias and Parker (2001).

reduction in the incidence of child labour (Ravallion and Wodon, 2000). Studies on Bangladesh's Food for Education programme find that the reduction in child labour time was less than proportionate to the rise in schooling (Ahmed and del Ninno, 2002). In Mexico's *Oportunidades*, evidence of a rise in enrolment and attendance among participant children is stronger and more compelling than the evidence that education subsidies reduced child labour (Skoufias and di Maro, 2008; Skoufias and Parker, 2001; Skoufias, Unar and González-Cossío, 2008). The success of Brazil's Programme for the Eradication of Child Labour in reducing child labour owed in large measure to the requirement that participating children spend time in after-school activities (Yap, Sedlacek and Orazem, 2002).[23]

Social pensions and other transfers targeted at older people are likely to reduce their labour supply even in the absence of inactivity tests as a requirement of eligibility. Social pensions in developing countries very rarely include inactivity tests as an eligibility requirement – a feature that distinguishes them from non-contributory pensions in developed countries (Barrientos, 2006). Labour force participation rates for those eligible to receive a pension are very low in South Africa, and decline rapidly when individuals reach the age of pension entitlement (Lam, Leibbrandt and Ranchhod, 2004). This is to be expected, as the combination of the generosity of the pension benefit and the means test provides strong incentives for withdrawal from the labour market.

Given the high incidence of co-residence for pensioners and their extended households in developing countries, and evidence of widespread pension income sharing, it is of some interest whether labour supply effects of social pensions can also be observed among non-pensioners. This has been investigated in some detail in South Africa. Bertrand, Mullainathan and Miller (2003) suggest that the effects of pension income on hours of work and employment of fifteen- to fifty-year-olds co-residing with pension beneficiaries in South Africa can be significant. Using 1993 cross-section data from three-generation African households, they estimate that fifteen- to fifty-year-old co-residents with a pension-eligible person undertake on average 6.4 fewer hours of work and have a 4.3 per cent lower probability of being in employment. They also find that the labour supply effect is

---

[23] The transfer component of this programme has been integrated into *Bolsa Família*.

strongly significant for co-residing males, but not significant among co-residing females. Critically, though, this study samples co-residents only, and misses out non-resident household members.

Posel, Fairburn and Lund (2004) note that a high proportion of household members of working age migrate to urban centres in search of work; as many as 30 per cent of rural households in South Africa have a migrant. Replicating the work of Bertrand, Mullainathan and Miller, but now including migrant household members, Posel, Fairburn and Lund find that the negative association between pension receipt and labour supply in that study becomes positive, and conclude that fifteen-to fifty-year-old individual members of a household with a pension-eligible person have a 3.2 per cent higher probability of employment. Disaggregating by gender, they find no significant effect associated with pension income received by male pensioners on the labour supply of adult household members, but a strong and positive effect when the pension recipient is female. They suggest that pension income received by women is particularly important for rural households, 'not only because it helps prime-age women overcome income constraints to migration, but also because it makes it possible for grandmothers to support grandchildren' (24). A recent study has confirmed this finding with longitudinal data helping track household changes around pension receipt (Ardington, Case and Hosegood, 2009). Similar findings have been reported for Chile's *Chile Solidario* (Carneiro, Galasso and Ginja, 2008).

Overall, the findings of the literature on the labour supply effects of transfers can be summarised as follows. First, anti-poverty transfers lead to a reduction in the labour supply of children and older people, especially when education subsidies or social pensions target these groups specifically. The effects are stronger where social assistance programmes include schooling conditions for children or inactivity tests on older people. Second, the reduction in labour supply from these groups is often compensated for by changes in the labour supply of other household members. To the extent that social transfers lift credit and care constraints, they could have the effect of encouraging additional labour supply from other household members, as appears to have been the case in South Africa and Chile. In these circumstances, the impact of social transfers on labour supply could well be positive.[24]

---

[24] Some studies find marginal shifts in employment to non-farm activities; see Skoufias and di Maro (2008) and Skoufias, Unar and González-Cossío (2008).

Third, there is scant evidence that social transfers have large adverse labour supply effects on beneficiaries and their households. It will be important to reassess this finding in the future, especially as transfer programmes expand their coverage, improve the level and generosity of transfer levels and implement stricter recertification procedures. Attention will also need to be paid to structuring pathways to employment among beneficiaries of transfer programmes.

Conclusions

The main objective of this chapter was to discuss three processes associated with social assistance programmes supporting assessments of their effectiveness. The chapter focused on the three 'I's: incidence, implementation and impact.

The incidence and reach of anti-poverty transfer programmes provide valuable information on their effectiveness. The extent to which transfers are directed to households in extreme poverty (incidence) and the extent to which they reach a majority of households in extreme poverty provide primary information on the likelihood that these programmes will be effective in reducing poverty. To date, the literature on 'targeting' has focused largely on identifying and measuring leakages to the population not in poverty. Although this approach has dominated the evaluation of social assistance programmes, its limitations are well understood. Removing the bias introduced by targeting approaches has stimulated research into more comprehensive measures of incidence. It has also thrown light on the need to focus on the core processes of beneficiary selection, which combine to determine the incidence of anti-poverty transfer programmes.

Compared with issues of design, analysis of the implementation of social assistance programmes has lagged behind, despite compelling evidence as to its significance. There are indications that the 'project' approach that informed early developments in social assistance in the South is gradually being replaced by research and policy concerns with institutions and institution building. Poverty eradication requires strong, stable and more or less permanent institutions, and there is much to be learned from the way institutionalisation is unfolding in developing countries. This chapter focused on processes of institutionalisation and on the role of information. A discussion on vertical and horizontal coordination issues highlighted challenges in the

implementation of social assistance programmes in large federal countries. A brief discussion on the role of information in the implementation of anti-poverty transfer programmes placed in sharp relief issues of
capacity and accountability.

Research on the impact of social assistance has grown in leaps and
bounds. A feature of the spread of social assistance in the South has
been the emphasis on developing monitoring and evaluation processes,
often encouraged by the need to shore up political support among
policymakers, international partners and the general public. The vast
and growing evaluation literature required a strong focus on core and
intermediary programmes objectives, namely poverty, consumption
and productive capacity; and on benchmarking the size and
direction of these effects. Well-designed and well-implemented social
assistance programmes can demonstrate strong effects on poverty,
especially on the poverty gap and the poverty gap squared. The
evidence base on the consumption effects of transfers confirms a strong
correlation between income transfers and improvements in food
consumption among participant households. The rise in consumption,
and especially food consumption, largely tracks the value of the
transfers. Evidence as to the impact of transfers on the productive
capacity of households is significant across a range of programmes
and contexts. This is true whether programmes target human or physical assets. Increasingly, research is focusing on ascertaining the
medium- and longer-term impacts of anti-poverty transfers. There is a
strong expectation that short- and medium-term improvements in the
productive capacity of households in poverty can lead to long-term
gains.

ADDITIONAL NOTES A6

A6.1 Measures of incidence

This brief note provides a more detailed description of the main measures of incidence used in the chapter and the literature.

Let us define Cp as the coverage rate of eligible people participating in
a social assistance programme. N stands for the number of people; D
denotes participation status as $D = 1$ if participating and $D = 0$ if not;
and eligibility is defined by the requirement that people have a welfare
indicator y_i with a value less than a threshold z; Cp can be written as

$$Cp = N[D = 1; y_i < z]/N[D = 1] \qquad (6.A1.1)$$

This could be replicated to enquire into the share of the programme budget *B* that goes to eligible people. Assuming a uniform transfer *t*, this can be written as

$$Bp = tN[D = 1; y_i < z]/tN[D = 1] \qquad (6.A1.2)$$

Type II incidence errors and budget 'leakages' are given by $(1 - Cp)$ and $(1 - Bp)$, respectively. Changing the denominator to $N[y_i < z]$ in 6.A1.1 and 6.A1.2 generates measures of 'undercoverage' and budget insufficiency, respectively. These measures are widely used (Ravallion, 2007).

The Coady, Grosh and Hoddinott measure (2004) normalises *Bp* by the share of the population in poverty *q*, the latter capturing the share of the budget going to people in poverty under a uniform transfer. Under a uniform transfer, the budget *B* is allocated evenly to the population regardless of their poverty status. This measure can be written as CGH = *Bp/q*. Values for the CGH above 1 indicate that the share of the budget going to people in poverty is greater than the share generated by a uniform transfer. Values for the CGH below 1 indicate that the share of the budget going to people in poverty is less than the share generated by a uniform transfer.

Concentration curves $C(p)$ provide graphical measures of incidence. They have the advantage of de-emphasising a particular poverty line. Ranking individuals by their welfare indicator from poorest to richest, concentration curves show the cumulative share of transfers *T* going to the poorest percentile of the population. With $T(x)$ denoting the transfers going to quantile *x*, and t^* denoting the mean transfer, $C(p)$ can be written as

$$C(p) = \frac{1}{t*} \int_0^p T(x) dx \qquad (6.A1.3)$$

The concentration index *CI* provides a measure of the gap existing between the concentration curve and the diagonal. The latter provides a benchmark in which everyone in the population receives a uniform transfer t^*. The concentration index can be written as

$$CI = 2 \int_0^1 C(p) dp - 1 \qquad (6.A1.4)$$

The concentration curve and index have been used to compare the incidence of different programmes within a country, and the incidence of programmes across countries (Medeiros, Britto and Soares, 2008; Soares *et al.*, 2007).

Skoufias and collaborators (Coady and Skoufias, 2004; Skoufias and Coady, 2007; Skoufias, Lindert and Shapiro, 2010) have developed the distributional characteristics index (DCI), a welfarist measure of incidence that has the advantage of making more transparent the value judgements embedded in the benchmark adopted. They start from a standard Bergson–Samuelson social welfare *W* function as

$$W = V^1\left(p, y^1\right), \ldots, V^i\left(p, y^i\right), \ldots, V^N\left(p, y^N\right) \qquad (6.A1.5)$$

With *V*(.) denoting indirect utility functions for a population *N*, *p* are prices and *y* is a welfare indicator. A transfer programme can be described by a vector T as T $= [t^1, \ldots, t^i, \ldots, t^N]$, where $t^i > 0$ for participating individuals and $t^i = 0$ for non-participating households.

The impact of the programme on social welfare is

$$dW = \sum_i^N \frac{\partial W}{\partial V_i} \frac{\partial V_i}{\partial t_i} t^i \equiv \sum_i^N \beta^i t^i \qquad (6.A1.6)$$

Here, β^i is interpreted as a welfare weight attaching to transfers to individual *i*. Multiplying and dividing the right-hand side by the transfers budget *B* ($= \Sigma\, t^i$) yields

$$dW = \sum_i^N \beta^i \frac{t^i}{\sum_i^N t^i} \sum_i^N t^i \equiv \lambda B \qquad (6.A1.7)$$

λ is the DCI of the programme, the sum of the fraction of the budget going to each individual multiplied by each individual's welfare weight. It can be interpreted as the 'number of units of social welfare generated per dollar transferred' (Skoufias, Lindert and Shapiro, 2010: 123). Skoufias proposes a specification of the welfare weights as $\beta^i = (y^k/y^i)^\epsilon$, where *k* indexes a reference household and ϵ captures aversion to inequality, which rises with the value of ϵ. If $\epsilon = 0$, there is no aversion to inequality; if ϵ approaches infinity, aversion to inequality comes close to a Rawlsian maximin.

A6.2 Difference-in-difference measures of impact

The challenge for researchers aiming to estimate the impact of anti-poverty transfer programmes is to identify and isolate with precision the outcomes that can be attributed directly to the intervention. Programme design, implementation and data availability often determine the quality and precision of this attribution (Ravallion, 2005). A range of techniques are available to support the estimation of impact in different conditions (Blundell and Costa Dias, 2000; Imbens and Wooldridge, 2009). Here, the focus is on providing a little more detail on difference-in-difference estimates of the impact of anti-poverty transfers.

A good starting point is to consider potential outcomes from a single policy intervention, assuming that individual responses are heterogeneous and selection is exogenous. D is the treatment indicator, with $D = 1$ if an individual i participates in the programme and $D = 0$ if not. Potential outcomes are y_i^1 and y_i^0 for the treated and non-treated scenarios, respectively, and can be written as

$$y_i^1 = \alpha + \beta_i + \mu_i$$
$$y_i^0 = \alpha + \mu_i$$
(6.A2.1)

where α is the intercept parameter and β_i is the effect of the treatment on individual i; μ_i is the unobservable component of y_i. The observed outcome is

$$y_i = \alpha + \beta_i D + \mu_i$$
(6.A2.2)

The population average treatment effect is therefore $\beta^{\text{ATE}} = E(\beta_i)$, while the average treatment effect on the treated is $\beta^{\text{ATT}} = E(\beta_i|D = 1)$. In an experimental setting, it might be possible to estimate these effects directly. Randomisation is aimed at ensuring that the treated and the not-treated are equal in all respects apart from the treatment status. With heterogeneous responses, this involves maintaining two key assumptions: (a) that unobservables do not influence selection; in other words, that selection is fully exogenous – that is, $E[u_i|D = 1] = E[u_i|D = 0] = [u_i]$; and (b) that selection on idiosyncratic gains from treatment that could mimic the randomisation process can be ruled out – that is, $E[\beta_i|D = 1] = E[\beta_i|D = 0] = [\beta_i]$.

In the context of anti-poverty transfer programmes, experimental methods are difficult to implement, especially when consideration is given to their ethical implications. In non-experimental settings, particular attention needs to be paid to selection problems and the assignment rule, and it cannot be guaranteed that the assumptions above hold.

Difference-in-difference estimates of impact rely on naturally occurring phenomena capable of inducing randomisation in the eligibility or assignment to the programmes (Blundell and Costa Dias, 2000). In the case of Mexico's *Progresa*, eligibility was determined before the start of the programme in 1997, partly on the basis of available census data. Constraints on the capacity of the relevant agency to roll out the programmes led to a delayed incorporation into the programme of a fraction of beneficiaries in randomly selected communities. This provided an opportunity to implement a difference-in-difference approach to estimating the impact of the programme, by comparing the outcome of interest before and after the implementation of the programme and also across the treated and untreated groups. For observations at time $t0$ and $t1$, the assumption (a) above is expected to hold in first differences – that is, that $E[u_{i1} - u_{i0}|D = 1] = E[u_{i1} - u_{i0}|D = 0] = [u_{i1} - u_{i0}]$. Because the difference-in-difference approach cannot maintain assumption (b), it can identify the average treatment only on the treated effect. The difference-in-difference estimator can be written as

$$\hat{\beta}^{DID} = [\bar{y}_{t1}^1 - \bar{y}_{t0}^1] - [\bar{y}_{t1}^0 - \bar{y}_{t0}^0] = \beta^{ATT} \qquad (6.A2.2)$$

7 | Budgets, finance and politics

Financing is often held to be one of the main constraints on the extension of social assistance in developing countries. Demonstrably, developing countries have high poverty incidence and limited resources to address it. This is particularly true of low-income countries. It is hard to underestimate the very real financial constraints operating in developing countries, but a one-sided focus on financing as a constraint has driven research and policy discussions on financing social assistance in developing countries away from a firm understanding of the issues involved. The organising argument in this chapter is that financing social assistance is 'politics by other means', and requires at least as much attention to issues of legitimacy and incentives as to the issue of resource mobilisation, which has dominated discussions to date.[1]

In policy discussions, the glare of financing constraints can blind both supporters and detractors of anti-poverty transfers. Detractors often rely on concerns over finance to argue that direct transfers to households in poverty are not affordable in developing countries. Furthermore, it is argued, they could be counterproductive if resources that would otherwise support infrastructure such as schools and clinics are diverted to social assistance (Ravallion, 2006; Smith and Subbarao, 2003). Among advocates of direct transfers, concerns over financing are often framed in resource mobilisation terms: finding additional resources to finance the extension of social assistance. All too directly, the resource mobilisation approach leads to proposals for additional international aid to support the extension of anti-poverty transfers in the South (Pogge, 2004; Townsend, 2009). Admittedly, trade-offs in social spending and international aid are substantive issues and highly relevant to the extension of social assistance in the South. Separated out from the broader political canvas, a narrow consideration of these two issues often distracts from a deeper understanding of the financing of anti-poverty transfers.

---

[1] This follows from the discussion in Chapters 2, 3 and 4.

In this context, this chapter has much work to do. The materials in the chapter address three main questions. What is the size of the budgets required to support assistance programmes in developing countries? How should these budgets be financed? How does financing influence the legitimacy and sustainability of social assistance institutions?

The starting point of the chapter is an attempt to assess the size of the budgets required. Chapter 4 reviewed theoretical approaches to identifying an optimal budget size for transfers. The discussion in this chapter adopts an empirical approach to assessing budgets in practice, taking, sequentially, a positive approach and a normative approach to assessing the required size of social assistance budgets. The positive approach examines available data for a range of developing and developed countries and provides estimates of the size of their social assistance budgets. Data restrictions are significant, but rough estimates suggest that the majority of countries in the sample allocate between 1 and 2 per cent of their GDP to social assistance. Many low-income countries spend a fraction of this figure. Normative approaches start instead from a needs assessment, based on estimating the costs of providing transfers to categories of people, or to individuals and households in poverty. The normative approach arrives at significantly larger budgets than those identified through the positive approach, especially in low-income countries.

How should the social assistance budget be financed? To date, policy discussions and research on financing social assistance have been dominated by resource mobilisation approaches, especially in the context of low-income countries. The financing issue becomes one of finding additional finance. Given well-documented resource constraints in developing countries, finding additional resources often leads to foreign aid. The discussion in this chapter departs from this approach in at least two important respects. First, in most developing countries, the resources required for assistance programmes are collected from a combination of different sources: tax revenues, expenditure switching, revenue from natural resources, debt cancellation, payroll taxes and foreign aid. In a dynamic context, the focus must be on the financing mix, as opposed to individual sources of finance. Second, it is essential that discussions of financing incorporate an understanding of the scope and functions of the financing mix. In addition to collecting the resources required for an extension of social protection, the financing mix generates a pattern of incentives for all stakeholders. Taxes and transfers generate behavioural responses from stakeholders. Foreign aid generates incentives for elites in recipient countries. The extent to which the pattern of incentives generated through the financing of social assistance is consistent with policy objectives and priorities will in large measure define the effectiveness and sustainability of social assistance. The implications from this insight are far-reaching. The financing mix also has implications for the shape and legitimacy of social assistance and social protection institutions.

This leads directly to the third question for this chapter: how does financing influence the legitimacy and sustainability of social assistance? Political support for social assistance programmes is essential for their introduction and for their longer-term sustainability. To an important extent, issues of financing social assistance hinge on political factors. Financing social assistance is 'politics by other means'. The final section of the chapter provides a discussion on the political factors facilitating or constraining the spread of social assistance in developing countries. This section provides an empirical counterpart to the basic analysis of tax transfer schemes in Chapter 4, by examining the emergence of 'fiscal pacts' in developing countries.

The main conclusion of this chapter is that, properly understood, the financing of social assistance is much less of a barrier to the spread of anti-poverty transfers in developing countries than is commonly perceived. Rather, it can be seen as the fulcrum of opportunity in shaping appropriate and effective institutions in the South capable of securing a significant reduction in – and eventually the eradication of – extreme poverty.

Social assistance budgets

The main objective of this section is to assess the size of social assistance budgets, in order to provide some order of magnitude of the resources required. The literature on this issue, which is scarce, commonly employs two approaches. One is to examine existing practice across a range of countries and then arrive at some estimate through an inductive process (Besley, Burgess and Rasul, 2003; Baulch, Weber and Wood, 2008). This is a positive approach, and it has the advantage of enabling a discussion on the factors influencing the level of the budget across countries. A different approach is to start from an assessment of needs and then estimate the budget required to address the needs gap

(Behrendt, 2008; Kakwani and Subbarao, 2007; Kakwani, Soares and Son, 2006). This is a normative approach, often based on a technical assessment of country conditions, but taking no account of potential constraints on the size of budgets. This section explores estimates from these two approaches sequentially.

Social assistance expenditure in developing countries

Social assistance expenditure is hard to establish on a comparative basis. Until recently the guidelines for reporting social expenditures in national income accounts did not identify social protection expenditure and social assistance as separate components.[2] In European countries, and more generally Organisation for Economic Co-operation and Development countries, efforts to measure the size of the welfare state and its components have led to improvements in the relevant data collection and enabled estimates of social assistance expenditure (Adema and Ladaique, 2009). In developing countries, the relative underdevelopment of social assistance institutions has been matched by paucity in the collection of appropriate data by national govern-ments.[3] This is rapidly changing, as social assistance programmes have mushroomed in the past decade. A stronger focus on social assistance has stimulated efforts to measure budgetary flows supporting relevant programmes and policies that can be described as social assistance. This is work in progress, but data culled from a handful of sources can be used to provide a rough picture of social assistance expenditures glob-ally in the mid-2000s. Figure 7.1 presents this information.

Keeping firmly in mind the lack of consistency in the country data, some stylised facts emerge from the figure. The mean value for social assistance expenditure as a proportion of GDP is 1.3 per cent, although the median is lower, at 1.1 per cent. Only twenty out of the 133 countries in the figure spend more than 2 per cent. Forty-five countries spend 1 per cent on social assistance or less, and fifty-seven countries spend 1 to 2 per cent. The range of social assistance expenditure across developed and developing countries is narrow.[4]

---

[2] For a description of recent guidelines on data collection and reporting by multilaterals, see Barrientos (2010c: annex 3).

[3] For a benchmarking exercise, see Besley, Burgess and Rasul (2003).

[4] In fact, the variation in the social assistance expenditure data across countries is significantly narrower than the variation shown by higher-level aggregates such as

A resource constraint hypothesis would suggest that, controlling for country social preferences for redistribution to groups in poverty, high-income countries would show higher levels of social assistance expenditure than low-income countries, simply because of the tighter resource constraints in the latter. The ranking of countries in Figure 7.1 appears to rule out the possibility of a linear relationship between the level of economic development and the level of social assistance expenditure. Among the countries with social assistance expenditure above 2 per cent, it is possible to find high-income countries together with very low-income countries, and former Soviet Union countries. The data do not necessarily rule out the resource constraint hypothesis. Low-income countries are conspicuous among the countries with very low social assistance expenditures; and the low-income countries among the high spenders on social assistance are supported by large foreign aid flows. Nonetheless, resource constraints appear not to be the primary factor explaining social assistance expenditures.

It is also possible to rule out the existence of a direct relationship between 'need' and the level of social assistance expenditure. Low-income countries with higher poverty incidence tend to bunch towards the right-hand side of the figure, not the left-hand side of the figure. High-income countries with low poverty incidence show relatively high levels of social assistance expenditure compared with low-income countries with high poverty incidence. This does not mean that need factors are not relevant. It is perhaps the way that needs are understood and intermediated within national political and policy processes that has greater influence.

Other factors could be explored in this context, including institutional structures and the influence of path dependence. The legacy of ideological factors, as much as regional factors, can account for the relatively high levels of social assistance expenditure in former Soviet Union countries.

Noting the narrow variation in the data on social assistance expenditure, Weigand and Grosh (2008: 11) suggest that it might confirm the proposition that 'societies agree that a certain floor of safety nets is required, but that they also have reservations about making the safety nets too large'. This is an interesting hypothesis to explore, but the narrow range can also be partially explained by institutional factors. Perhaps influenced by modernisation theory, some authors have argued

social protection expenditure or social expenditure. This has been noted by Weigand and Grosh (2008).

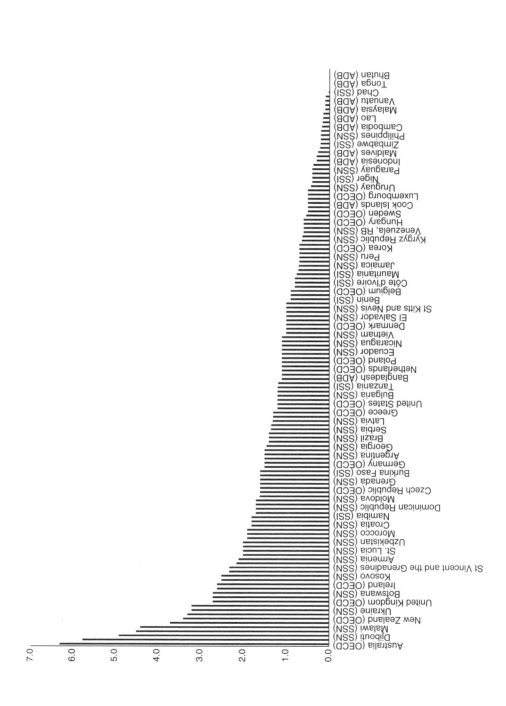

Figure 7.1 Social assistance expenditure as percentage of GDP

Notes: 'OECD' data refer to social expenditure on income-tested programmes addressing the needs of the unemployed, families, the elderly and the disabled, but excluding expenditure on active labour market programmes and expenditure on health care. 'SSN' ('Social safety nets' database) data include public expenditure on non-contributory transfer programmes targeted at the poor and vulnerable, and international aid flows in support of these programmes. Ethiopia's domestically financed expenditure stands at only 0.5 per cent of its GDP. 'ADB' (Asian Development Bank) data include public expenditure on welfare and social services targeted at the sick, the poor, orphans, disabled and other vulnerable groups; subsidised health care costs; targeted utility and staple food subsidies; fee exemptions; and cash and in-kind transfers. 'SSI' ('Social security inquiry' survey) data include public expenditure on social insurance and social assistance. The data extracted from this series mainly cover low-income sub-Saharan African countries with limited social insurance provision and therefore limited public expenditure on social insurance. The data must be interpreted as the upper ceiling for social assistance expenditure. Countries with large public social insurance schemes, such as the Seychelles and Liberia, are left out.

Sources: Adema and Ladaique (2009) ('OECD'), Weigand and Grosh (2008) ('SSN'), Baulch, Weber and Wood (2008) ('ADB') and ILO (2010) ('SSI').

that economic development generates a 'tipping point', beyond which countries grow social insurance institutions that take over some of the functions of social assistance (Barry, 1990; Lindert, 2002), effectively placing an upper ceiling on the latter's expansion. This stylised dynamic of social protection expenditure cannot be taken for granted. Australia, New Zealand and South Africa provide examples of a different institutional dynamics. In these countries, social insurance has not fully replaced social assistance institutions. The scarce literature on the institutional dynamics of social protection in developing countries provides little support for the modernisation hypothesis (Gough *et al.*, 2004; Haggard and Kaufman, 2008). Latin American countries are, in fact, in the process of strengthening social assistance institutions after decades of institutional investment in social insurance (Barrientos and Santibañez, 2009a).

The data in Figure 7.1 do not provide clues as to the effectiveness of social assistance expenditure. If high spenders are inefficient in reducing poverty and low spenders are efficient, the range in effective social assistance expenditure could be even narrower. The reverse is also a possibility.

Needs assessments of social assistance expenditure

A different approach to identifying orders of magnitude for social assistance budgets is to start from a needs assessment and then cost the budgets for appropriate interventions. There are many examples available of this type of approach, including feasibility studies commissioned by multilaterals and bilaterals in low-income developing countries. These begin by measuring the incidence and depth of poverty, then propose specific instruments to address poverty and related objectives and simulate both the size of the budgets required to finance these instruments and their expected impact on poverty. The findings from needs assessment exercises are an essential input into policy formulation and programme design.

Two studies, by Kakwani, Soares and Son (2006) and Kakwani and Subarrao (2007), use data sets from several low-income sub-Saharan Africa countries to study ex ante the poverty reduction effectiveness of human development transfer programmes and non-contributory pensions. They employ standard methodologies for simulating policy changes on representative household data, and also employ national poverty lines.[5] Figure 7.2 summarises the results of a simulation of

---

[5] The findings are roughly in line with those from other studies (Behrendt, 2008; Gassman and Behrendt, 2006).

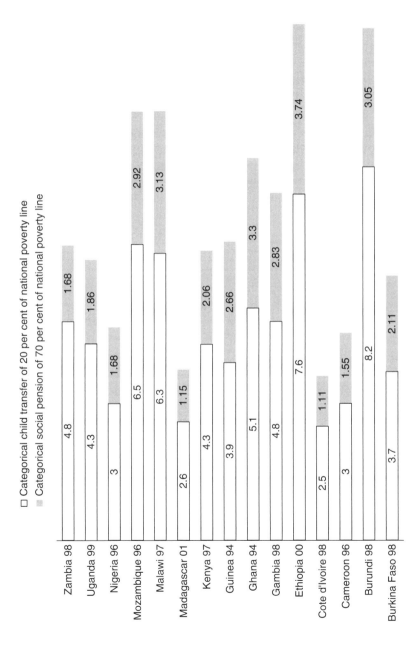

□ Categorical child transfer of 20 per cent of national poverty line

▓ Categorical social pension of 70 per cent of national poverty line

Country	Child transfer	Social pension
Zambia 98	4.8	1.68
Uganda 99	4.3	1.86
Nigeria 96	3	1.68
Mozambique 96	6.5	2.92
Malawi 97	6.3	3.13
Madagascar 01	2.6	1.15
Kenya 97	4.3	2.06
Guinea 94	3.9	2.66
Ghana 94	5.1	3.3
Gambia 98	4.8	2.83
Ethiopia 00	7.6	3.74
Cote d'Ivoire 98	2.5	1.11
Cameroon 96	3	1.55
Burundi 98	8.2	3.05
Burkina Faso 98	3.7	2.11

Figure 7.2 Simulated budgets of categorical transfers to children and older people in selected countries in sub-Saharan Africa
Sources: Kakwani, Soares and Son (2006) and Kakwani and Subbarao (2007).

categorical transfers to all children of school age (five to sixteen years of age), equivalent to 20 per cent of the national poverty line, and a transfer to older people (women aged sixty and over, males aged sixty-five and over), equivalent to 70 per cent of the national poverty line. The demographic structure of sub-Saharan African countries is such that children make up a significant portion of the population, and therefore categorical transfers, even at relatively low levels, would absorb a significant amount of resources. In the figure, they range from 2.5 per cent of GDP in Côte d'Ivoire to 8.2 per cent in Burundi. On the other hand, the same demographic structure means that only a small proportion of the population is old. The budgets required to finance a transfer equivalent to 70 per cent of the national poverty line to all older people are smaller than less generous transfers to children, but still substantial. They range from 1.1 per cent of GDP in Côte d'Ivoire to 3.7 per cent in Ethiopia. From these figures, it is possible to obtain some order of magnitude of the budgets required to provide categorical transfers to children and older people. They range from 3.7 per cent of GDP in Madagascar to 11.3 per cent in Ethiopia.

The studies also explore the costs of providing selective transfers, either fixed-level transfers only to groups in poverty or variable transfers covering the estimated poverty gap for households. Figure 7.3 shows the budgets required to finance non-contributory pensions equivalent to 70 per cent of the national poverty line only to older people in poor households, and those needed to finance a variable transfer equivalent to the poverty gap of households with older people.[6] Even though a minority of households in these countries have older people, the required budgets are large. Fixed transfers would require between 0.5 per cent of GDP in Côte d'Ivoire and 2.2 per cent in Malawi; variable transfers would absorb from 1.2 per cent in Côte d'Ivoire to 9.1 per cent in The Gambia. A similar exercise to assess the required budgets for children would generate much larger figures, given demographic factors.

Comparing the social assistance budgets generated by adopting a positive approach with those resulting from taking a normative approach is very informative. First, the budgets generated by the normative approach are several times larger than those identified in the positive approach. Even restricting the normative budgets to

---

[6] The share of households with older people ranges between 12.9 per cent in Burundi and 46 per cent in The Gambia.

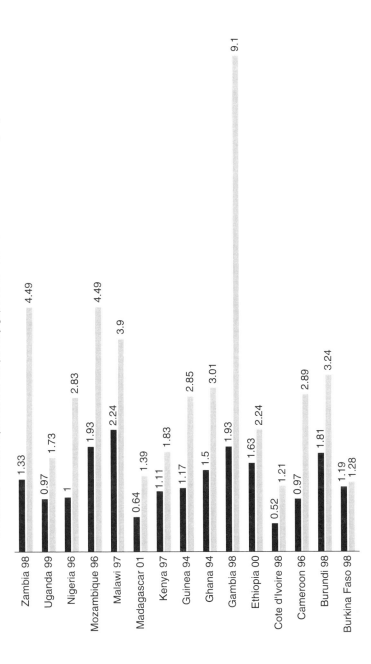

■ Selective pension of 70 per cent of national poverty line

▨ Selective transfer equivalent to the poverty gap in extended households with older people

Figure 7.3 Comparison of simulated budgets for a selective pension of 70 per cent of national poverty line and a transfer equivalent to the poverty gap in extended households with older people as a percentage of GDP in selected sub-Saharan African countries
Source: Kakwani and Subbarao (2007).

interventions for children and older people, and leaving aside other groups in poverty, it is apparent that in low-income countries the budgets arrived at from a needs assessment are not affordable. Normative budgets are useful in highlighting deficits in social assistance provision and in throwing light on the budgetary implications of alternative programme design and reach. Second, a positive approach to assessing social assistance budgets fails to indicate an 'optimal' level, although it does suggest that the range is fairly narrow, with most countries located in the range of 1 to 2 per cent of GDP. Third, it is hard to disagree with the conclusion reached by Weigand and Grosh (2008) for a smaller sample of countries, namely that the policy focus in developing countries should be on achieving a moderate rise in social assistance budgets, while making a strong effort to improve the effectiveness of expenditure.

Financing anti-poverty transfers

In order to extend social protection in developing countries, national governments need to pay attention to their financing (Barrientos, 2008b). Experience and lessons from the expansion of social protection in European countries are unlikely to provide feasible models for developing countries to follow.[7] European countries largely financed the construction of their welfare states after 1950 through a rapid expansion of social security payroll taxes. Globalisation places strong pressure on the capacity of developing countries to raise revenues. The size and significance of informality in the South in particular limits the scope of social security payroll taxation (Tanzi, 2000). The issue of how to finance the extension of social protection in developing countries calls for hard-headed, innovative responses.

The revenue mobilisation approach and its drawbacks

Debates on how to finance the extension of anti-poverty transfers in developing countries have been dominated by the revenue mobilisation

---

[7] On the emergence of welfare states in developed countries, see Lindert (2004). On the financing of social protection, see Cichon *et al.* (2004). De Kam and Owens (1999) and Sjöberg (1999) discuss the evolution of the financing of the welfare state expansion in European countries.

approach – the view that what is needed is to find 'new money' to finance anti-poverty transfer programmes. In the context of developing countries, and of low-income countries in particular, this approach privileges a search for additional aid flows. The dominance of the revenue mobilisation approach largely reflects the focus of multilaterals and bilaterals on the issue of poverty reduction. Although identifying additional sources of finance for development is an important issue in its own right,[8] a one-sided focus on resource mobilisation in the context of the extension of social assistance has in fact prevented the proper formulation and understanding of the challenges for developing countries on this issue. The revenue mobilisation approach goes hand in hand with a short-term timeframe unsuited to longer-term institution building. It focuses on anti-poverty transfers mainly as expenditure, rather than as investment in human development. It often takes it for granted that existing budget allocations are both efficient and desirable, and as a result ignores the variable effectiveness of existing social assistance expenditure and social protection more generally. It favours a 'resourcist' and 'projectised' approach to poverty reduction, which overlooks the dominant role of politics in determining social assistance budgets at the national level.

A fuller understanding of the issues associated with the financing of anti-poverty transfers requires a more comprehensive approach. Two parameters of such an approach are important. First, the unit of analysis has to be the *financing mix*, including a range of potential sources of finance and their change over time. Second, it is essential to approach the financing of anti-poverty transfers as performing three tasks: (a) generating an appropriate level of resources for social assistance programmes; (b) ensuring that the pattern of incentives generated by the financing mix is consistent with poverty reduction and other policy objectives and priorities; and (c) ensuring that the financing mix progressively supports the legitimacy and sustainability of social assistance policies and institutions. The last two parameters add greater complexity to the analysis of financing issues when compared with the resource mobilisation approach, but they also have the effect of taking us closer to a sound understanding of the fundamental issues involved.

---

[8] See Atkinson (2005) for a comprehensive discussion on innovative sources of finance for development.

Further complications need to be factored in. Public expenditure on social assistance is a relatively small fraction of government expenditure, as we know from the discussion at the start of the chapter. National income accounts report social assistance under social protection expenditures, which in turn are reported within the social expenditures category, comprising expenditure on health, education and social protection. With most available data, it is difficult to separate out the different components of social protection, especially social insurance and social assistance. However, as we know from the handful of studies able to make this identification in household survey data, the distributional impacts of social insurance and social assistance in developing countries are chalk and cheese (Skoufias, Lindert and Shapiro, 2010). Empirically, accurate measures of social assistance expenditure across developing countries over time are hard to construct. Analytically, the financing of social assistance is not separable from the full government financial envelope. There are examples when the political processes leading to an extension of social assistance claim that the associated expenditure is earmarked from a specific source of finance. This 'strategic earmarking' can influence the shape of social assistance institutions, and it therefore merits study.

Accordingly, the discussion that follows begins by examining the financing mix in developing countries. It then considers the issue of incentives, before looking into cases of strategic earmarking and considering issues of legitimacy.

Financing mix and trends

Governments' revenues are, essentially, fungible; what is spent on one programme is not spent on another. Even in circumstances in which sources of funds are earmarked, the main purpose of this is most often political rather than financial. In assessing the financing of social assistance, it is necessary therefore to gain a perspective on the entire government financial envelope. In order to analyse the main sources of government revenue, a distinction is made between domestic sources, including tax and non-tax revenues, and external sources, including aid and borrowing.

Tax revenues represent the most significant source of government revenue in developing countries. In low- and lower middle-income countries, taxes represent about 80 per cent of government revenues, followed by revenues from property income, sales of goods and services, grants from foreign governments and international organisations and property income (IMF, 'Government finance statistics' database). In middle-income countries, taxes make up 90 per cent of government revenues, followed by other revenues and social security contributions.

Taxes on income include personal income tax and corporate income tax. In developing countries, taxes on personal income apply mainly to wealthier groups and contribute a very small share of tax revenues. Revenues from taxes on corporations make a larger, and rising, contribution to government revenues. Taxes on consumption have been on the rise in developing countries, and include value-added tax, general sales tax and excise duties. General sales tax applies to the sale of goods and services normally calculated as a proportion of the value of sales, ad valorem. Value-added tax has been adopted in the majority of countries because it prevents the 'cascading' effect of general sales taxes (Bird and Gendron, 2011). It applies to the value of sales minus the value of inputs, to the value added between two transactions. Excises are charged on commodities with inelastic demand, such as cigarettes and alcohol. Revenue from consumption taxes accounts for the majority of tax revenues in developing countries.

Governments in the South used to rely on revenues from trade taxes, but these have declined over time. Property taxes can be charged on landholdings in rural or urban areas and are used most commonly to finance local government expenditure. In developing countries, the revenues accruing to government from the exploitation of natural resources constitute the bulk of non-tax revenue category. The rise in commodity prices, especially oil and mineral resources, has increased their contribution to government revenues (Jiménez and Gómez Sabaini, 2009). Depending on country reporting practices, revenues from the exploitation of natural resources, a rising source of government revenue in resource-rich countries in the South, can be accounted for as taxes on corporations or non-tax revenues.

Among external sources of government revenues, foreign aid is especially important in low-income countries. In recent years the role and structure of aid has changed a great deal. The traditional aid modalities, project or programme aid, have been complemented by sector-wide assistance programmes and general budget support. Donor agreements on aid harmonisation have proved difficult to implement. The increasing influence of large emerging economies, such as the BRICs (Brazil,

Russia, India, China and South Africa), has opened up wider opportunities for international partnerships among developing countries. A focus on poverty reduction among multilateral and bilateral donors, encouraged by the Millennium Development Goals and poverty reduction strategies at the national level, has given greater visibility to expenditure on anti-poverty transfer programmes. Government borrowing is seldom a sensible option for financing social assistance programmes, but debt cancellation, as through the Heavily Indebted Poor Countries initiative, has provided participating governments with additional funds. This can be looked upon as 'negative borrowing' (Keen and Mansour, 2009).

Changes in the financing mix over time vary across developing regions and countries, but some overall trends can be observed in the past two decades. There has been a sustained rise in the share of gross domestic product accounted for by government revenues since the 1990s. This trend reflects the influence of several factors: economic growth and development; rising commodity prices and demand for natural resources; tax reform aimed at expanding the tax base and simplifying tax structures; and an improvement in the administrative capacity to collect taxes. For Africa as a whole, government revenues as a share of GDP rose from 22 per cent in 1990 to 27 per cent in 2007 (AfDB and OECD Development Centre, 2010). In Latin America, they rose from 14.8 per cent in 1990 to 21 per cent in 2008 (Jiménez and Gómez Sabaini, 2009). The strength of the rise varies markedly across countries within these two developing regions, but, overall, the trends have been positive in the last two decades.

Recent trends in the relative contribution of revenue sources are particularly relevant in the context of the growth in anti-poverty transfer programmes. The main trends in the components of the financing mix include the following.

- A reduction in the contribution of trade taxes to government revenues. This change has been strongly advocated by international organisations as a means of facilitating the integration of developing economies with the world economy. This is perhaps the most significant change in the structure of government revenues across the developing world.
- A stronger contribution from consumption taxes, especially in Latin America. In some countries in the region, consumption taxes provide

the bulk of government revenues. In Africa, the contribution of consumption taxes to the government financial envelope is important, but has changed little in the past decade.

- With few exceptions, personal income taxes make a very limited contribution to financing governments in the South. Corporate taxes, on the other hand, have increased recently, driven mainly by commodity prices. The share of income taxes in government revenue in developing countries is small, especially when compared with OECD countries.
- Aid flows make a very significant contribution to financing government expenditure in many low-income countries in sub-Saharan Africa, but show a diminishing role in middle-income countries.
- The contribution to government revenues from natural resources, oil and non-oil, has risen, especially in Africa, where they are responsible for the bulk of the rise in total revenues.

The rise in government revenues as a share of GDP and the changes in the financing mix in developing countries define the fiscal space within which to examine the financing of anti-poverty transfers.

The financing mix and social assistance

The rise in government revenues as a share of GDP is an important factor facilitating the extension of anti-poverty transfer programmes.[9] The extent to which social expenditure levels are correlated with low or high growth has been studied in a cross-country setting mainly for advanced economies.[10] Among developing countries, there is a strong positive correlation between the recent growth of government revenues and the growth in social expenditures (ECLAC, 2009). In Latin America, the growth of the first has led to a more than proportionate increase in public expenditure. This is an explicit policy response to the

[9] See the advice of the International Monetary Fund (IMF, 2009: 39) to sub-Saharan African governments in the context of the impact of the global financial crisis: '[O]n the expenditure side, it would be desirable, with external support, to adopt and gradually scale up safety net programs, targeting them carefully and building in countercyclical properties. Existing programs that are performing well should be scaled up first; in the short run, though the capacity of Sub-Saharan African countries to set up new programs is limited.'

[10] This literature is summarised by Atkinson (1999). See also Arjona, Ladaique and Pearson (2001).

impact of the 1980s 'lost decade' and the structural adjustment that followed on social expenditures, which Latin Americans aptly describe as 'social debt' (*deuda social*). Linking the rise in government revenue as a proportion of GDP to the rise in social assistance is more difficult to establish in a cross-country setting given data restrictions. It was noted above that national income accounts fail to report social assistance expenditure separately from social protection, which also includes expenditure on social insurance. The hypothesis tested in these studies is that social protection transfers encourage growth. For Latin American countries: a strong correlation between growth and expenditure on social protection has been observed for the last two decades (Cornia, 2010).[11] The expansion of the financial envelope of developing country governments is likely to have facilitated investment in social assistance, but at this stage this remains a strong hypothesis.

It is even harder to disentangle the extent to which changes in the financing mix can facilitate or constrain investment in social assistance programmes. Figure 7.4 provides a comparison of changes in the composition of fiscal revenues in Latin America and Africa. The comparison indicates that, while both regions have experienced growth in government revenues, in Africa revenues from natural resources have driven this growth, whereas in Latin America consumption taxes, and taxes on the income of corporations, have constituted the main source of growth in fiscal revenues. To what extent could the observed changes in the finance mix offer an explanation for the stronger extension of anti-poverty transfers in Latin America?

Current research on the extension of social assistance in developing countries does not support a full answer to this question, but the literature on the politics and political economy of taxation can throw some light on the issue. The literature on revenue bargaining in developing countries argues that there is a link between the extent to which governments are dependent on revenues raised from taxation and constraints on state power (Mahon, 2005; Moore, 2004). Governments able to rely on other sources of financing, such as rents from natural resources or international aid, have greater autonomy with respect to their citizens' needs and preferences. Moore describes revenue

---

[11] Several studies have noted the link between the rise in tax revenues and social assistance. See Barreix, Villela and Roca (2007), Breceda, Rigolini and Saavedra (2009) and Cubero and Vladkova Hollar (2010).

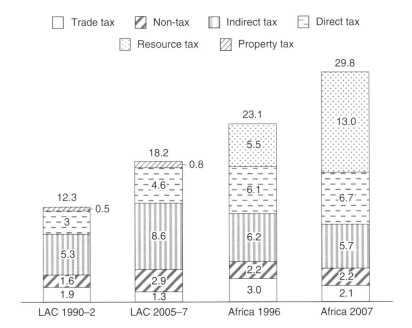

Figure 7.4 Government revenue in Latin America and the Caribbean and Africa regions as a percentage of GDP
Notes: The Latin American and Caribbean ('LAC') data are based
on ECLAC's data series, and are a simple average. The data for Africa
reflect a GDP-weighted average. The data are not strictly comparable across regions, but are consistent within a region.
Sources: Jiménez and Gómez-Sabaini (2009) (Latin America and the Caribbean) and AfDB and OECD Development Centre (2010) (Africa).

bargaining as a 'beautiful story – about the creation of state capacity of various kinds, the expansion of the authority of political representation and the establishment of accountability to citizens and limits to autocratic state power' (M. Moore, 2008: 48). Fiscal contracts or pacts are examples of revenue bargaining.

There are alternative ways to model the parameters of revenue bargaining and the plurality of parties to the agreement. This can be described as direct bargaining between government and citizens over the scope and reach of taxes and services (D'Arcy, 2011). The focus here is on the tax burden and the overall fiscal envelope. An extension of the revenue bargaining model focuses on negotiations between the government and specific income groups. In this model of revenue bargaining, the tax mix could have a bearing on the level and composition of government spending (Lindert, 2004; Timmons, 2005). This is particularly relevant to our concern with identifying alternative tax–transfer linkages associated with anti-poverty transfers. Timmons (2005) puts forward the hypothesis that, in a context in which (a) governments find it necessary to engage citizens in bargaining over the level and incidence of taxation, as opposed to relying on coercion or on autonomous revenue sources such as aid or rents from natural resources, and in which (b) citizens are divided in their preferences for government service provision, revenue bargaining will make it possible for government to act as a discriminating monopoly and ensure that citizens pay for the services they value. This assumes an advantage in public provision arising from, say, economies of scale in information gathering and/or provision or, alternatively, insurance. In this situation, transfers and service provision will match the preferences of different citizens' groups. To the extent that the government relies on the direct taxation of wealthier groups, transfers and services will be focused on these groups. Alternatively, if the government relies on regressive taxes, it will need to ensure that services reach non-wealthy groups.

In this approach, government transfers and services follow taxes in a fairly direct fashion. This could be relaxed in a context in which the government can rely on a broad-based agreement among the main civil society groups. Kato (2003) argues that the expansion of the welfare state in advanced economies eventually had to rely on expanding indirect taxes. In her analysis of advanced economies, she finds that governments that were able to diversify away from payroll taxes as a means to finance welfare provision earlier on also managed to sustain the expansion in provision during the retrenchment in the 1980s and 1990s. Governments that did not diversify their financing by recourse to indirect taxation met hard limits to the expansion of the welfare state. This explains a bifurcation of advanced economies into high tax/high transfers and low tax/low transfers. Beramendi and Rueda (2007) take this approach further by including attention to partisanship. They note that rule by social democratic governments in advanced economies can be associated with a rising share of consumption taxes. They hypothesise that corporatist structures limit social democratic governments' capacity to raise income taxes. Trade unions and business will eventually come to oppose further increases in income taxes. To sustain welfare provision directly benefiting their labour supporters, they must rely increasingly on consumption taxes.

Revenue bargaining can provide a partial explanation for the differences in the spread of social assistance in Africa and Latin America. This appears to be less to do with the overall level of taxes and transfers, and more with the observed differences in the changes in the financing mix. This is a very rough and ready hypothesis, which would need to be developed and tested further. There are many complications arising from observing conditions in the two regions; these would need to be ironed out before the hypotheses could gain purchase. In sub-Saharan countries, pilot anti-poverty programmes have been financed mostly from foreign aid, and have been influenced strongly in their design and scope by international donors. In Latin America, governments reliant on natural resources to finance their expenditure – Bolivia, Chile and Mexico, to name a few – have expanded their anti-poverty transfer programmes as much as non-resource rich countries have done. Few, if any, Latin American countries show signs of corporatist structures in place. This hypothesis is considered further in the following sections, and especially in the section on legitimacy. Its introduction here is useful in providing a strong justification for examining issues of incentives and legitimacy in the context of financing social assistance.

Incentives

A full understanding of the financing of social assistance transfers requires consideration of the extent to which the incentives that alternative forms of financing generate are consistent with poverty reduction objectives. At the limit, financing could generate adverse incentives of a magnitude sufficient to undermine seriously any beneficial effects of anti-poverty transfers. In the context of the extension of social assistance in developing countries, two general concerns need to be considered. First, it is important to pay attention to the impact of financing on the strategic incentives of policymakers. This is particularly relevant in the context of anti-poverty transfers being financed by foreign aid or natural resource revenue. As Chapter 6 discussed, the expansion of social assistance in developing countries involves significant institution building, extending over the medium and longer term. This imposes limits on the role of foreign aid in financing it. Second, the behavioural and political responses of economic agents to alternative financing streams could have implications for the evolution of anti-poverty transfers. The discussion below takes up each of these issues in turn.

Foreign aid has played an important role in supporting the introduction of anti-poverty transfer programmes in low-income countries. This is critical in the early stages of institutional development, especially as the initial costs involved can be large. To the extent that set-up costs are a barrier to the adoption of effective anti-poverty transfer programmes, or the reform of existing programmes, international assistance can be extremely useful. International assistance was crucial, for example, in facilitating the introduction of Mexico's *Progresa*, especially as the government was facing a financial crisis, which restricted its fiscal space, while at the same time political instability made it difficult to switch expenditures from existing non-performing poverty programmes (Levy, 2006). In sub-Saharan Africa, international assistance has made possible the introduction of pilot anti-poverty transfer programmes in several countries (Niño-Zarazúa *et al.*, 2012). There is also a prima facie case for using international aid to support knowledge generation and dissemination relating to anti-poverty transfers. In particular, monitoring and evaluation processes in anti-poverty transfer programmes support and generate knowledge on poverty reduction in the countries involved and, more generally, in countries with similar conditions. To the extent that much of the knowledge on poverty reduction that these programmes generate constitutes a global public good, there is a strong case for international assistance financing.[12]

The case for using foreign aid to fund anti-poverty transfers, as opposed to the design, implementation or reform of these programmes, is weaker and substantially more complex.[13] There is an extensive literature documenting and discussing the adverse impact of aid dependence on state formation in developing countries. With regard to taxation, and governance in general, a strong case can be presented to demonstrate that there is an institutional dividend from the domestic financing of government expenditure. This follows from concerns that aid might actually reduce the incentives for elites to respond to citizens'

---

[12] A good example is the South–South Learning on Social Protection initiative by the International Policy Centre for Inclusive Growth in Brasilia, financed jointly by the government of Brazil and the United Kingdom's Department for International Development; see http://south-south.ipc-undp.org.

[13] Holmqvist (2010 examines these complexities very lucidly.

preferences and demands (Brautigam and Knack, 2004; M. Moore, 2004; 2008). Holmqvist (2010) discusses the extensive literature on the adverse impact of aid on institutional development more generally. Aid could act to slow down or prevent institutional development, and make elites less responsive to their citizens. The concern is that external financing extending beyond the specific areas identified above could have the effect of undermining the emergence and long-term sustainability of social assistance institutions.

Other factors come into play too. The term structure of aid is normally too short to support effective institution building for social assistance. This helps explain the reluctance on the part of governments in low-income countries to embark on large-scale anti-poverty transfer programmes financed with international aid, and their preferences for small-scale pilots (Niño-Zarazúa *et al.*, 2012). Establishing longer-term partnerships between governments and donors can provide a way to overcome this problem. This was the insight supporting a drive towards budget support, which gives medium-term stability to aid, provided that national governments and donors share common objectives.[14] Structured efforts to strengthen the revenue collection capacity of national governments, in combination with aid-supported anti-poverty transfers, might provide another viable strategy to address this problem. Setting targets for 'budget graduation', through decreasing aid-to-revenue ratios, can be useful in ensuring that national governments are committed to achieving financial sustainability in the medium and longer term.[15] Even if these proposals could be agreed and implemented, the core incentive compatibility issues remain. Aside from helping developing countries overcome the large initial costs of introducing social assistance programmes anew, foreign aid is a very limited instrument for financing effective social assistance.

The same incentive issues apply to proposals to finance anti-poverty transfers with global taxes or with natural resources rents. Townsend (2009), for instance, has proposed the introduction of a global child benefit, which could be financed through a Tobin-type tax – a tax on

---

[14] Interestingly, budget support was never fully embraced by Development Assistance Committee donors, in part because it was difficult to persuade electorates of their benefits.

[15] The ILO's 'Global social trust' programme, for example, envisages the provision of start-up capital and knowhow for open-ended projects, with a gradual withdrawal of the trust after ten years.

exchanges of foreign currency. The global financial crisis has rekindled interest in Tobin-type taxes. Proponents claim that there are potential benefits from such a tax, including greater financial stability in the global economy resulting from the disincentives for short-term currency exchange associated with the tax. However, a recent study is sceptical of the benefits for the global economy of a foreign currency tax, and suggests that the actual funds that might be made available would not be significant (Matheson, 2011). From the perspective of anti-poverty transfers, additional factors would need to be considered. Most proposals envisage the tax as applying to the four main currencies used in the foreign exchanges, but this would probably endow the relevant countries with a dominant influence over the scheme and the distribution of the funds raised. Proposals linking anti-poverty transfers to revenues from natural resources face similar incentive problems (Moss, 2011).

The likely effects of regular external income flows from developed countries on the economies of developing countries cannot be covered here. However, they could be substantial. A recent study simulated the impact on taxes and employment of a global welfare state, understood as one in which optimal taxation, as Chapter 4 described, is applied to all people, without reference to nation states (Kopczuk, Slemrod and Yitzhaki, 2005). The authors conclude that such a scheme would generate significant transfers from taxpayers in the wealthy parts of the world to the low-income population of the world, located mainly in developing regions. The global welfare state would also significantly raise unemployment in low-income regions of the world, because of skills differentials. In the same way that welfare states enforce high unemployment among low-skilled individuals in developed countries, a global welfare state would replicate these effects on a global basis.

There is an extensive literature focused on the impact of the domestic financing of transfers on economic incentives, particularly with regard to taxpayers and beneficiaries.[16] The main issue is the extent to which the financing of anti-poverty transfer programmes distorts incentives to work and save among agents in the economy, and the relative effect of alternative forms of finance. The public finance literature suggests that there

---

[16] This is at the core of the optimal taxation literature covered in Chapter 4 (Mirrlees, 1971).

are costs to a market economy of raising revenue through taxation.[17] Payroll taxes may reduce work incentives for marginal workers, and taxes on non-labour income may reduce incentives to save.[18] This implies that, in order to finance US$1 of anti-poverty transfers, it may be necessary to raise, say, US$1.25 in revenue. In this scenario, the marginal cost of social funds would be greater than the amount needed for expenditure.[19] Warlters and Auriol (2005) estimate the marginal costs of social funds for African countries to be in the order of US$1.17.[20] If the marginal costs of financing transfers are different across the different components of the finance mix, it might then be less costly to finance anti-poverty transfers at the margin with, say, consumption taxes than with payroll taxes. Few studies have tackled this issue empirically,[21] mainly because the financing of social assistance is not earmarked within government revenues, and also because determining the final incidence of taxation is complex. The findings from studies simulating the distributional, rather than the welfare, effects of different ways of financing anti-poverty transfers suggest that the former are not an important concern.[22]

The effects from introducing anti-poverty transfer programmes on overall incentives in the economy can be minimised if expenditure is

---

[17] To the extent that increased taxation provides a corrective instrument for market imperfections that cause inefficiencies, the tax 'burden' associated with financing anti-poverty transfer programmes could become a 'dividend'. For a discussion, see Atkinson (2005).

[18] In addition, there are costs associated with the administration and enforcement of tax rules.

[19] The marginal cost of public funds is 'the multiplier to be applied to the direct resource cost in order to arrive at the socially relevant shadow price of resources to be used in the public sector' (Sadmo, 1998: 367).

[20] A test for the efficiency of taxing to spend on transfers is to compare the marginal cost of funds with estimates of marginal benefits from expenditure. Estimates of a global average return to education are in the order of 26.6 per cent, 17.0 per cent and 19.0 per cent for primary, secondary and high school levels, respectively. However, for sub-Saharan African countries, the returns to education for the same levels of schooling jump to 37.6 per cent, 24.6 per cent and 27.8 per cent, respectively. See Psacharopoulos and Patrinos (2004).

[21] One study tackling this issue in a general equilibrium setting concludes that there are gains for developing countries in combining tax reforms and anti-poverty transfers; see Coady and Harris (2004).

[22] Cubero and Vladkova Hollar (2010), for example, conclude that the distributional effects of raising an additional 1 per cent of GDP to distribute through transfers in Central America are not that different whether they are financed through value-added tax or through a composite tax.

financed by switching expenditure from underperforming poverty programmes. The opportunities for financing transfer programmes in this
way vary from country to country. In low-income countries with low
levels of social assistance expenditure, the opportunities are bound to be
more limited. In low-income countries in sub-Saharan Africa, there is
scope from shifting expenditure from emergency aid to investment in
stable institutions addressing persistent poverty and vulnerability
(Barrett, Holden and Clay, 2005). In fact, the donor advocacy of anti-
poverty transfer programmes in low-income countries is often motivated by a perceived need to find more effective means of reducing
poverty than recurrent emergency assistance (Gilligan, Hoddinott and
Seyoum Taffesse, 2008). In middle-income countries, and especially in
Latin America, switching public subsidies from social insurance
schemes for the better off to social assistance is likely to deliver both
distributional and efficiency gains (Barrientos, 2011b; Ferreira and
Robalino, 2010; Levy, 2008). On the tax side, studies suggest that a
policy focus on reducing tax privileges and exemptions, as well as
tackling tax evasion through improved administration, can generate
fiscal space without the need for tax reforms (AfDB and OECD
Development Centre, 2010; Jiménez, Gómez Sabaini and
Podestá, 2010). Tax exemptions are common in developing countries
and tend to benefit the better off, while at the same time diminishing the
tax base.

This extended discussion leads to four main conclusions. First, it is
important to evaluate the impact of tax and transfer policies on incentives. Second, the role of aid in financing anti-poverty transfers is
limited, in part because it generates strategic incentives away from
institution building and sustainable financing. Similar arguments
apply to other sources of finance, such as global taxes and natural
resource rents. Foreign aid has an important role in financing the
large set-up costs associated with the introduction of social assistance
and in supporting knowledge and capacity. Third, it is hard to
obtain reliable measures of the incentive effects of alternative forms of
financing anti-poverty transfers from domestic taxation, but available
studies suggest that this is not a huge issue. Fourth, there is significant
scope for financing anti-poverty transfers from improved efficiency in
social protection expenditure and from minimising tax exemptions and
evasion.

Legitimacy

The conventional view is that the level of economic development, the structure of the economy and administrative capacity influence fiscal structures. Increasingly, attention is being paid to the central role that politics and institutions play in defining both the tax and expenditure structures of developing countries. An emerging literature focuses on the linkages existing between tax and state formation and development (Brautigam, Fjeldstad and Moore, 2008; DiJohn, 2010). More recently, research has taken the further step of connecting the politics of taxation and expenditure (Bird, 2005; Timmons, 2005). These authors emphasise how important it is to develop an understanding of the third function of financing in the context of the extension of social assistance: to endow emerging social assistance institutions with a measure of legitimacy.[23]

Current discussions on the role of anti-poverty transfer programmes as part of social pacts or social contracts in developing countries help frame this discussion. The significance and scope of social pacts and social contracts is discussed explicitly among Latin American researchers (Breceda, Rigolini and Saavedra, 2009; Lora, 2008; Machinea, 2006) and among South African researchers (Nattrass and Seekings, 2001). The absence of social pacts has been noted as a factor in the slow spread of anti-poverty transfers in sub-Saharan Africa (Hickey, 2008). The enlargement of the fiscal space in Africa has created the conditions for further consideration of the fiscal structure their populations expect (D'Arcy, 2011).

It is easy to agree at a conceptual level that fiscal pacts combining agreement around taxes and transfers are central to the emergence of social assistance institutions in developing countries, but there are considerable challenges involved in identifying appropriate empirical counterparts. It is therefore important to start with a simple approach and a limited set of objectives. The discussion below adopts a two-stage approach. The first stage is to map out and analyse 'narratives' of social assistance financing. As argued above, analytically the financing of social assistance should be linked to the full financial envelope available to national governments. However, there are several instances in which

---

[23] There is a highly relevant literature on the link between the growth of welfare states in advanced economies, the role of indirect taxation and politics (Beramendi and Rueda, 2007; Kato, 2003).

policymakers have sought to make an explicit link between a source of finance and the expansion of social assistance programmes. Ostensibly, this has been done to make a political point, with the objective of lending legitimacy to decisions on taxation and expenditure. They have the effect of constructing a 'narrative' about fiscal structures. Below, several such narratives are identified and studied. The second stage provides a preliminary analysis of these narratives with the aim of establishing differences and similarities. A particular interest is to throw some light on the extent to which these 'narratives' influence legitimacy and encourage social contracts.

In most cases, social assistance programmes financed from domestic resources are supported from general government revenues, and no explicit link is made between anti-poverty transfers and specific sources of financing. However, in a number of cases, policymakers explicitly make such a link. It is useful to consider some of these cases.

- Chile's return to democracy after seventeen years of dictatorship was led by a centre-left coalition of parties. The transition was fraught with danger, as General Pinochet, who remained head of the army, and the business community, which had benefited greatly from his rule, exercised considerable power. The coalition was committed to expanding social expenditure, especially poverty reduction. This was financed by a rise of 2 per cent in the tax burden, distributed across rises in corporate taxes, personal income taxation and value-added tax. In particular, a 2 percentage point rise in the value-added tax rate, from 16 to 18 per cent, was explicitly linked to the financing of poverty reduction programmes. The package was negotiated success-fully with the business sector. According to Boylan (1996), the ear-marking narrative had three advantages: (a) it reduced uncertainty over the tax transfer plans of the new coalition government; (b) it reassured the public about the new government's commitment to fiscal responsibility; and (c) it undermined potential opposition from the business sector and trade unions.
- In 1994 Bolivia was poised to privatise state-owned enterprises, especially in the energy sector. To facilitate public consent, the gov-ernment proposed maintaining one-half of the shares in the privatised enterprises in a Special Fund (Gray-Molina, Pérez de Rada and Yañez, 1999). The returns from this fund were to be used to finance a regular transfer to the adult cohort (aged twenty-one years or over

in 1995). After further debate, the transfer became a non-contributory pension, the *Bono de Solidaridad*, payable from the age of sixty-five. There were several modifications to the transfer, as the fund was insufficient to support the required budget (Aponte *et al.*, 2007). The government of Evo Morales extended entitlement to the transfer to all Bolivians on reaching sixty years of age. As he intended the energy sector to be brought back into public control, its finance was linked to a new hydrocarbons tax (Barrientos, 2009c).

- The 1988 constitution in Brazil – after twenty years of dictatorship had ended in 1985 – embedded a new social contract, with explicit recognition of the right to social protection as a key principle (Jaccoud, Hadjab and Chaibub, 2009). This acknowledged social assistance as a key pillar embodied in two programmes: a new means-tested non-contributory pension, the *Benefício de Prestação Continuada*, providing benefits to older people in extreme poverty; and the extension of social insurance provision to informal workers in rural areas, the *Prêvidencia Social Rural*. Enabling legislation established a transitional period of ten years for workers in this situation to regularise their contribution histories. In effect, contributory requirements for social insurance pensions have never been enforced for these workers, and, in the apt description of Brazilian researchers, this remains a quasi-contributory transfer. Enabling legislation established that financing for this transfer was to come from a 2 per cent tax on agricultural sales, and the rest from social insurance funds. The earmarking helped legitimise the programme as an instrument of solidarity with rural workers, as agreed in the constitution. In practice, the sales tax raises a very small fraction of the estimated costs of the programme, the majority of which is funded from government revenues (Schwarzer and Querino, 2002).
- Non-contributory pension programmes introduced in Lesotho (2004) and Swaziland (2006) are linked to revenues from the Southern African Customs Union, which some researchers consider a mechanism for South Africa to provide financial support to member countries (Ulriksen, 2011).
- Anti-poverty transfer programmes in Ethiopia, Uganda and Zambia are financed by bilateral aid, through a memorandum of understanding between donors and the government channelling funds through the budget. In Kenya and Mozambique, governments and donors co-finance anti-poverty transfer programmes; in the case of

Mozambique, donors specifically finance an extension in the number of beneficiaries. In Ghana, the initial financing of the Livelihood Empowerment against Poverty programme was linked to debt cancellation under the Heavily Indebted Poor Countries initiative, but bilateral donors also contributed (Niño-Zarazúa *et al.*, 2012).

There is a great deal in common in the narratives for Latin American countries, which embed widely shared perceptions that structural adjustment resulted in high and persistent poverty as well as social exclusion, creating a welfare deficit (*deuda social*). Linking finance sources to expenditure on anti-poverty transfers underlines government efforts to reduce social protection exclusion.[24] Democratisation processes often provide the context against which financing narratives are constructed. Narratives embody the emerging social pacts or social contracts. In important respects, the connections made by these narratives go beyond essentially redistributive mechanisms and include elements of inclusion and fairness.

The narratives in sub-Saharan African countries tend to be more diverse and lack reference to social pacts. To an important extent, this is because they link anti-poverty transfer programmes primarily to external funding. They do not emphasise social assistance as a means of inclusion, nor as embodying national aspirations and priorities. The likely exceptions are Kenya and Mozambique, because the contribution by the national governments to the financing of these programmes is capable of generating such connections in the future.[25] Mozambique's extension of social assistance was grounded in new legislation, the Social Security Law, passed in 2007, including as one of its components 'Basic social protection', which governs anti-poverty programmes.

Despite variation in the strength or accuracy of the financing narratives, there is some evidence to support the view that they do influence the evolution of the relevant programmes. This is clearest in the case of aid-financed anti-poverty transfer programmes. Their lifespan is tied to the term structure of the financing, especially when no provision has been made for the medium- or longer-term financing. In some of the

---

[24] In Argentina, this strategy is entitled the Social Protection and Inclusion System; see Maurizio (2009).

[25] The paths of the two countries might well turn out to be different. The government of Kenya has stated its intention to raise its contribution to finance a further extension of the Orphans and Vulnerable Children Programme.

examples from Latin America, the evolution of programmes has managed to overcome this time restriction and achieve full institutionalisation. However, this was not the case in Nicaragua, where a donor-funded programme was not continued after the funding window had closed.

The narratives are interesting in revealing the influence of political processes around the issue of financing. They are also able to influence institution building in positive ways (sustainability) as well as in negative ways (projectised time windows). They flesh out the connection between financing and the legitimacy of anti-poverty transfer expenditure. They also leave open the question of whether there are underlying explanations linking tax and transfers in a more fundamental way.

This leads to four main conclusions. First, the financing of anti-poverty transfer programmes has implications for their legitimacy. The narratives examined above help make this point, by making explicit reference to linkages between financing sources and anti-poverty transfer expenditure. Earmarking financing for anti-poverty transfer expenditure is in the main a political intervention, a means by which to legitimise tax–transfer linkages. They are important because they have the capacity to influence programme design and sustainability. They also have the capacity to signal the emergence of social pacts or social contracts. Second, consideration of narratives of financing does not imply abandoning the search for underlying explanations; on the contrary, they help throw light on the scope and reach of revenue bargaining. Third, it is helpful to consider narratives in terms of the contrast in the expansion of social protection between Africa and Latin America. In Latin America, where the main revenue sources are consumption taxes and natural resource rents, there has been a rapid expansion of anti-poverty transfer programmes. In Africa, where revenues from natural resources have dominated the rise in tax revenues, the expansion of anti-poverty transfer programmes has been slow. Narratives in Latin America highlight the role of consumption taxes and domestically captured natural resource rents, but narratives in Africa tend to emphasise external sources of revenue, or, at least, they fail to emphasise domestic sources of revenue. Fourth, in explaining the development of social assistance in developing countries, narratives suggest that an understanding of the politics connecting taxation and spending is essential.

Conclusions

This chapter has focused on the financing of anti-poverty transfer pro-grammes in developing countries. It began by noting that an under-standing of this issue has been hampered by a focus on resource mobilisation. Financing social assistance is about a great deal more than simply collecting additional resources for countries to invest in anti-poverty policies, important though this is. The financing mix has a strong influence on the effectiveness and sustainability of anti-poverty transfer programmes, through its effects on incentives and on legiti-macy. Three main questions helped focus and organise the materials in this chapter. It is time to review the answers provided.

What is the size of the budgets required to support assistance pro-grammes in developing countries? A positive approach to determining the size of social assistance programmes concludes that the majority of countries spend between 1 and 2 per cent of their GDP on anti-poverty transfer programmes. A few countries – a mix of high- and low-income countries – spend in excess of this amount. The group of countries spending less than 1 per cent of GDP on social assistance includes mainly low-income countries. The figures do not appear to support a direct positive link between the level of development and the size of social assistance budgets. They do raise the possibility that expenditure on social assistance has a ceiling, and they highlight the important role of path dependence. Normative approaches measure the costs of addressing a needs assessment in each country, and result in signifi-cantly higher, and perhaps unachievable, social assistance budgets.

How should these budgets be financed? This depends on the financing mix of government revenues, especially tax revenues. The size and the composition of a country's tax revenues provide the main parameters of the fiscal space within which decisions on the size of the social assistance budget are made. The growth of social assistance in developing coun-tries has been supported by recent growth in the share of government revenues as a proportion of GDP in developing countries. Arguably, the rise of consumption tax revenues and natural resource rents within the financing mix could explain the stronger growth in social assistance in Latin America. By contrast, the growth in government revenues in sub-Saharan Africa is mainly a factor of natural resource rents. This suggests a need to pay attention to incentives in the financing of social assistance. Future research needs to examine in some detail the poverty reduction incentives generated by variations in the size and composition of the financing mix.

How does financing influence the legitimacy and sustainability of social assistance? There are important implications in this regard. Earmarking of the financing of anti-poverty transfers, when explicit, makes it possible to examine the linkages between financing and anti-poverty transfer design and expenditure. Anti-poverty transfer programmes are often the outcome of emerging social pacts or social contracts, and contribute to reinforcing them. Their financing has a large influence over their sustainability, suggesting that an understanding of the politics connecting taxation and spending is essential to explaining the growth of social assistance in developing countries.

PART IV

Conclusion

8 | *The future of social assistance in developing countries*

The book has examined the emergence and rapid growth of social assistance in developing countries. In a very short period of time anti-poverty programmes have expanded to reach a large number of households in poverty in the South, estimated at between 0.74 and 1 billion people. The scale of the expansion of social assistance in the South demonstrates its potential to make a large contribution to the reduction, prevention and eradication of world poverty. Previous chapters have highlighted innovation and diversity in the design and implementation of anti-poverty programmes in developing countries. Income maintenance forms of social assistance are the norm in developed countries, but the exception in developing countries. Income maintenance approaches to social assistance apply only partially to the Minimum Living Standard Guarantee schemes in China and South Korea. A classification of social assistance programmes in developing countries in Chapter 5 identified three main types: programmes providing pure income transfers; programmes providing income transfers in combination with asset accumulation; and integrated anti-poverty programmes, in which income transfers are a relatively small component and for which social and economic inclusion constitute the primary objective. There are, clearly, visible linkages between poverty research and social assistance. The findings from impact evaluation studies point to the effectiveness of these programmes, but are also a tool to redesign and reform them. In middle-income countries in particular, social assistance programmes are extending their reach and strengthening their institutionalisation.

Where do we go from here? This closing chapter looks into the evolution of social assistance in developing countries in the next decade. The rapid growth in anti-poverty transfer programmes over the past decade is unlikely to abate in the years ahead. The discussion below focuses on the main challenges ahead and on the factors shaping the dynamics of anti-poverty programmes.

Main challenges ahead

There are important challenges to the expansion of social assistance in developing countries. The discussion below focuses on what are arguably the three most significant: the limited reach of anti-poverty transfers, the institutionalisation of social assistance and its financing. In discussing these three main challenges, it is important to distinguish between middle- and low-income countries.

Despite the rapid expansion of anti-poverty transfers in the South, there remain large gaps in the reach of these programmes. Social assistance fails to reach an important number of households in extreme poverty. It also fails to reach significant numbers of households in moderate poverty and vulnerability. Extending the reach of social transfer programmes, especially in low-income countries, remains a considerable challenge.

In middle-income countries, the scaling up of social assistance programmes is proceeding in leaps and bounds. Among the 'pioneer' countries – certainly Brazil, Mexico and South Africa, and perhaps China – social transfer programmes now cover large sections of the population, and reach beyond households in poverty and extreme poverty to include those considered vulnerable to falling into poverty.[1] In South Africa, one in every two households has a member receiving a grant; Mexico's *Oportunidades* and Brazil's *Bolsa Família* reach around a quarter of their respective populations. The extension of the Minimum Living Standards Guarantee to rural areas, and the extension of pension and health insurance schemes, implies that social assistance will continue its rapid expansion. Gao (2010) notes that a 2008 Panel of Experts in China predicted that universal social protection coverage will be achieved by 2049. In India, there is a lively debate on proposals for consolidating and expanding anti-poverty transfer programmes (Ghosh, 2011; Narayanan, 2011).

In Latin America, the Economic Commission for Latin America and the Caribbean has estimated the reach of human-development-conditional

---

[1] See the discussion on *Bolsa Família* targeting in Chapter 6 (Soares, Ribas and Soares, 2009).

transfer programmes based on household survey responses. The estimates are presented in Figure 8.1. In the more advanced economies in the Southern Cone, social assistance transfers reach all the population in extreme poverty and also extend to a large share of the population in poverty.[2] For countries in the Andean region, the reach of social assistance programmes is less extensive but growing. Ecuador's *Bono de Desarrollo Humano* reaches all the population in extreme poverty and a significant share of the population in poverty. In Central American countries, the reach of human development programmes is much lower, and rapid scaling up is required.

In low-income countries in sub-Saharan Africa, the reach of anti-poverty programmes is significantly lower. Ethiopia's Productive Safety Net Programme, the largest among low-income countries in the region, reaches around 11 per cent of households – a fraction of the population in extreme poverty. Mozambique's Food Security Benefit, the oldest social assistance programme among low-income countries in the region, targets older people and people with disabilities in poverty. It reached over 100,000 direct beneficiaries in 2008, less than one-half of the target population. In fact, the majority of anti-poverty transfer programmes in low-income countries in the region consist of pilot programmes, explic-itly intended to reach a minority of households in extreme poverty.

There are several explanations for the gaps in the reach of social assistance programmes in developing countries, but they can be grouped under two main headings: (a) programme design and implementation; and (b) resources and politics. Extending the reach of social assistance will involve addressing the constraints present in these two areas.

In many developing countries, programme designers have focused explicitly on a subset of households in poverty. Categorical pro-grammes, such as social pensions or child and family allowances, focus on specific groups considered to be especially vulnerable.[3] In low-income countries, groups targeted by social assistance are some-times defined more finely, such as HIV/AIDS-affected families in pov-erty, or orphans and vulnerable children. A focus on vulnerable groups inevitably leads to gaps in the reach of the programmes. At the same

---

[2] The agency defines the population in extreme poverty as including those with per capita household income insufficient to purchase a basic basket of food; the population in poverty includes those with per capita household income below the cost of a basic basket of food and non-food items.

[3] See the discussion on vulnerable groups in Chapter 5.

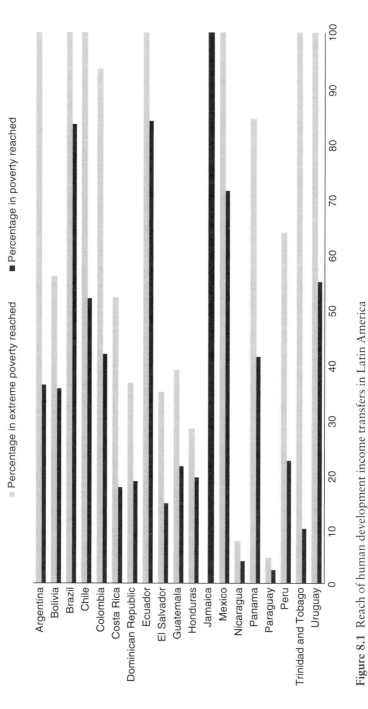

Figure 8.1 Reach of human development income transfers in Latin America
Source: ECLAC (2009).

time, the sharing of transfers within households in poverty extends the reach of categorical programmes beyond direct beneficiaries. Studies on social pensions demonstrate that transfers are shared within households (Barrientos and Lloyd-Sherlock, 2003; Møller and Sotshongaye, 1996), to the extent that it is more appropriate to describe social pensions as income transfers to households in poverty containing older people. In the context of low-income countries in sub-Saharan Africa, demographic profiles show that many households in poverty do not have an older person, with the implication that social pensions alone are likely to have a limited reach (Kakwani and Subbarao, 2007). Child benefits are also shared, more often with non-beneficiary children,[4] and the share of households in poverty with children in sub-Saharan Africa is considerably greater. The reach of a categorical child transfer is likely to be significantly larger in sub-Saharan Africa, but few low-income countries in the region have large-scale child-focused transfers. While taking into account the fact that anti-poverty transfers are shared within households, it remains the case that categorical anti-poverty transfers, in the absence of supplementary programmes, lead to gaps in the reach of social assistance.

Increasingly, programmes focus on households in poverty, as opposed to categories of individuals. A large proportion of these programmes target households in extreme or persistent poverty. Some programmes have a geographic or sectoral focus, such as the rural focus of the Mahatma Gandhi National Rural Employment Guarantee scheme in India. In south Asia, the rural focus of anti-poverty transfer programmes often leads to a comparative neglect of urban poverty. These restrictions, though perhaps effective in focusing scarce anti-poverty budgets on groups in greater need of assistance, lead to large gaps in the reach of the programmes. The challenge in this case is how to extend this reach.

In low-income countries, the limited reach of anti-poverty transfer programmes is explained by a combination of high poverty incidence and resource restrictions, including delivery capacity and budgetary restriction. Capacity constraints are acute among these countries. Social assistance programmes are often managed by agencies with limited

---

[4] The earlier evaluations of Mexico's *Progresa* noted that nutrition supplements aimed at infants were sometimes shared with older children (see Coady, 2003). In Africa, assistance programmes aimed at orphans are less effective if they do not also reach other children in the households where orphans live (Levine, 2001).

policy formulation and delivery capacity, especially by comparison with stronger and better-resourced ministries of health or education. Moreover, in lower-income countries in sub-Saharan Africa, two-thirds of programmes are managed outside government agencies (Garcia and Moore, 2012). The revenue-raising capacity of governments in low-income countries is a hard constraint on their capacity to support social assistance, but budgetary restrictions in part reflect the lack of political support for anti-poverty transfers among governing elites. The scale of the programmes is often insufficient even to reach the population in extreme poverty.

In low-income countries in sub-Saharan Africa, the reluctance of political elites to introduce social assistance programmes, motivated to an extent by a fear of rapid escalation, has resulted in the spread of pilot transfer programmes. Anti-poverty transfer programmes were originally introduced as pilot programmes in Ghana, Kenya, Liberia, Malawi, Nigeria, Tanzania, Uganda and Zambia. To an extent, political factors can also help explain the introduction of pilots in lower middle-income countries in Latin America. Human-development-conditional transfer programmes were introduced as pilot programmes in the Dominican Republic, Honduras, Nicaragua, Panama and Paraguay. On paper, most anti-poverty transfer programmes should be piloted to allow programme agencies to test their capacity and to identify design and implementation flaws. This applies particularly to low-income countries. It is crucial to ascertain whether anti-poverty transfer programmes could be implemented successfully in settings with low implementation and delivery capacity, and with more limited budgetary resources. In practice, a stronger motivation for the introduction of pilots has been to try to overcome the reluctance of domestic elites, especially in sub-Saharan Africa (Niño-Zarazúa *et al.*, 2012). As a consequence, pilot programmes are not implemented to generate valuable lessons for subsequent scaling up but, instead, to achieve 'demonstration' effects. Inevitably, insufficient attention has been paid to monitoring and evaluation processes in the design of pilot programmes, limiting the learning they can generate on the barriers to effective design and implementation.[5] This approach also serves to limit the reach of

---

[5] Pilots have not been designed, by and large, to serve as the first phase of a fully scaled-up programme. Few have made the necessary investment in information systems, delivery capacity and monitoring and evaluation processes.

these programmes, at least in the short and medium terms. Pilot programmes, by design, focus on a small subset of potential beneficiaries and therefore involve large shortfalls in reach. In most countries in west and central Africa, social assistance is almost non-existent (Niño-Zarazúa *et al.*, 2012).

Another major challenge is institutionalisation. Social assistance programmes in developing countries have emerged in a variety of contexts. Some have come from a deliberative process in which legislators set out a legal framework and priorities, with governmental agencies later embedding these in specific programmes. The principle underpinning Brazil's social pension, the *Benefício de Prestação Continuada*, for example, was included in the new 1988 constitution, and later implemented by the Brazilian government. Similarly, the National Rural Employment Guarantee Act in India provided the legal framework within which the scheme was later implemented. In developing countries, these examples of structured policy making are exceptional. The rule is for social assistance programmes to begin life as projects, as interventions with a limited time window, usually based on an executive decision. Mexico's *Progresa/Oportunidades*, for example, began life as a five-year project. Ethiopia's Productive Safety Net Programme also began life as a fixed-term intervention. In lower-income countries in particular, whether in sub-Saharan Africa or Central America, financing and advice from foreign aid agencies has precluded long-term planning and institutionalisation (Barrientos and Santibañez, 2009b; Niño-Zarazúa *et al.*, 2012). In some cases, the political environment has been such that programmes could be introduced only as short-term interventions (Sumarto, Suryahadi and Bazzi, 2008). In other cases, the process of policy formulation has been far from ideal (Pelham, 2007). An outcome of the project orientation of the birth and initial development of social assistance programmes in developing countries is that they are significantly under-institutionalised.

The weak institutionalisation of social assistance programmes places important constraints on their sustainability and effectiveness. This is especially the case when their funding is regulated outside normal budgeting processes; when their normative basis is not embedded in legislation but, instead, ruled by governmental discretion; when their operations and disbursements are not accountable to parliament; and when decisions on eligibility are not subject to adequate appeal and review processes. In most cases, institutionalisation emerges through a gradual process. Over time, fixed-term interventions are extended, and legal frameworks are eventually developed to account for them in budgetary processes. Later on, an established dedicated agency or ministry is given responsibility for programme implementation, and entitlements are recognised and protected by law. Governance structures are eventually made permanent. This process of institutionalisation is essential to the sustainability and effectiveness of social assistance.

Appropriate institutionalisation is a real challenge, especially as there are important trade-offs involved. Legislative or constitutional recognition is essential to establishing that access to social assistance is an entitlement, and not subject to the discretion of government officials. However, it is important that social assistance institutions are able to adapt to changing economic, social and demographic conditions. An important lesson from pension reforms, for example, is that changes in the labour market, life expectancy and structure of households can turn an effective pension scheme into an ineffective albatross (Gill, Packard and Yermo, 2004). Entitlements to social assistance can be stronger if they are protected by the constitution, but it is important that parliament is able to reflect changing conditions in the design and implementation of these entitlements (Seekings, 2008a). These can be difficult balances to achieve in conditions in which political processes aggregate preferences imperfectly, often to the detriment of lower-income groups' full participation in political decisions.

The institutionalisation of social assistance also involves appropriate mechanisms for the horizontal and vertical integration of anti-poverty programmes. Horizontal integration is important in circumstances in which there is a proliferation of separate but overlapping programmes. Vertical integration is important in the context of federal and decentralised government structures. Achieving an effective integration of anti-poverty programmes involves in practice difficult trade-offs between the relative power of central and local government agencies and across ministries. More recently, attention has been paid to the need to improve process dimensions in social assistance programmes. Rights-based approaches emphasise the need to ensure that social assistance programmes meet three main requirements: non-discrimination; participation; and accountability (Sepúlveda Carmona, 2009). It is important that social assistance programmes do not discriminate among eligible beneficiaries – that is, that the operation of the programme ensures horizontal equity among beneficiaries. Few social assistance programmes ensure participation by beneficiaries in the formulation and operation of the programme. Moreover, the parliamentary scrutiny of programme agencies requires that they are institutionalised appropriately in the first place.

The third main challenge concerns the financing of social assistance programmes, especially in low-income countries. This was discussed in some detail in Chapter 7. The dominance of the resource mobilisation approach, among aid agencies in particular, has prevented a fuller understanding of the issues involved. This approach focuses on finding additional sources of finance to support the expansion of transfer programmes. Its main disadvantages were noted. Financing the extension of social assistance as stable institutions charged with eradicating poverty requires that attention also be paid to incentives and legitimacy. A more comprehensive approach to financing emphasises the important role of domestic taxation in the financing mix needed to support transfers. Furthermore, linking social assistance and its financing is essential. There will be considerable diversity in the way in which countries face the financing challenge. From the discussion in Chapter 7, it is apparent that there are significant trade-offs involved. Financing the extension of social assistance through resource revenues requires hard consideration to avoiding a fiscal resource curse, preventing revenue diversification and the strengthening of the tax system. Financing the extension of social assistance from regressive taxation needs a balance between the benefits of fiscal inclusion and the adverse impact of taxes on standards of living among low-income households. In low-income countries, ensuring that foreign aid does not undermine the legitimacy of poverty reduction strategies is essential.

How best to address these major challenges requires urgent consideration by researchers and policymakers in developing countries. The way these challenges are addressed will shape the evolution of social assistance in the South.

Evolution of social assistance

The rate of growth of social assistance in developing countries has been a focal point of this book. Programmes are expanding rapidly in scale and scope. Knowledge and practice relating to their design and implementation continue to be extended and refined. It is interesting to speculate on how social assistance will evolve over the next two decades. It will be useful to review briefly the main factors shaping the dynamics of anti-poverty transfer programmes in the South.

Poverty research and social assistance

A feature of the expansion of social assistance in developing countries to date has been the interconnectedness of poverty research and knowledge with the design and implementation of anti-poverty transfers. The discussion in the last two chapters identified four core areas of programme design in which poverty research has strongly influenced programme design: incentives; multidimensionality; poverty rankings; and evaluation. These areas are covered below. At the same time, social assistance programmes in developing countries have made important contributions to knowledge about poverty. Findings from impact evaluation studies throw light on the factors keeping people in poverty, for example. This interconnectedness of knowledge and practice will have a strong influence on the future evolution of social assistance.

Conventional social assistance relied largely on income transfers to fill in the gap in consumption experienced by households in poverty. This is the basis for income maintenance schemes, which dominate social assistance in high-income countries. The impact of income maintenance transfers operated largely through income effects, and transfers were perceived in the main as compensatory. Emerging social assistance programmes in developing countries pay much more attention to the incentive effects of transfers than conventional income maintenance schemes. Conditions in human development transfer programmes, for example, emphasise the role of substitution effects as much as that of income effects. Further research on this is likely to influence the design and implementation of social assistance in the future.[6] This should not be taken to mean that the incidence of conditions in anti-poverty programmes will increase. There may well be diminishing returns to conditions in anti-poverty programmes, as the example of the early introduction of the Programme of Advancement through Health and

---

[6] As noted in Chapter 5, the knowledge base on the design and effectiveness of conditions is expanding rapidly, albeit from a low base (Baird, McIntosh and Özler, 2011; Barrientos, 2011a).

Education in Jamaica demonstrated.[7] Instead, what will merit further attention and refinement are the quality and role of co-responsibilities and conditions in enhancing income effects.[8] This is an area in which linkages between research and practice can produce future gains in programme effectiveness and poverty knowledge (Baird, Mcintosh and Özler, 2011).

Human-development-conditional income transfers explicitly adopt a multidimensional perspective on poverty. They seek to combine and integrate interventions along several dimensions, but especially those likely to strengthen productive capacity among children when they reach adulthood. This reflects not just lessons from past anti-poverty programmes but also the main findings from the literature on the multi-dimensional nature of poverty in developing countries (Thorbecke, 2007). In Latin America, in particular, the need to address intergenerational poverty persistence was a driving force behind these programmes. An equally important driver was an understanding that investment in children's nutrition, schooling and health was essential for programmes that could successfully address the duration dimension of poverty (Levy, 2006). A focus on the many dimensions of poverty, but duration in particular, has direct implications for crucial, but insufficiently researched, issues around the optimal length of participation and exit conditions. In many respects, the recent focus on exit strategies is extending the application of the literature on poverty duration and on poverty transitions into programme design (Villa, 2008).

Another important feature of emerging anti-poverty programmes in the South is the attention paid to differences between households in poverty. Strategies for beneficiary selection increasingly aim to rank households from the poorest to the moderately poor, extending perhaps to households not currently in poverty but highly vulnerable to fall into poverty. Registries of potential beneficiaries, such as *Sisbén* in Colombia or the *Cadastro Único* in Brazil, include all these groups. Increasingly, households in poverty are no longer bunched together as an undifferentiated group, with identification reduced to a binary indicator (poor/not poor). Instead, a ranking of households in poverty

---

[7] It was designed to include nine conditions, but after implementation they were revised down to three.

[8] For a discussion on co-responsibilities and 'hard' and 'soft' conditions in Latin American human-development-conditional transfer programmes, see Cecchini and Madariaga (2011).

enables a clearer differentiation to be made with regard to the depth and intensity of poverty. The discussion on the reach of social assistance programmes in Chapter 6 concluded that the appropriate size of the target population is often larger than that in poverty at one point in time. Poverty rankings have the great advantage of significantly enlarging the options available to policymakers and to the agencies engaged in implementing anti-poverty programmes. Over time, as resources become available, programme agencies can extend the reach of social assistance programmes.[9] An important advantage is that the ethical judgements made by programme designers acquire greater visibility in the context of poverty rankings.

A third important feature of the current design of transfer programmes in developing countries relates to monitoring and evaluation processes. Compared with most other types of policy interventions in the context of poverty and poverty reduction, anti-poverty transfers have been designed with a stronger regard for monitoring and evaluation. These are important not only in the context of assessing the effectiveness of budget allocations but also in that of programme development and refinement. The presence of clearly defined monitoring and evaluation protocols is apparent among more recently introduced transfer programmes. To the extent that these protocols are well designed, effectively implemented and cost-effective, attention to monitoring and evaluation will lead to self-reflective and self-improving interventions. Monitoring and evaluation features make this possible in the context of large-scale programmes. This goes hand in hand with social assistance programmes becoming examples of institutional building, as opposed to short-term development projects.

It is hard to overestimate the significance of the interconnectedness of poverty research with the practice of anti-poverty programmes. The four areas discussed provide examples of the significance of the links between research and practice. The time lag from theory to practice and vice versa is comparatively short for social assistance in developing countries, and this is a key factor shaping its future evolution.

---

[9] Poverty rankings enabled a faster response to the 2008 global financial crisis, as countries with established social assistance programmes had the option to expand the target population (Barrientos and Niño-Zarazúa, 2011).

Evolution in programme design

The analysis of anti-poverty programmes identified several areas in which programme design has evolved over time. It will be useful to discuss design trends briefly and speculate on the future evolution of social assistance. The approach adopted is to generalise from the experience of current programmes.[10]

To begin with a rough and ready generalisation, there are many examples of progression in pension programme design, from pure income transfers to income transfers combined with basic services. Most examples of progression in social assistance programmes are in the direction of integrating additional services and transfers. There are fewer cases of programmes migrating towards integrated anti-poverty programmes.

Countries relying on pure income transfers often experience constraints in introducing reforms to extend the scope of programmes, but there are examples of pure income transfers incorporating service provision and/or conditions. South Africa's social pension offers no additional services, but schooling conditions as part of the Child Support Grant, following a debate on their likely effectiveness.[11] There are long-standing examples of family or child subsidies in Latin America, mainly in the context of social insurance schemes, but they lacked any linkages to services. Argentina's recently introduced child subsidy, the *Asignación Universal por Hijo*, does introduce explicit linkages to service provision through conditions (Gasparini and Cruces, 2010). Mexico's non-contributory pension *70 y más* combines cash transfers and health care. Health care services are particularly important for this age group.

Mexico's *Oportunidades* has over time extended the reach of the programmes to other rural areas, and to urban areas. It has also expanded the range of interventions packaged into the programmes to include savings plans and retirement savings plans, microenterprise training, transfer components for older people, college support and scholarships and, more recently, income supplements to reduce the

---

[10] For an analysis of the evolution of human-development-conditional transfer programmes in Latin America, see Cecchini and Madariaga (2011).

[11] The domestic debate around the introduction of conditions has probably detracted from a debate on the effectiveness of linking income and service provision. See Lund (2011) and van der Berg and Siebrits (2010).

impact of food prices rises (SEDESOL (Secretaría de Desarrollo Social), 2003). Brazil's *Bolsa Família* emerged as a means of integrating several transfer programmes, and has in time expanded to include a range of complementary services and intermediation for beneficiaries (Jaccoud *et al.*, 2010). Most human-development-conditional transfer programmes in Latin America show an expansion in the range of interventions packaged over time.

Among low-income countries, there are fewer experiences of programmes enhancing the range of interventions in the package. This is most likely to be a reflection of resource and capacity restrictions. The impact evaluation of Ethiopia's Productive Safety Net Programme, for example, finds that the strongest evidence on impacts on food security gains is for the groups of beneficiaries who, in addition to participating in the employment guarantee scheme, also benefited from the agricultural extension component (Gilligan, Hoddinott and Seyoum Taffesse, 2008).

There are two areas likely to experience substantive change in the future: intermediation and economic inclusion. Chile's *Chile Solidario* focused on overcoming social exclusion through intermediation. Households participating in the programme were assigned a social worker, who coordinated government programmes and transfers and tailored these to the specific needs of households along seven dimensions of well-being (Barrientos, 2010a). This component of the programme was considered crucial to addressing the social exclusion experienced by households in extreme poverty in Chile. Intriguingly, the impact evaluations for this programme did not find strong evidence on income and employment growth among these households, but the intermediation component of the programme has not been evaluated directly. Despite the mixed impact evaluation outcomes of *Chile Solidario*, and its reform in 2012, several human-development-conditional transfer programmes are attempting to adapt its intermediation component. This applies, for example, to Brazil's *Bolsa Família*, Colombia's *Familias en Acción* and a small social transfer programme in one of Cairo's low-income settlements, *Ain Sera*.

Exit strategies focused on economic inclusion are being actively studied and experimented on in many social assistance programmes. They include components improving the employability of beneficiaries; self-employment or microenterprise training and asset transfers; and employment subsidies and incentives. Economic inclusion will be a crucial area for experimentation and development in transfer programmes in the next decade.[12]

Primacy of national governments

National governments have taken a leading role in the growth of social assistance to date. This is likely to continue in the future, and it is crucial that the organising role in the expansion of social assistance remains with them.

Throughout the book the respective roles of different stakeholders have been identified and assessed. It might be worth recapitulating on these. The introduction of extended social assistance is predicated on national governments playing a dominant and enabling role, in terms of collecting and allocating the necessary resources, designing the programmes and managing their implementation. The role of research and knowledge creation and application was noted as an important driver in the growth of social assistance in the South. Research and knowledge are essential to poverty eradication. The important but limited role of multilateral and bilateral donors was noted above. For the future, South–South policy diffusion and cooperation should acquire a more prominent role. The role of civil society and the private sector in supporting social assistance has not been studied in any depth in the literature and constitutes a significant knowledge gap.

Chapter 7 raised several concerns regarding the potentially adverse effects arising from a reliance on foreign aid to finance anti-poverty transfer programmes in the South. The 2008 financial crisis has renewed interest in the potential contribution of international sources of finance, especially taxes on financial transactions, as a means to finance anti-poverty programmes. However, the limitations of international aid as a driver for the extension of social assistance in developing countries have cropped up at different points in the book. Foreign aid can help kick-start social assistance, but it also has the potential to

---

[12] There are also several initiatives to link up transfers and financial inclusion. See Proyecto Capital, at www.proyectocapital.org/index.php/en, and the Consultative Group to Assist the Poor's Graduation Programme, at www.cgap.org/p/site/c/template.rc/1.26.1467.

undermine the emergence of fiscal pacts, and thus the sustainability and legitimacy of anti-poverty transfer programmes.

For similar reasons, 'cosmopolitan' social assistance – as in proposals advocating global anti-poverty transfer programmes – is problematic, in that it weakens social contracts at the national level. Well-intentioned cosmopolitan proposals often fail to take into account the institution building that is at the basis of the extension of social assistance in developing countries.[13] There is also a second concern with these proposals. In Chapter 4, a brief discussion of non-linear optimal taxation suggested that combining redistribution to low-income groups through the tax system with adequate work incentives among high-income taxpayers would require high marginal rates of tax for those at the bottom of the income distribution. This in turn would imply a high incidence of unemployment among lower-productivity groups. A global optimal tax scheme is likely to improve welfare among workers in low-income countries, but also to generate high levels of unemployment among them (Kopczuk, Slemrod and Yitzhaki, 2004). There are limits to the globalisation of social assistance, which the international policy literature commonly ignores. On close inspection, cosmopolitan social assistance might well turn out not to be advantageous for groups in extreme poverty in the South.

Linking taxes and transfers

The dynamics of financing are of significant interest for the evolution of social assistance in developing countries in the next two decades. The discussion in the book has contributed three main points. First, based on the analysis of current social assistance expenditure in developing countries, the financing requirement for most countries lies between 1 and 2 per cent of gross domestic product. As these figures were arrived at inductively, they do not provide an indication of what countries ought to spend. Second, the focus of financing discussions should be on the financing mix, not on individual sources of finance. This implies variation between countries in the way that the financing requirement is going to be covered. In developing countries, the financing mix is likely to vary across regions and countries. However, and with a focus on the evolution of direct transfers in the coming decades, the contribution of

[13] See, for example, Milanovic (2007) and Townsend (2009).

domestic taxation will be fundamental. As discussed in Chapter 7, the tax/GDP ratio and the tax mix are equally important. The tax/GDP ratio and resource revenues define government's financial envelope. In a revenue bargaining context, the mix of the components of government revenue influences the share of the budget allocated to social protection and social assistance. The tax mix, direct and indirect taxation and resources revenues, and their evolution over time will effectively shape social assistance in the coming decades.

In particular, the relative weight of consumption and resource revenues will strongly influence the scale and scope of anti-poverty programmes. Personal income taxes are unlikely to play a major role, given their low profile in developing countries. A key difference between the rapid expansion of social assistance in Latin America and the slower – and, arguably, weaker – extension of social assistance in sub-Saharan Africa is that, in the latter, resource revenues have constituted the most dynamic source of government revenues, and most anti-poverty transfer programmes have been financed by foreign aid. This could help explain the prevalence of pilot programmes, and the project orientation of social assistance. In Latin America, resource revenues have also been significant, and foreign aid has helped kick-start large-scale anti-poverty transfer programmes, but consumption taxes have been the most dynamic component of the tax mix. Gradually, domestic revenues have replaced foreign aid as the main source of funding for anti-poverty transfer programmes. Resource revenues alone have proved too volatile as financial support for these programmes. In many countries, 'narratives' surrounding the extension of social assistance often link consumption taxes to social assistance expenditure. In a revenue bargaining context, whether social assistance expenditure is financed through natural resource revenues, foreign aid or consumption taxes has implications for the effectiveness and legitimacy of poverty reduction. The composition of the tax mix will play a significant role in shaping the extension of social assistance in the two regions.

The consideration of international aid flows is particularly relevant to low-income countries. The contribution of official development assistance to supporting anti-poverty programmes has been studied in some detail. Over the past decade international assistance has been applied to the financing of pilot programmes in sub-Saharan Africa, Asia and Latin America. It has an important role to play in helping to reduce the initial set-up costs of social assistance programmes, including analytical work, feasibility studies, baseline and evaluation data collection and analysis, information systems and administrative capacity building. These can be significant, and as a result they constitute a barrier to the introduction of social assistance.

Research and practice in connection with anti-poverty transfer programmes will in the future need to include careful consideration of the links between taxes and transfers.

Social contracts

The discussion on the linkages between taxes and transfers poses the intriguing question as to whether the growth of social assistance in developing countries contributes to the formation or consolidation of social contracts. The analysis in previous chapters reflected on the influence of democratisation processes in the growth of social assistance. The question here is whether the spread of institutions addressing poverty, vulnerability and social exclusion in developing countries can contribute to the emergence or renewal of social contracts.

The term 'social contract' opens up a range of possible interpretations. The term is not used in the classic sense of a compact between conflicting interests or between individuals and government, as with Rousseau, Locke and Hobbes. Instead, it is employed in the more restricted Rawlsian sense of an overlapping consensus, emerging in pluralistic societies with economic structures generating inequalities, around the equal distribution of primary goods and priority for the least advantaged (Rawls, 2001).[14] It echoes European, but perhaps not Anglo-Saxon, perspectives on the 'social' underlying welfare states, which include both provisioning institutions and a political commitment to ensuring appropriate levels of well-being for all (Leisering, 2003).

In practice, the development of social assistance in Brazil, South Africa and, arguably, India is grounded in variants of a 'social contract'. In Brazil and South Africa, as discussed in Chapters 5 and 7, social

---

[14] It is more about commitment than about bargaining. As Freeman (2007: 33) puts it, 'The agreement is not a compromise among essentially conflicting interests. Instead, it represents a joint commitment to certain shared ends or ideal models of interaction which each desires as regulative of his own pursuit of his particular purposes.' With Rawls, the social contract provides the basis for his concern with the 'strains of commitment', which justifies a social minimum; see Chapter 2.

contracts were embedded in new constitutions, which enshrined rights to social protection. Insofar as anti-poverty transfer programmes are perceived to be effective in reducing poverty and exclusion, and therefore strengthening equity and justice, they can in turn strengthen social contracts in the sense defined in the previous paragraph.[15] In this context, anti-poverty transfers are capable of having feedback effects that embed, and strengthen, new social contracts.[16] The rise of social protection in Brazil and South Africa is a case in point (Barrientos, 2011c). This is an important topic for further research. To an important extent, social contracts are underpinned by fiscal contracts, constituting the nexus of revenue and social policy bargaining. Research on tax transfer systems in developing countries provides another route to study potential feedback effects from the growth of social assistance in developing countries (Lustig, 2011).

Ten findings

It is time to summarise the main contributions of the analysis in the book. These are organised around the following ten questions.

What is the (ethical) value of assisting those in poverty? This is a foundational question for the analysis of anti-poverty transfers. The analysis in Chapter 2 led to the conclusion that it makes sense to justify assistance to those in poverty on the basis of justice – or, more precisely, on a political conception of justice that grants greater value to assisting the worst off because their lives have not gone as well as they might. From this perspective, priority should be attached to assisting those in poverty, because they experience the largest gap between how their lives might have gone and how they have gone in practice. Embedding the priority principle in appropriate institutions implies paying attention to social assistance.

Do we really need poverty lines? Chapter 2 discussed the concern that priority is too demanding, and examined sufficiency as a means to limit this principle. On closer examination, sufficiency thresholds are found to be intrinsically ad hoc. The examination of the role of poverty lines in

[15] On South Africa, see Seekings (2008a). On Brazil, see Jaccoud *et al.* (2009) and Melo (2007).

[16] On the fast-growing literature on the political feedback effects of antipoverty transfers, see De La O (2013) and Zucco (2008).

Chapter 3 provided further support for this view. Poverty measures rely on a particular threshold to assess how much poverty there is in a household or community, but dominance analysis was found to be required precisely because of the discretionary nature of poverty thresholds. The analysis in Chapter 4 on optimal transfers in a non-welfarist setting provided further confirmation of this point. The analysis of existing anti-poverty transfer programmes in Part II of this book supported the conclusion that poverty lines are benchmarks rather than substantive thresholds. Increasingly, beneficiary selection is based on poverty rankings, with poverty thresholds acting as benchmarks, which can be adjusted in line with societal priorities and available budgets. In middle-income countries with large-scale transfer programmes, the population that these programmes target extends beyond those in extreme poverty, and can include households in moderate poverty, or even households not in poverty but considered to have high vulnerability to falling into poverty. Poverty lines are not essential for effective poverty reduction strategies.

Are there optimal transfer programmes? The discussion on optimal transfer programmes in Chapter 4 helped identify the main parameters of effective anti-poverty transfers. In a non-welfarist context – that is, when the objective of policy is to achieve a minimum standard of living – the key parameters of anti-poverty programme design and implementation are ethical judgements, budget constraints, incentives and information. In a welfarist context – that is, when the objective of policy is to achieve a minimum level of utility – ethical judgements and incentives dominate. The optimal transfer literature points to the need to take full account of incentives, as well as political economy issues, in our understanding of existing anti-poverty transfer programmes.

Does targeting matter? Targeting and targeting strategies contribute towards minimising the cost of anti-poverty programmes, but are only one of the factors determining poverty reduction effectiveness. The targeting literature has focused one-sidedly on type I errors, and disregarded the significance of type II errors. Well-targeted programmes can be relatively ineffective in reducing poverty, and poorly targeted programmes can have large effects on poverty. It is time to move away from this one-sided focus on targeting and consider more comprehensive measures of incidence and reach. From a perspective of programme effectiveness, it is essential to take a process approach to beneficiary selection. This necessitates attention being paid to the identification, eligibility, registration, enrolment and recertification of programme participants. A process approach to the selection of programme participants is essential to enhancing the effectiveness of social assistance.

Do conditions matter? Well-designed and well-implemented conditions do matter, because they add a substitution effect to the income effects associated with participation in anti-poverty transfers. Conditions can ensure that social assistance has effects over and above the purchasing power transferred to participants. This does not mean that conditions are desirable or effective in all circumstances, or that all types of conditions have substitution effects. Substitution effects from poorly designed conditions could actually reduce, rather than amplify, income effects – as when conditions increase uncompensated compliance costs for beneficiaries. Because conditions bind at the margins, it is hard to identify and measure their effects accurately. The effects of conditions will be greater the larger the number of households on the margins, and the less costly it is for households to comply with conditions. In addition, conditions can also have positive externalities on the effectiveness of programme implementation. Conditions can also have a positive influence on agency coordination. Appropriately designed and implemented, they can trigger additional services and interventions for households unable to comply with them.

What is the appropriate size of social assistance budgets? Most countries – high-, medium- and low-income countries alike – spend between 1 and 2 per cent of their GDP on social assistance. A minority of countries spend in excess of 2 per cent. These include high-income countries relying on social assistance to a greater extent than social insurance, such as Australia and New Zealand; middle-income countries in the same situation, such as South Africa; and low-income countries able to tap substantial levels of international aid, such as Ethiopia and Malawi. Most low-income countries spend less than 1 per cent of GDP on social assistance. It is unclear how much countries *should* spend on social assistance, as this depends on the range of welfare programmes and policies they have in place, and – crucially – on their effectiveness. Over the past decade and a half social assistance budgets have risen as a proportion of GDP in most countries.

Why is there an obsession with resource mobilisation, and why is this wrong? The dominance of resource mobilisation approaches to the financing of anti-poverty programmes is explained largely by the influence of donors in international poverty policy debates. It should not be

surprising that aid donors tend to overestimate the scope and effectiveness of foreign aid. However, in the context of the growth of social
assistance in developing countries, a one-sided focus on resource mobilisation can be counterproductive. It is problematic to finance an expansion of social assistance mainly through foreign aid, especially as the
objective is to develop long-term institutions capable of eradicating
poverty. There is a role for international aid in supporting countries in
their efforts to establish, reform or scale up anti-poverty transfers.
International aid also has a role in supporting knowledge generation
and dissemination, as this knowledge constitutes a global public good.
However, overreliance on international aid to finance transfers can
weaken domestic revenue bargaining and policy prioritisation, and
delay the emergence of social contracts. To a large extent, the extension
of social assistance in the South has been financed domestically, often
from existing anti-poverty budgets. Focusing on the financing mix
capable of supporting anti-poverty transfers can bring a deeper and
more effective understanding of how the expansion of social assistance
in the South can be financed. There is a role for aid in the short term, and
a role for reallocating expenditure in the short to medium term, but a
focus on taxation is essential in the medium and longer term. Attention
to incentive and legitimacy issues associated with the financing of anti-
poverty transfer programmes is vital to ensure their sustainability and
effectiveness.

*Why is so little attention being paid to politics and institutionalisa-
tion?* It is difficult to account for the limited attention paid to these two
areas, which are central to the extension of social assistance in developing countries. In large part, it owes to the influence of technocratic
and project approaches to anti-poverty transfers. It is to be hoped that
the analysis in this book has made a case for the view that institutionalisation is the primary challenge in the extension of social assistance in
the South. Research on the politics of long-term, sustainable and legit-
imate social assistance institutions in developing countries is urgently
needed.

Do transfers have long-term effects? At this point in time the evidence
base is insufficient to identify and measure these effects with accuracy.
To date, studies on this issue have concentrated on a handful of anti-
poverty transfer programmes, mainly Mexico's *Oportunidades*. This
owes to the continuous and consistent efforts by the Mexican government to evaluate this programme. However, the available studies on this

issue strongly suggest that effective anti-poverty transfer programmes can indeed achieve long-term improvements in the productive capacity of beneficiary households. Further research is needed to generalise these findings for other programmes and other contexts.

Is it possible to 'grow' comprehensive social protection systems out of social assistance? This will be tested by the current expansion of social assistance in developing countries. Expectations about the path to be followed by developing countries in constructing comprehensive social protection systems are often coloured by the experience of European countries in establishing their own welfare states. They presume a focus on contribution-financed social insurance. For a variety of reasons discussed in the book – including the incidence of informality, the dominance of international markets by advanced economies and the absence of corporatism – the European path is unlikely to be feasible or appropriate for developing countries. Countries in the South will need to find alternative routes to developing welfare institutions appropriate to their conditions and ambition. The analysis in this book has demonstrated that examples of alternative paths are available. It is feasible to build welfare institutions from social assistance, especially when the emphasis is not only to secure minimum levels of consumption but also to ensure full productive lives for all. It will be necessary to think through the kind of social insurance institutions that might be appropriate and sustainable in developing countries, and how social assistance and social insurance institutions develop in tandem. In all likelihood, the growth of social assistance institutions in developing countries will put to the test diverse routes towards building appropriate welfare institutions in the South.

The main objective in writing this book was to provide a comprehensive analysis of the emergence of social assistance institutions in developing countries. It is my strong belief, based on years of research and engagement with this topic, that the eradication of poverty in the world needs much more than social assistance to become a reality, but that it is unlikely ever to happen without it. Readers will make their own judgements on whether the book has achieved this objective, but it is my hope that they feel stimulated to reflect on, and engage with, the greatest challenge for this century.

References

Adema, W. 2006. 'Social assistance policy development and the provision of a decent level of income in selected OECD countries', Social, Employment and Migration Working Paper no. 38. OECD, Paris.

Adema, W., and Ladaique, M. 2009. 'How expensive is the welfare state? Gross and net indicators in the OECD Social Expenditure Database (SOCX)', Social, Employment and Migration Working Paper no. 92. OECD, Paris.

AfDB and OECD Development Centre. 2010. *African Economic Outlook 2010*. Paris: OECD.

Aguero, J. M., Carter, M. R., and Woolard, I. 2007. 'The impact of unconditional transfers on nutrition: the South African Child Support Grant', Working Paper no. 39. Brasilia: International Poverty Centre (IPC).

Ahmad, E., Drèze, J., Hills, J., and Sen, A. (eds.) 1991. *Social Security in Developing Countries*. Oxford: Clarendon Press.

Ahmed, A. U., and del Ninno, C. 2002. 'Food for Education programme in Bangladesh: an evaluation of the impact on educational attainment and food security', Discussion Paper no. 138. International Food Policy Research Institute (IFPRI), Washington, DC.

Ahmed, A. U., Rabbani, M., Sulaiman, M., and Das, N. C. 2009. 'The impact of asset transfer on livelihoods of the ultra poor in Bangladesh', Research Monograph no. 39. BRAC, Dhaka.

Akerlof, G. A. 1978. 'The economics of "tagging" as applied to optimal tax, welfare programs, and manpower planning'. *American Economic Review* 68: 8–19.

Alkire, S., and Foster, J. E. 2011. 'Counting and multidimensional poverty measurement'. *Journal of Public Economics* 95: 476–87.

Altimir, O. 1997. 'Desigualdad, empleo y pobreza en America Latina: efectos del ajuste y del cambio en el estilo de desarrollo'. *Desarrollo Económico* 37: 3–29.

Alzúa, M. L., Cruces, G., and Ripani, L. 2010. 'Welfare programs and labour supply in developing countries: experimental evidence for Latin America', Working Paper no. 95. Centro de Estudios Distributivos Laborales y Sociales (CEDLAS), University of La Plata, Argentina.

Angelucci, M., and Attanasio, O. 2009. 'Oportunidades: program effect on consumption, low participation, and methodological issues'. *Economic Development and Cultural Change* 57: 479–506.

Aponte, G., Jemio, L. C., Laserna, R., Martinez, S., Molina, F., Schulze, E., and Skinner, E. 2007. *La inversión prudente: Impacto del Bonosol sobre la familia, la equidad social y el crecimiento económico.* La Paz: Fundación Milenio.

Ardington, C., Case, A., and Hosegood, V. 2009. 'Labour supply responses to large social transfers: longitudinal evidence from South Africa'. *American Economic Journal: Applied Economics* 1: 22–48.

Arjona, R., Ladaique, M., and Pearson, M. 2001. 'Growth, inequality and social protection', Labour Market and Social Policy Working Paper no. 51. OECD, Paris.

Arneson, R. J. 2000. 'Luck egalitarianism and prioritarianism'. *Ethics* 110: 339–49.

2002. 'Why justice requires transfers to offset income and wealth inequalities'. *Social Philosophy and Public Policy* 19: 172–200.

2004. 'Moral limits on the demands of beneficence?', in Chatterjee, D. K. (ed.), *The Ethics of Assistance: Morality and the Distant Needy*, 33–58. Cambridge University Press.

Arroyo Ortiz, J. P., Ordaz Diaz, J. L., Li Ng, J. J., and Zaragoza López, M. L. 2008a. 'A diez años de intervención en zonas rurales', evaluation report. SEDESOL, Mexico City.

2008b. *Evaluación externa del programa Oportunidades 2008: A diez años de intervención en zonas rurales (1997–2007): Estudio sobre los efectos de Oportunidades a diez años de intervención, en el consumo e inversión de las familias beneficiarias en zonas rurales, con base en la encuesta de evaluación de los hogares rurales 2007.* Mexico City: SEDESOL.

Atkinson, A. B. 1987. 'On the measurement of poverty'. *Econometrica* 55: 749–64.

1995. 'On targeting and family benefits', in *Incomes and the Welfare State: Essays on Britain and Europe*, 233–61. Cambridge University Press.

1999. *The Economic Consequences of Rolling Back the Welfare State.* Cambridge, MA: MIT Press.

(ed.) 2005. *New Sources of Development Finance.* Oxford University Press.

2009. 'Welfare economics and giving for development', in Basu, K., and Kanbur, R. (eds.), *Arguments for a Better World: Essays in Honor of Amartya Sen*, vol. I, *Ethics, Welfare, and Measurement*, 489–500. Oxford University Press.

Attanasio, O. 2003. *Baseline Report on the Evaluation of Familias en Acción.* London: Institute for Fiscal Studies (IFS).

Attanasio, O., Battistin, E., Fitzsimons, E., and Mesnard, A. 2005. 'How effective are conditional cash transfers?', Briefing Note no. 54. IFS, London.

Azevedo, V., Bouillon, C. P., and Irarrázaval, I. 2011. 'La efectividad de las redes de protección social: el rol de los sistemas integrados de información social en seis países de America Latina', Technical Note no. 233. Inter-American Development Bank (IADB), Washington, DC.

Azevedo, V., and Robles, M. 2009. 'Multidimensional targeting: identifying beneficiaries of poverty reduction programmes', mimeo. IADB, Washington, DC.

Baird, S., McIntosh, C. and Özler, B. 2011. 'Cash or condition? Evidence from a cash experiment'. *Quarterly Journal of Economics* 126: 1709–53.

Barreix, A., Villela, L., and Roca, J. 2007. 'Fiscal policy and equity: estimation of the progressivity and redistributive capacity of taxes and social public expenditure in the Andean countries', mimeo. IADB, Washington, DC.

Barrett, C.-B., and Carter, M. R. 2010. 'The power and pitfalls of experiments in development economics: some non-random reflections'. *Journal of Economic Perspectives and Policy* 32: 515–48.

Barrett, C.-B., and Maxwell, D.-G. 2005. *Food Aid after Fifty Years: Recasting Its Role*. Abingdon: Routledge.

Barrett, C. R., Holden, S., and Clay, D. C. 2005. 'Can food-for-work programmes reduce vulnerability?', in Dercon, S. (ed.), *Insurance against Poverty*, 361–86. Oxford University Press.

Barrientos, A. 2004. 'Latin America: towards a liberal-informal welfare regime', in Gough, I., Wood, G., Barrientos, A., Bevan, P., David, P., and Room, G. (eds.), *Insecurity and Welfare Regimes in Asia, Africa and Latin America*, 121–68. Cambridge University Press.

2006. 'Pensions for development and poverty reduction', in Clark, G. L., Munnell, A. H., and Orszag, M. (eds.), *Oxford Handbook of Pensions and Retirement Income*, 781–98. Oxford University Press.

2007. 'Tax-financed social security'. *International Social Security Review* 60: 99–117.

2008a. 'Cash transfers for older people reduce poverty and inequality', in Bebbington, A. J., Dani, A. A., de Haan, A., and Walton, M. (eds.), *Institutional Pathways to Equity: Addressing Inequality Traps*, 169–92. Washington, DC: World Bank.

2008b. 'Financing social protection', in Barrientos, A., and Hulme, D. (eds.), *Social Protection for the Poor and Poorest: Concepts, Policies and Politics*, 300–12. London: Palgrave Macmillan.

2009a. 'Introducing basic social protection in low income countries: lessons from existing programmes', in Townsend, P. (ed.), *Building Decent*

Societies: Rethinking the Role of Social Security in Development, 253–73. London: Palgrave Macmillan.

2009b. 'Labour markets and the (hyphenated) welfare regime in Latin America'. *Economy and Society* 38: 87–108.

2009c. 'Social pensions in low income countries', in Holzman, R., Drobalino, D., and Takayama, N. (eds.), *Closing the Coverage Gap: The Role of Social Pensions and Other Retirement Transfers*, 73–84. Washington, DC: World Bank.

2010a. 'Protecting capabilities, eradicating extreme poverty: *Chile Solidario* and the future of social protection'. *Journal of Human Development and Capabilities* 11: 579–97.

2010b. 'Should poverty researchers worry about inequality?', Working Paper no. 118. Brooks World Poverty Institute (BWPI), University of Manchester.

2010c. 'Social protection and poverty', Social Policy and Development Paper no. 42. UN Research Institute for Social Development, Geneva.

2011a. 'Conditions in antipoverty programmes'. *Journal of Poverty and Social Justice* 19: 15–26.

2011b. 'On the distributional implications of social protection reforms in Latin America', Working Paper no. 2011/69. World Institute for Development Economics Research, UN University, Helsinki.

2011c. 'The rise of social assistance in Brazil', mimeo. BWPI, University of Manchester.

2012. 'Social transfers and growth: what do we know? What do we need to find out?' *World Development* 40: 11–20.

Barrientos, A., and DeJong, J. 2006. 'Reducing child poverty with cash transfers: a sure thing?' *Development Policy Review* 24: 537–52.

Barrientos, A., Gorman, M., and Heslop, A. 2003. 'Old age poverty in developing countries: contributions and dependence in later life'. *World Development* 3: 555–70.

Barrientos, A., and Hulme, D. 2009. 'Social protection for the poor and poorest'. *Oxford Development Studies* 37: 439–56.

Barrientos, A., and Lloyd-Sherlock, P. 2003. 'Non-contributory pensions and poverty prevention: a comparative study of Brazil and South Africa'. Institute of Development and Policy Management and HelpAge International, Manchester.

Barrientos, A., and Niño-Zarazúa, M. 2011. 'Financing social protection for children through crises'. *Development Policy Review* 29: 601–18.

Barrientos, A., Niño-Zarazúa, M. and Maitrot, M. 2010. 'Social assistance in developing countries database: version 5.0'. BWPI, University of Manchester.

Barrientos, A., and Santibañez, C. 2009a. 'New forms of social assistance and the evolution of social protection in Latin America'. *Journal of Latin American Studies* 41: 1–26.

2009b. 'Social policy for poverty reduction in lower-income countries in Latin America: lessons and challenges'. *Social Policy and Administration* 43: 409–24.

Barry, B. 1990. 'The welfare state versus the relief of poverty'. *Ethics* 100: 503–29.

Bastagli, F. 2008. 'Conditionality in public policy targeted to the poor: promoting resilience?' *Social Policy and Society* 8: 127–40.

Baulch, B. 2011. 'Household panel data sets in developing and transition countries (version 2)'. CPRC, University of Manchester.

Baulch, B., and Hoddinott, J. 2000. 'Economic mobility and poverty dynamics in developing countries'. *Journal of Development Studies* 36: 3–40.

Baulch, B., Weber, A., and Wood, J. 2008. *Social Protection Index for Committed Poverty Reduction, vol. II, Asia*. Manila: ADB.

Behrendt, C. 2008. 'Can low income countries in sub-Saharan Africa afford basic social protection? First results of a modelling exercise', in Barrientos, A., and Hulme, D. (eds.), *Social Protection for the Poor and Poorest: Concepts, Policies and Politics*, 282–99. London: Palgrave Macmillan.

Beramendi, P., and Rueda, D. 2007. 'Social democracy constrained: indirect taxation in industrialized democracies'. *British Journal of Political Science* 37: 619–41.

Bérgolo, M., Cruces, G., Gasparini, L., and Ham, A. 2010. 'Vulnerability to poverty in Latin America: empirical evidence from cross-sectional data and robustness analysis with panel data', Working Paper no. 170. CPRC, University of Manchester.

Bertrand, M., Mullainathan, S., and Miller, D. 2003. 'Public policy and extended families: evidence from pensions in South Africa'. *World Bank Economic Review* 17: 27–50.

Besley, T. 1997. 'Political economy of alleviating poverty: theory and institutions', in Bruno, M., and Pleskovic, B. (eds.), *Annual World Bank Conference on Development Economics 1996*, 117–34. Washington, DC: World Bank.

Besley, T., Burgess, R., and Rasul, I. 2003. 'Benchmarking government provision of social safety nets', Social Protection Discussion Paper no. 0315. World Bank, Washington, DC.

Besley, T., and Coate, S. 1992. 'Workfare versus welfare: incentive arguments for work requirements in poverty-alleviation programs'. *American Economic Review* 82: 249–61.

1995. 'The design of income maintenance programmes'. *Review of Economic Studies* 62: 187–221.

Besley, T., and Kanbur, R. 1988. 'Food subsidies and poverty alleviation'. *Economic Journal* 98: 701–19.

1990. 'The principles of targeting', Policy Research Working Paper no. 385. World Bank, Washington, DC.

Bibi, S. 2002. 'On the impact of better targeted transfers on poverty in Tunisia', Working Paper no. 02–03. Centre interuniversitaire sur le risque, les politiques économiques et l'emploi, Montreal.

Bird, R. M. 2005. 'Evaluating public expenditures: does it matter how they are financed?', Working Paper no. 0506. University of Toronto.

Bird, R. M., and Gendron, P.-P. 2011. *The VAT in Developing and Transitional Countries*. Cambridge University Press.

Bitler, M., and Hoynes, H. 2010. 'The state of the safety net in the post-welfare reform era', Working Paper no. 16504. National Bureau of Economic Research (NBER), Cambridge, MA.

Blackorby, C., and Donaldson, D. 1988. 'Cash versus kind, self-selection, and efficient transfers'. *American Economic Review* 78: 691–700.

Blundell, R., and Costa Dias, M. 2000. 'Evaluation methods for non-experimental data'. *Fiscal Studies* 21: 427–68.

Bossert, W., Chakravarty, S. R., and D'Ambrosio, C. 2008. 'Poverty and time', Working Paper no. 2008–87. Society for the Study of Economic Inequality, Palma de Mallorca.

Bourguignon, F. 2005. 'Development strategies for more and better jobs', paper presented at conference 'Help wanted: more and better jobs in a globalized economy'. Washington, DC, 14 April.

Bourguignon, F., Ferreira, F., and Leite, P. 2003. 'Conditional cash transfers, schooling and child labor: micro-simulating Brazil's Bolsa Escola program'. *World Bank Economic Review* 17: 229–54.

Bourguignon, F., and Fields, G. 1990. 'Poverty measures and anti-poverty policy'. *Recherches Economiques de Louvain* 56: 409–27.

1997. 'Discontinuous losses from poverty, generalized Pα measures and optimal transfers'. *Journal of Public Economics* 63: 155–75.

Bourguignon, F., and Pereira da Silva, L. A. (eds.) 2003. *The Impact of Economic Policies on Poverty and Distribution: Evaluation Techniques and Tools*. Washington, DC: World Bank.

Boylan, D. M. 1996. 'Taxation and transition: the politics of the 1990 Chilean tax reform'. *Latin American Research Review* 31: 7–31.

Bradbury, B. 2004. 'Targeting social assistance'. *Fiscal Studies* 25: 305–24.

Brautigam, D., Fjeldstad, O.-H., and Moore, M. 2008. *Taxation and State-Building in Developing Countries: Capacity and Consent*. Cambridge University Press.

Brautigam, D., and Knack, S. 2004. 'Foreign aid, institutions, and governance in sub-Saharan Africa'. *Economic Development and Cultural Change* 52: 255–86.

Breceda, K., Rigolini, J., and Saavedra, J. 2009. 'Latin America and the social contract: patterns of social spending and taxation'. *Population and Development Review* 35: 721–48.

Brewer, M., Saez, E., and Shephard, A. 2010. 'Means-testing and tax rates on earnings', in Mirrlees, J. A., Adam, S., Besley, T., Blundell, R., Bond, S., Chote, R., Gammie, M., Johnson, P., Myles, G., and Poterba, J. (eds.), *Dimensions of Tax Design: The Mirrlees Review*, 90–173. Oxford University Press.

Broome, J. 1995. *Weighing Goods: Equality, Uncertainty and Time*. Oxford: Basil Blackwell.

Forthcoming. 'Equality versus priority: a useful distinction', in Wikler, D., and Murray, C. J. L. (eds.), *Fairness and Goodness in Health*. Geneva: World Health Organization (WHO).

Brown, C. 2006. 'Priority or sufficiency...or both?'. *Economics and Philosophy* 21: 190–220.

Caldés, N., Coady, D., and Maluccio, J. A. 2006. 'The cost of poverty alleviation transfer programs: a comparative analysis of three programs in Latin America'. *World Development* 34: 818–37.

Camacho, A., and Conover, E. 2009. 'Manipulation of social program eligibility: detection, explanations and consequences for empirical research', Research Paper no. 2009–19. Department of Economics, University of the Andes, Bogotá.

Cardoso, E., and Portela Souza, A. 2003. 'The impacts of cash transfers on child labor and school attendance in Brazil', mimeo. Department of Economics, University of São Paulo.

Carneiro, P., Galasso, E., and Ginja, R. 2008. 'The impact of providing psycho-social support to indigent families and increasing their access to social services: evaluating Chile Solidario', mimeo. University College London.

Case, A., and Deaton, A. 1998. 'Large scale transfers to the elderly in South Africa'. *Economic Journal* 108: 1330–61.

2003. 'Consumption, health, gender and poverty', Policy Research Working Paper no. 3020. World Bank, Washington, DC.

Case, A., and Paxson, C. 2008. 'Stature and status: height, ability and labor market outcomes'. *Journal of Political Economy* 116: 499–532.

Case, A., and Wilson, F. 2000. 'Health and well-being in South Africa: evidence from the Langeberg survey', mimeo. Princeton University, NJ.

Castaneda, T., and Lindert, K. 2005. 'Designing and implementing household targeting systems: lessons from Latin America and the United

States', Social Protection Discussion Paper no. 0526. World Bank, Washington, DC.

Cecchini, S., and Madariaga, A. 2011. 'La trayectoria de los programas de transferencia con corresponsabilidad (PCT) en América Latina y el Caribe', report. ECLAC, Santiago.

Cecchini, S. and Martínez, R. 2011. *Protección social inclusiva en América Latina: Una mirada integral, un enfoque de derechos*. Santiago: ECLAC.

Chakravarty, S. R. 2009. *Inequality, Polarization and Poverty: Advances in Distributional Analysis*. New York: Springer.

Chakravarty, S. R., Deutsch, J., and Silber, J. 2008. 'On the Watts multidimensional poverty index and its decomposition'. *World Development* 36: 1067–77.

Chakravarty, S. R., and Silber, J. 2008. 'Measuring multidimensional poverty: the axiomatic approach', in Kakwani, N., and Silber, J. (eds.), *Quantitative Approaches to Multidimensional Poverty Measurement*, 192–209. Basingstoke: Palgrave Macmillan.

Chatterjee, D. K. (ed.) 2004. *The Ethics of Assistance: Morality and the Distant Needy*. Cambridge University Press.

Chaudhuri, S. 2003. 'Assessing vulnerability to poverty: concepts, empirical methods and illustrative examples'. Department of Economics, Columbia University, New York.

Chen, J., and Barrientos, A. 2006. 'Extending social assistance in China: lessons from the Minimum Living Standard Scheme', Working Paper no. 67. CPRC, University of Manchester.

Chen, S., and Ravallion, M. 2004. 'How have the world's poorest fared since the early 1980s?'. *World Bank Research Observer* 19: 141–69.

2009. 'The impact of the global financial crisis on the world's poorest'. Vox: www.voxeu.org/article/impact-global-financial-crisis-world-s-poorest.

2012. 'An update to the World Bank's estimates of consumption poverty in the developing world', briefing note. World Bank, Washington, DC.

Cichon, M., Scholz, W., van de Meerendonk, A., Hagemejer, K., Bertranou, F., and Plamondon, P. 2004. *Financing Social Protection*. Geneva: ILO.

Coady, D. P. 2003. 'Alleviating structural poverty in developing countries: the approach of Progresa in Mexico', mimeo. IFPRI, Washington, DC.

2004. 'Designing and evaluating safety nets: theory, evidence, and policy conclusions', Food Consumption and Nutrition Division (FCND) Discussion Paper no. 172. IFPRI, Washington, DC.

Coady, D. P., Grosh, M., and Hoddinott, J. 2004. *Targeting of Transfers in Developing Countries: Review of Lessons and Experience*. Washington, DC: World Bank.

Coady, D. P., and Harris, R. L. 2004. 'Evaluating transfer programmes within a general equilibrium framework'. *Economic Journal* 114: 778–99.

Coady, D. P., and Morley, S. A. 2003. *From Social Assistance to Social Development: Targeted Education Subsidies in Developing Countries.* Washington, DC: IFPRI.

Coady, D. P., and Skoufias, E. 2004. 'On the targeting and redistributive efficiencies of alternative transfer instruments'. *Review of Income and Wealth* 50: 11–27.

Cornia, G. A. 2010. 'Income distribution under Latin America's new left regimes'. *Journal of Human Development and Capabilities* 11: 86–114.

Cornia, G. A., and Stewart, F. 1995. 'Two errors of targeting', in van de Walle, D., and Nead, K. (eds.), *Public Spending and the Poor: Theory and Evidence*, 350–86. Baltimore: Johns Hopkins University Press.

Cortez Reis, M., and Camargo, J. M. 2007. 'Rendimientos domiciliáres com aposentadorias e pensôes e as decisôes dos jovens quanto à educacão e a participação na forca de trabalho', Discussion Paper no. 1262. Instituto de Pesquisa Econômica Aplicada (IPEA), Rio de Janeiro.

CPRC. 2005. *The Chronic Poverty Report 2004–05.* Manchester: CPRC.

Crisp, R. 2003. 'Equality, priority, and compassion'. *Ethics* 113: 745–63.

Cubero, R., and Vladkova Hollar, I. 2010. 'Equity and fiscal policy: the income distribution effects of taxation and social spending in Central America', Working Paper no. 10/112. IMF, Washington, DC.

Currie, J. 2004. 'The take-up of social benefits', Discussion Paper no. 1103. Forschungsinstitut zur Zukunft der Arbeit (IZA), Bonn.

Currie, J., and Gahvari, F. 2007. 'Transfers in cash and in kind: theory meets the data', Working Paper no. 13557. NBER, Cambridge, MA.

D'Arcy, M. 2011. 'Why do citizens assent to pay tax? Legitimacy, taxation and the African state', Working Paper no. 126. Afrobarometer, Accra.

Das, J., Do, Q.-T., and Özler, B. 2005. 'Reassessing conditional cash transfer programs'. *World Bank Research Observer* 20: 1–28.

Daude, C., and Melguizo, A. 2010. 'Taxation and more representation? On fiscal policy, social mobility and democracy in Latin America', Working Paper no. 294. OECD Development Centre, Paris.

Davis, S. P. 1979. 'The concept of poverty in the Encyclopaedia Britannica from 1810 to 1975'. *Labor History* 21: 91–101.

De Barros, R. P., de Carvalho, M., Franco, S., and Mendonça, R. 2008. 'A importância das cotas para a focalização do Programa Bolsa Família', Discussion Paper no. 238. Fluminense Federal University, Niterói, Brazil.

De Brauw, A., and Hoddinott, J. 2011. 'Must conditional cash transfers programs be conditioned to be effective? The impact of conditioning transfers on school enrollment in Mexico'. *Journal of Development Economics* 96: 359–70.

De Carvalho, I. E. 2008a. 'Household income as a determinant of child labour and school enrollment in Brazil: evidence from a social security reform', Working Paper no. 08/241. IMF, Washington, DC.

2008b. 'Old-age benefits and the labour supply of rural elderly in Brazil'. *Journal of Development Economics* 86: 129–46.

De Castro, J. A., and Modesto, L. (eds.). 2010. *Bolsa Família 2003–2010: Avanços e desafios*. Brasilia: IPEA.

De Janvry, A., Finan, F., Sadoulet, E., and Vakis, R. 2006. 'Can conditional transfer programs work as safety nets in keeping children at school and from working when exposed to shocks?'. *Journal of Development Economics* 79: 349–73.

De Kam, F., and Owens, J. 1999. 'Financing social protection in the 21st century', mimeo. Ministry of Social Affairs and Health, Helsinki.

De La O, A. L. 2013. 'Do conditional cash transfers affect electoral behavior? Evidence from a randomized experiment in Mexico'. *American Journal of Political Science* 57: 1–14.

Deaton, A. 1997. *The Analysis of Household Surveys: A Microeconometric Approach to Development Policy*. Baltimore: Johns Hopkins University Press.

2001. 'Counting the world's poor: problems and possible solutions'. *World Bank Research Observer* 16: 125–47.

Delgado, G. C., and Cardoso, J. C. (eds.). 2000. *A universalização de direitos sociais no Brasil: A Prêvidencia Rural nos anos 90*. Brasilia: IPEA.

Dercon, S. 2002. 'Income risk, coping strategies, and safety nets'. *World Bank Research Observer* 17: 141–66.

2006. 'La vulnerabilite: une perspective microeconomique'. *Revue d'Economie du Developpement* 20: 79–118.

Diamond, P. 1967. 'Negative taxes and the poverty problem: a review article'. *National Tax Journal* 21: 288–303.

Diamond, P., and Saez, E. 2011. 'The case for a progressive tax: from basic research to policy recommendations', Working Paper no. 3548. Center for Economic Studies, Ifo Institute and CESifo GmbH, Munich.

DiJohn, J. 2010. 'Taxation, resource mobilization and state performance', Working Paper no. 2. London School of Economics.

Dilnot, A., and Stark, G. (eds.). 1989. *The Poverty Trap, Tax Cuts and the Reform of Social Security*. Oxford: Clarendon Press.

Drèze, J., and Sen, A. 1991. 'Public action for social security: foundations and strategy', in Ahmad, E., Drèze, J., Hills, J., and Sen, A. (eds.), *Social Security in Developing Countries*, 1–40. Oxford: Clarendon Press.

Duclos, J.-Y. 2002. 'Vulnerability and poverty: measurement issues for public policy', Social Protection Discussion Paper no. 0230. World Bank, Washington, DC.

Duclos, J.-Y., and Araar, A. 2004. *Poverty and Equity: Measurement, Policy and Estimation with DAD.* Dordrecht: Kluwer Academic Publishers.

Duflo, E. 2003. 'Grandmothers and granddaughters: old age pensions and intrahousehold allocation in South Africa'. *World Bank Economic Review* 17: 1–25.

Duflo, E., and Kremer, M. 2003. 'Use of randomization in the evaluation of development effectiveness', mimeo. World Bank, Washington, DC.

Dutta, I., Roope, L., and Zank, H. 2010. 'A new class of inter-temporal poverty measures', mimeo. University of Manchester.

Dye, R. A., and Antle, R. 1986. 'Cost-minimizing welfare programs'. *Journal of Public Economics* 30: 259–65.

ECLAC. 2009. *Social Panorama of Latin America 2009.* Santiago: ECLAC. 2010. *Social Panorama of Latin America 2010.* Santiago: ECLAC.

Edmonds, E. 2006. 'Child labor and schooling responses to anticipated income in South Africa'. *Journal of Development Economics* 81: 386–414.

Elbers, C., and Gunning, J. W. 2003. 'Estimating vulnerability', mimeo. Free University, Amsterdam.

Escobar Latapí, A., and González de la Rocha, M. 2009. *Evaluacion cualitativa del programa Oportunidades: Etapa urbana 2003.* Mexico City: Centro de Investigaciónes y Estudios Superiores en Antropología Social (CIESAS) – Occidente.

Esping-Andersen, G. 1990. *The Three Worlds of Welfare Capitalism.* Cambridge: Polity Press.

Feldstein, M. 1987. 'Should social security benefits be means tested?'. *Journal of Political Economy* 95: 468–84.

Ferreira, F. H. G., and Robalino, D. 2010. 'Social protection in Latin America: achievements and limitations', Policy Research Working Paper no. 5305. World Bank, Washington, DC.

Ferro, A., and Nicollela, A. 2007. 'The impact of conditional cash transfer programmes on household work decisions in Brazil', mimeo. Pontifical Catholic University, Rio de Janeiro.

Fiszbein, A. 2005. 'Beyond truncated welfare states: quo vadis Latin America?', mimeo. World Bank, Washington, DC.

Fiszbein, A., and Schady, N. 2009. *Conditional Cash Transfers: Reducing Present and Future Poverty.* Washington, DC: World Bank.

Fleurbaey, M. forthcoming. 'Equality versus priority: how relevant is this distinction?', in Wikler, D., and Murray, C. J. L. (eds.), *Fairness and Goodness in Health.* Geneva: WHO.

Foguel, M. N., and Paes de Barros, R. 2008. 'The effects of conditional cash transfer programmes on adult labour supply: an empirical analysis using a time series cross section sample of Brazilian municipalities', mimeo. IPEA, Rio de Janeiro.

Foster, J. E. 1984. 'On economic poverty: a survey of aggregate measures', in Basmann, R. L., and Rhodes, G. F. (eds.), *Advances in Econometrics*, vol. III, 215–51. Hartford, CT: JAI Press.

2009. 'A class of chronic poverty measures', in Addison, T., Hulme, D., and Kanbur, R. (eds.), *Poverty Dynamics: Interdisciplinary Perspectives*, 59–76. Oxford University Press.

Foster, J. E., Greer, J., and Thorbecke, E. 1984. 'A class of decomposable poverty measures'. *Econometrica* 52: 761–5.

Foster, J. E., and Sen, A. 1997. '*On Economic Inequality* after a quarter century', in Sen, A. (ed.), *On Economic Inequality*, 107–220. Oxford: Clarendon Press.

Frankfurt, H. 1987. 'Equality as a moral ideal'. *Ethics* 98: 21–43.

Freeman, S. 2007. *Justice and the Social Contract: Essays on Rawlsian Political Philosophy*. Oxford University Press.

Freije, S., Bando, R., and Arce, F. 2006. 'Conditional transfers, labour supply, and poverty: microsimulating Oportunidades'. *Economía* 7: 73–124.

Gahvari, F., and Mattos, E. 2007. 'Conditional cash transfers, public provision of public goods, and income redistribution'. *American Economic Review* 97: 491–502.

Galasso, E. 2006. '"With their effort and one opportunity": alleviating extreme poverty in Chile', mimeo. World Bank, Washington, DC.

Gangopadhyay, S., and Subramanian, S. 1992. 'Optimal budgetary intervention in poverty alleviation schemes', in Subramanian, S. (ed.), *Themes in Development Economics: Essays in Honour of Malcolm Adiseshiah*, 216–41. Delhi: Oxford University Press.

Gao, Q. 2010. 'Redistributive nature of the Chinese social benefit system: progressive or regressive?'. *The China Quarterly* 201: 1–19.

Gao, Q., Zhai, F., and Garfinkel, I. 2009. 'How does public assistance affect family expenditures? The case of urban China'. *World Development* 38: 989–1000.

Garcia, M., and Moore, C. M. T. 2012. *The Cash Dividend; The Rise of Cash Transfer Programs in Sub-Saharan Africa*. Washington, DC: World Bank.

Gasparini, L., and Cruces, G. 2010. 'Las asignaciones universales por hijo: impacto, discusión y alternativas', Working Paper no. 102. CEDLAS, University of la Plata, Argentina.

Gassmann, F., and Behrendt, C. 2006. 'Cash benefits in low income countries: simulating the effects on poverty reduction for Senegal and Tanzania', Discussion Paper no. 15. ILO, Geneva.

Ghosh, J. 2011. 'Cash transfers as the silver bullet for poverty reduction: a sceptical note'. *Economic and Political Weekly* 46: 67–71.

Gill, I. S., Packard, T., and Yermo, J. 2004. *Keeping the Promise of Social Security in Latin America*. Stanford University Press.

Gilligan, D. O., Hoddinott, J., and Seyoum Taffesse, A. 2008. 'The impact of Ethiopia's Productive Safety Net Programme and its linkages'. *Journal of Development Studies* 45: 1684–706.

Gough, I. 2004. 'Welfare regimes in development contexts: a global and regional analysis', in Gough, I., Wood, G., Barrientos, A., Bevan, P., Davis, P., and Room, G. (eds.), *Insecurity and Welfare Regimes in Asia, Africa and Latin America*: 15–48. Cambridge University Press.

Gough, I., Bradshaw, J., Ditch, J., Eardley, T., and Whiteford, P. 1997. 'Social assistance in OECD countries'. *Journal of European Social Policy* 7: 17–43.

Gough, I., Wood, G., Barrientos, A., Bevan, P., Davis, P., and Room, G. (eds.). 2004. *Insecurity and Welfare Regimes in Asia, Africa and Latin America*. Cambridge University Press.

Gray-Molina, G., Pérez de Rada, E., and Yañez, E. 1999. 'La economía política de reformas institucionales en Bolivia', Working Paper no. 350. IADB, Washington, DC.

Grosh, M., del Ninno, C., Tesliuc, E., and Ouerghi, A. 2008. *For Protection and Promotion: The Design and Implementation of Effective Safety Nets*. Washington, DC: World Bank.

Haddad, L., and Kanbur, R. 1990. 'How serious is the neglect of intrahousehold inequality?'. *Economic Journal* 100: 866–81.

Haggard, S., and Kaufman, R. R. 2008. *Development, Democracy, and Welfare States: Latin America, Asia, and Eastern Europe*. Princeton University Press.

Harvey, P. 2005. 'Cash and vouchers in emergencies', Humanitarian Policy Group discussion paper. Overseas Development Institute, London.

Haughton, J., and Khandker, S. R. 2009. *Handbook of Poverty and Inequality*. Washington, DC: World Bank.

Hausman, D. M. forthcoming. 'Equality versus priority: a badly misleading distinction', in Wikler, D., and Murray, C. J. L. (eds.), *Fairness and Goodness in Health*. Geneva: WHO.

Hickey, S. 2008. 'Conceptualising the politics of social protection in Africa', in Barrientos, A., and Hulme, D. (eds.), *Social Protection for the Poor and Poorest: Concepts, Policies and Politics*, 247–63. London: Palgrave Macmillan.

Hoddinott, J., and Kinsey, B. 2001. 'Child health in the time of drought'. *Oxford Bulletin of Economics and Statistics* 63: 409–36.

Hoddinott, J., and Skoufias, E. 2004. 'The impact of PROGRESA on food consumption'. *Economic Development and Cultural Change* 53: 37–61.

Hojman, D., and Kast, F. 2009. 'On the measurement of poverty dynamics', Faculty Research Working Paper no. 09–035. John F. Kennedy School of Government, Harvard University, Boston.

Holmqvist, G. 2010. 'External financing of social protection: opportunities and risks', mimeo. Nordic Africa Institute, Uppsala.

Holtung, N. 2007. 'Prioritarianism', in Holtung, N., and Lippert-Rasmussen, K. (eds.), *Egalitarianism: New Essays on the Nature and Value of Equality*, 125–56. Oxford: Clarendon Press.

Holtung, N., and Lippert-Rasmussen, K. (eds.). 2007. *Egalitarianism: New Essays on the Nature and Value of Equality*. Oxford: Clarendon Press.

Holzmann, R., and Jorgensen, S. 1999. 'Social protection as social risk management: conceptual underpinnings for the social protection strategy paper'. *Journal of International Development* 11: 1005–27.

Hubbard, R. G., Skinner, J., and Zeldez, S. P. 1995. 'Precautionary savings and social insurance'. *Journal of Political Economy* 103: 360–99.

Hulme, D. 2010. *Global Poverty: How Global Governance is Failing the Poor*. London: Routledge.

ILO. 2010. *World Social Security Report 2010/11: Providing Coverage in Times of Crisis and Beyond*. Geneva: ILO.

Imai, K., and Gaiha, R. 2004. 'Vulnerability, shocks and persistence of poverty: estimates for semi-arid rural south India'. *Oxford Development Studies* 32: 261–81.

Imbens, G., and Wooldridge, J. M. 2009. 'Recent developments in the econometrics of program evaluation'. *Journal of Economic Literature* 47: 5–86.

IMF. 2009. *Regional Economic Outlook Oct. 09: Sub-Saharan Africa: Weathering the Storm*. Washington, DC: IMF.

Immonen, R., Kanbur, R., Keen, M., and Toumala, M. 1998. 'Tagging and taxing: the optimal use of categorical and income information in designing tax/transfer schemes'. *Economica* 65: 179–92.

Jaccoud, L., Hadjab, P. D. E.-M., and Chaibub, J. R. 2009. 'Assistência social e segurança alimentar: entre novas trajetórias, vehlas agendas e recentes desafíos (1988–2008)', in Diretoría de Estudos e Políticas Sociais (ed.), *Políticas sociais: Acompanhamento e análise 17*, 175–250. Brasilia: IPEA.
  2010. 'The consolidation of social assistance in Brazil and its challenges, 1988–2008', Working Paper no. 76. IPC, Brasilia.

Jalan, J., and Ravallion, M. 2001. 'Is transient poverty different? Evidence for rural China'. *Journal of Development Studies* 36: 82–99.

Jiménez, J. P., and Gómez Sabaini, J. C. 2009. 'The role of tax policy in the context of the global crisis: consequences and prospects', report. ECLAC, Montevideo.

Jiménez, J. P., Gómez Sabaini, J. C., and Podestá, A. 2010. 'Tax gap and equity in Latin America and the Caribbean', Fiscal Study no. 16. Deutsche Gesellschaft für Technische Zusammenarbeit, Eschborn.

Kakwani, N. 1980. 'On a class of poverty measures'. *Econometrica* 48: 437–46.

2003. 'Issues in setting absolute poverty lines', Poverty and Social Development Paper no. 3. ADB, Manila.

Kakwani, N., Soares, F. V., and Son, H. H. 2006. 'Cash transfers for school-age children in African countries: simulation of impacts on poverty and school attendance'. *Development Policy Review* 24: 553–69.

Kakwani, N., and Subbarao, K. 2007. 'Poverty among the elderly in sub-Saharan Africa and the role of social pensions'. *Journal of Development Studies* 43: 987–1008.

Kanbur, R. 1987. 'Measurement and alleviation of poverty'. *IMF Staff Paper* 34: 60–85.

1994. 'Optimal non-linear income taxation for the alleviation of income poverty'. *European Economic Review* 38: 1613–32.

2009. 'Poverty and distribution: twenty years ago and now', Working Paper no. 48918. Cornell University, Ithaca, NY.

Kanbur, R., and Keen, M. 1989. 'Poverty, incentives, and linear income taxation', in Dilnot, A., and Walker, I. (eds.), *The Economics of Social Security*, 100–15. Oxford University Press.

Kaplow, L. 2006. 'Optimal income transfers', Working Paper no. 12284. NBER, Cambridge, MA.

2007. 'Optimal income transfers'. *International Tax and Public Finance* 14: 295–325.

Kato, J. 2003. *Regressive Taxation and the Welfare State: Path Dependence and Policy Diffusion*. Cambridge University Press.

Keen, M. 1992. 'Needs and targeting'. *Economic Journal* 102: 67–79.

Keen, M., and Mansour, M. 2009. 'Revenue mobilization in sub-Saharan Africa: challenges from globalization', Working Paper no. 09/157. IMF, Washington, DC.

Kopczuk, W., Slemrod, J., and Yitzhaki, S. 2005. 'The limitations of decentralized world redistribution: an optimal taxation approach'. *European Economic Review* 49: 1051–79.

Lam, D., Leibbrandt, M. and Ranchhod, V. 2004. 'Labour force withdrawal of the elderly in South Africa', Centre for Social Science Research Working Paper no. 118. Southern Africa Labour and Development Research Unit, University of Cape Town.

Lanjouw, P., and Ravallion, M. 1995. 'Poverty and household size'. *Economic Journal* 105: 1415–34.

Leisering, L. 2003. 'Nation state and welfare state: an intellectual and political history: review essay'. *Journal of European Social Policy* 13: 175–85.

    2010. 'Social assistance in developed and developing countries: a case of global social policy?', FLOOR Working Paper no. 4. Zentrum für interdisziplinäre Forschung, University of Bielefeld.

Levine, A. 2001. 'Orphans and other vulnerable children: what role for social protection?', Social Protection Discussion Paper no. 0126. World Bank, Washington, DC.

Levy, S. 2006. *Progress against Poverty: Sustaining Mexico's Progresa-Oportunidades Program*. Washington, DC: Brookings Institution Press.

    2008. *Good Intentions, Bad Outcomes: Social Policy, Informality, and Economic Growth in Mexico*. Washington, DC: Brookings Institution Press.

Lindert, K., Linder, A., Hobbs, J., and de la Brière, B. 2007. 'The nuts and bolts of Brazil's Bolsa Família program: implementing conditional cash transfers in a decentralized context', Social Protection Discussion Paper no. 0709. World Bank, Washington, DC.

Lindert, K., Skoufias, E., and Shapiro, J. 2006. 'Redistributing income to the poor and the rich: public transfers in LAC', Social Protection Discussion Paper no. 0605. World Bank, Washington, DC.

Lindert, P. H. 2002. 'What drives social spending? 1780 to 2020', in Kapstein, E. B., and Milanovic, B. (eds.), *When Markets Fail: Social Policy and Economic Reform*, 185–214. New York: Russell Sage Foundation.

    2004. *Growing Public: Social Spending and Economic Growth since the Eighteenth Century*. Cambridge University Press.

Lora, E. 2008. 'El futuro de los pactos fiscales en América Latina', Working Paper no. 650. IADB, Washington, DC.

Lund, F. 2008. *Changing Social Policy: The Child Support Grant in South Africa*. Cape Town: HSRC Press.

    2011. 'A step in the wrong direction: linking the South Africa Child Support Grant to school attendance'. *Journal of Poverty and Social Justice* 19: 5–14.

Lustig, N. C. 2011. 'Fiscal policy and income redistribution in Latin America: challenging the conventional wisdom', mimeo. Tulane University, New Orleans.

Machinea, J. L. 2006. 'El financiamiento solidario de la protección social: condición indispensable para un pacto de cohesion social en América Latina', mimeo. ECLAC, Santiago.

Mahon, J. E. 2005. 'Liberal states and fiscal contracts: aspects of the political economy of public finance', mimeo. Williams College, Boston.

Maluccio, J. A. 2005. 'Coping with the "coffee crisis" in Central America: the role of the Nicaraguan Red de Protección Social', FCND Discussion Paper no. 188. IFPRI, Washington, DC.

Maluccio, J. A., and Flores, R. 2004. 'Impact evaluation of a conditional cash transfer program: the Nicaraguan *Red de Protección Social*', FCND Discussion Paper no. 184. IFPRI, Washington, DC.

Mankiw, G. N., Weinzierl, M., and Yagan, D. 2009. 'Optimal taxation in theory and practice'. *Journal of Economic Perspectives* 23: 147–74.

Matheson, T. 2011. 'Taxing financial transactions: issues and evidence', Working Paper no. 11/54. IMF, Washington, DC.

Maurizio, R. 2009. 'Políticas de transferencias monetarias en Argentina: evaluación de su impacto sobre la pobreza y la desigualdad, y evaluación de sus costos', in Keifman, S. (ed.), *Reflexiones y propuestas para mejorar la distribución de ingresos en Argentina*, 181–263. Buenos Aires: ILO.

McKerlie, D. 2002. 'Justice between the young and the old'. *Philosophy and Public Affairs* 30: 152–77.

2003. 'Understanding egalitarianism'. *Economics and Philosophy* 19: 45–60.

Medeiros, M., Britto, T., and Soares, F. 2008. 'Targeted cash transfer programmes in Brazil', Working Paper no. 46. IPC, Brasilia.

Melo, M. A. 2007. 'Unexpected successes, unanticipated failures: social policy from Cardoso to Lula', in Kingstone, P. R., and Power, T. J. (eds.), *Democratic Brazil Revisited*, 161–84. University of Pittsburgh Press.

Mesa-Lago, C. 1991. 'Social security in Latin America and the Caribbean: a comparative assessment', in Ahmad, E., Drèze, J., Hills, J., and Sen, A. (eds.), *Social Security in Developing Countries*, 356–94. Oxford: Clarendon Press.

Micklewright, J., Coudouel, A., and Marnie, S. 2004. 'Targeting and self-targeting in a new social assistance scheme', Discussion Paper no. 1112. IZA, Bonn.

MIDEPLAN. 2004. *Conceptos fundamentals: Sistema de protección social Chile Solidario*. Santiago: MIDEPLAN.

2009. 'Fundamentos para la operación de un sistema intersectorial de protección social', report. MIDEPLAN, Santiago.

Milanovic, B. 2007. 'Ethical case and economic feasibility of global transfers', Policy Research Working Paper no. 3775. World Bank, Washington, DC.

Mirrlees, J. A. 1971. 'An exploration in the theory of optimum income taxation'. *Review of Economic Studies* 38: 175–208.

2005. 'Global public economics', in Atkinson, A. B. (ed.), *New Sources of Development Finance*, 200–9. Oxford University Press.

Mirrlees, J. A., Adam, S., Besley, T., Blundell, R., Bond, S., Chote, R., Gammie, M., Johnson, P., Myles, G., and Poterba, J. 2011. 'Integrating personal taxes and benefits', in *Tax by Design: The Mirrlees Review*, 122–47. Oxford University Press.

Moffitt, R. A. 2002. 'Welfare programs and labor supply', in Auerbach, A. J., and Feldstein, M. (eds.), *Handbook of Public Economics*, vol. IV, 2393–430. Amsterdam: Elsevier Science.

2006. 'Welfare work requirements with paternalistic government preferences'. *Economic Journal* 116: F441–58.

Møller, V., and Sotshongaye, A. 1996. '"My family eats this money too": pension sharing and self-respect among Zulu grandmothers'. *Southern African Journal of Gerontology* 5: 9–19.

Molyneux, M. 2006. 'Mothers at the service of the new poverty agenda: Progresa/Oportunidades, Mexico's conditional transfer programme'. *Social Policy and Administration* 40: 425–49.

Moon, J. D. 1988. 'The moral basis of the democratic welfare state', in Gutmann, A. (ed.), *Democracy and the Welfare State*, 27–52. Princeton University Press.

Moore, C. 2008. 'Assessing Honduras' CCT programme PRAF, Programa de Asignación Familiar: expected and unexpected realities', Country Study no. 15. IPC, Brasilia.

Moore, M. 2004. 'Revenues, state formation, and the quality of governance in developing countries'. *International Political Science Review* 25: 297–319.

2008. 'Between coercion and contract: competing narratives on taxation and governance', in Brautigam, D., Fjeldstad, O.-H., and Moore, M. (eds.), *Taxation and State-Building in Developing Countries: Capacity and Consent*, 34–63. Cambridge University Press.

Morduch, J. 1998a. 'Between the state and the market: can informal insurance patch the safety net?'. *World Bank Research Observer* 14: 187–207.

1998b. 'Poverty, economic growth, and average exit from poverty'. *Economics Letters* 59: 385–90.

Moreno-Ternero, J., and Roemer, J. E. 2005. 'Impartiality and priority part 2: a characterization with solidarity', Discussion Paper no. 1477B. Cowles Foundation, Yale University, New Haven, CT.

Morley, S., and Coady, D. 2003. *From Social Assistance to Social Development: Targeted Education Subsidies in Developing Countries*. Washington, DC: Center for Global Development (CGD) and IFPRI.

Moss, T. 2011. 'Oil to cash: fighting the resource curse through cash transfers', Working Paper no. 237. CGD, Washington, DC.

Myles, J., and Picot, G. 2000. 'Poverty indices and poverty analysis'. *Review of Income and Wealth* 46: 161–79.

Nagel, T. 1991. *Mortal Questions*. Cambridge University Press.

Narayanan, S. 2011. 'A case for reframing the cash transfer debate in India'. *Economic and Political Weekly* 46: 41–8.

Nattrass, N., and Seekings, J. 2001. 'Democracy and distribution in highly unequal economies: the case of South Africa'. *Journal of Modern African Studies* 39: 471–98.

Neufeld, L., Sotres Alvarez, D., Gertler, P., Tolentino Mayo, L., Jimenez Ruiz, J., Fernald, L. C., Villapando, S., Shamah, T., and Rivera Donmarco, J. 2005. 'Impacto de Oportunidades en el crecimiento y el estado de nutrición de niños en zonal rurales', in Hernández Prado, B., and Hernández Avila, M. (eds.), *Evaluación externa de impacto del programa Oportunidades 2004: Alimentación*, 15–50. Cuernavaca, Mexico: Instituto Nacional de Salud Pública.

Nichols, A. L., and Zeckhauser, R. J. 1982. 'Targeting transfers through restrictions on recipients'. *American Economic Review* 72: 372–7.

Niño-Zarazúa, M., Barrientos, A., Hulme, D., and Hickey, S. 2012. 'Social protection in sub-Saharan Africa: getting the politics right'. *World Development* 40: 163–76.

Norman, R. 1988. 'The social basis of equality', in Mason, A. (ed.), *Ideals of Equality*, 37–51. Oxford: Basil Blackwell.

OECD. 1994. *The OECD Jobs Study: Evidence and Explanations*. Paris: OECD.

1999. *Implementing the OECD Jobs Strategy: Assessing Performance and Policy*. Paris: OECD.

2003. 'Benefits and employment, friend or foe? Interactions between passive and active social programmes', in *OECD Employment Outlook 2003: Towards More and Better Jobs*, 171–235. Paris: OECD.

Parfit, D. 1991. *Equality or Priority? The Lindley Lecture*. Kansas City, MO: University Press of Kansas.

1997. 'Equality and priority'. *Ratio* 10: 202–21.

Parker, S., and Behrman, J. R. 2008. 'Seguimiento de adultos jóvenes en hogares incorporados desde 1998 a Oportunidades: impactos en educación y pruebas de desempeño', in SEDESOL (ed.), *Evaluación externa del programa Oportunidades 2008: a diez años de intervención en zonas rurales (1997–2007)*, vol. I, *Efectos de Oportunidades en áreas rurales a diez años de intervención*, 199–238. Mexico City: SEDESOL.

Patten, A. 2005. 'Should we stop thinking about poverty in terms of helping the poor?'. *Ethics and International Affairs* 19: 19–27.

Pelham, L. 2007. 'The politics behind the non-contributory old age social pensions in Lesotho, Namibia and South Africa', Working Paper no. 83. CPRC, Manchester.

Pellissery, S. 2008. 'Process deficits in the provision of social protection in rural Maharashtra', in Barrientos, A., and Hulme, D. (eds.), *Social Protection for the Poor and Poorest: Concepts, Policies and Politics*, 227–46. London: Palgrave Macmillan.

Petersen, M., and Hansson, S. O. 2005. 'Equality and priority'. *Utilitas* 17: 299–309.

Pinto, S. M. 2004. 'Assistance to poor households when income is not observed: targeted in-kind and in-cash transfers'. *Journal of Urban Economics* 56: 536–53.

Pogge, T. W. 1989. *Realizing Rawls*. Ithaca, NY: Cornell University Press.

(ed.) 2001. *Global Justice*. Oxford: Basil Blackwell.

2002. *World Poverty and Human Rights*. Cambridge: Polity Press.

2004. '"Assisting" the global poor', in Chatterjee, D. K. (ed.), *The Ethics of Assistance: Morality and the Distant Needy*, 260–88. Cambridge University Press.

2008. *World Poverty and Human Rights: Cosmopolitan Responsibilities and Reforms*. Cambridge: Polity Press.

Polanyi, K. 1957. *The Great Transformation: The Political and Economic Origins of Our Time*. Boston: Beacon Press.

Ponce, J., and Bedi, A. S. 2010. 'The impact of a cash transfer program on cognitive achievement: the Bono de Desarrollo Humano of Ecuador'. *Economics of Education Review* 29: 261–81.

Posel, D., Fairburn, J. A., and Lund, F. 2004. 'Labour migration and households: a reconsideration of the effects of the social pension on labour supply in South Africa'. *Economic Modelling* 23: 836–53.

Pritchett, L. 2002. 'It pays to be ignorant: a simple political economy of rigorous program evaluation'. *Policy Reform* 5: 251–69.

Psacharopoulos, G., and Patrinos, H. A. 2004. 'Returns to investment in education: a further update'. *Education Economics* 12: 111–34.

Ravallion, M. 1988. 'Expected poverty under risk-induced welfare variability'. *Economic Journal* 98: 1171–82.

1996. 'Issues in measuring and modeling poverty', Policy Research Working Paper no. 1615. World Bank, Washington, DC.

2003. 'Measuring pro-poor growth'. *Economics Letters* 78: 93–9.

2005. 'Evaluating anti-poverty programs', Policy Research Working Paper no. 3625. World Bank, Washington, DC.

2006. 'Transfers and safety nets in poor countries: revisiting the trade-offs and policy options', in Banerjee, A. V., Bénabou, T., and Mookherjee, D. (eds.), *Understanding Poverty*, 203–30. Oxford University Press.

2007. 'How relevant is targeting to the success of an antipoverty program?', Policy Research Working Paper no. 4385. World Bank, Washington, DC.

2008. 'Mis-targeted or mis-measured?' *Economics Letters* 100: 9–12.

2011. 'The two poverty enlightenments: historical insights from digitized books spanning three centuries'. *Poverty and Public Policy* 3: 1–46.

Ravallion, M., and Datt, G. 1995. 'Is targeting through a work requirement efficient? Some evidence for rural India', in van del Walle, D., and Nead, K. (eds.), *Public Spending and the Poor: Theory and Evidence*, 413–44. Baltimore: Johns Hopkins University Press.

Ravallion, M., and Wodon, Q. 2000. 'Does child labour displace schooling? Evidence on behavioural responses to enrollment subsidy'. *Economic Journal* 110: C158–75.

Rawls, J. 1971. *A Theory of Justice*. Cambridge, MA: Harvard University Press.

2001. *Justice as Fairness: A Restatement*. Cambridge, MA: Belknap Press.

2005. *Political Liberalism*. New York: Columbia University Press.

Risse, M. 2005. 'Do we owe the global poor assistance or rectification?'. *Ethics and International Affairs* 19: 9–18.

Rofman, R., Lucchetti, L., and Ourens, G. 2008. 'Pension systems in Latin America: concepts and measurements of coverage', Social Protection Discussion Paper no. 0616. World Bank, Washington, DC.

Rosenthal, L. 1983. 'Subsidies to the personal sector', in Millward, R., Parker, D., Sumner, M. T., and Topham, N. (eds.), *Public Sector Economics*, 78–128. London: Longman.

Ross, T. W. 1991. 'On the relative efficiency of cash transfers and subsidies'. *Economic Enquiry* 29: 485–96.

Rubalcava, L., Teruel, G., and Thomas, D. 2002. 'Welfare design, women's empowerment and income pooling', mimeo. Centro de Investigación y Docencia Económicas, Mexico City.

Runciman, W. G. 1966. *Relative Deprivation and Social Justice*. Berkeley: University of California Press.

Sabates-Wheeler, R., and Devereux, S. 2010. 'Cash transfers and high food prices: explaining outcomes on Ethiopia's Productive Safety Net Programme'. *Food Policy* 35: 274–85.

Sadmo, A. 1998. 'Redistribution and the marginal cost of public funds'. *Journal of Public Economics* 70: 365–82.

Sadoulet, E., de Janvry, A., and Davis, B. 2001. 'Cash transfer programs with income multipliers: PROCAMPO in Mexico'. *World Development* 29: 1043–56.

Santibañez, C. 2005. 'The informational basis of poverty measurement: using the capability approach to improve the CAS proxy tool'. *European Journal of Development Research* 17: 89–110.

Scanlon, T. M. 1998. *What We Owe Each Other*. Cambridge, MA: Belknap Press.

Schady, N., and Araujo, M. C. 2006. 'Cash transfers, conditions, school enrolment, and child work: evidence from a randomized experiment in Ecuador', mimeo. World Bank, Washington, DC.

Schubert, B. 2008. 'Protecting the poorest with cash transfers in low income countries', in Barrientos, A., and Hulme, D. (eds.), *Social Protection for the Poor and Poorest: Concepts, Policies and Politics*, 211–24. London: Palgrave Macmillan.

Schwarzer, H. 2000. 'Impactos socioeconômicos do sistema de aposentadorias rurais no Brazil: evidências empíricas de un estudio de caso no estado de Pará', Discussion Paper no. 729. IPEA, Rio de Janeiro.

Schwarzer, H., and Querino, A. C. 2002. 'Beneficios sociales y los pobres en Brazil: programas de pensiones no convencionales', in Bertranou, F., Solorio, C., and van Ginneken, W. (eds.), *Pensiones no contributivas y asistenciales: Argentina, Brasil, Chile, Costa Rica y Uruguay*, 63–124. Santiago: ILO.

SEDESOL. 2003. 'Programa institucional Oportunidades 2002–2006', report. SEDESOL, Mexico City.

Seekings, J. 2008a. 'Deserving individuals and groups: the post-apartheid state's justification of the shape of South Africa's system of social assistance'. *Transformation* 68: 28–52.

2008b. 'The ILO and social protection in the global South, 1919–2005', draft paper. University of Cape Town.

Seidl, C. 1988. 'Poverty measurement: a survey', in Bös, D., Rose, M., and Seidl, C. (eds.), *Welfare and Efficiency in Public Economics*, 71–148. Heidelberg: Springer-Verlag.

Sen, A. 1976a. 'Poverty: an ordinal approach to measurement'. *Econometrica* 44: 219–31.

1976b. 'Welfare inequalities and Rawlsian axiomatics'. *Theory and Decision* 7: 243–62.

1985. *Commodities and Capabilities*. Amsterdam: North-Holland.

1997a. *Inequality Reexamined*. Cambridge, MA: Harvard University Press.

1997b. *On Economic Inequality*. Oxford: Clarendon Press.

1999. *Development as Freedom*. Oxford University Press.

2009. *The Idea of Justice*. London: Penguin Books.

Sen, A., and Williams, B. 1982. 'Introduction: utilitarianism and beyond', in Sen, A., and Williams, B. (eds.), *Utilitarianism and Beyond*, 1–22. Cambridge University Press.

Sepúlveda Carmona, M. 2009. 'Promotion and protection of all human rights, civil, political, economic, social and cultural rights, including the right to development', report A/HRC/11/9. UN, New York.

Shankar, S., Gaiha, R., and Jha, R. 2011. 'Information, access and targeting: the National Rural Employment Guarantee scheme in India'. *Oxford Development Studies* 39: 69–95.

Shorrocks, A. 1995. 'Revisiting the Sen index'. *Econometrica* 63: 1225–30.

Singer, P. 1972. 'Famine, affluence and morality'. *Philosophy and Public Affairs* 1: 231–2.

2002. *One World: The Ethics of Globalization*. New Haven, CT: Yale University Press.

Sjöberg, O. 1999. 'Financing social protection in Europe: an historical outline', in Ministry of Social Affairs and Health (ed.), *Financing Social Protection in Europe*, 15–35. Helsinki: Ministry of Social Affairs and Health.

Skoufias, E. 2001. *Progresa and Its Impacts on the Human Capital and Welfare of Households in Rural Mexico: A Synthesis of the Results of an Evaluation by IFPRI*. Washington, DC: IFPRI.

2005. 'Progresa and its impacts on the welfare of rural households in Mexico', Research Report no. 139. IFPRI, Washington, DC.

Skoufias, E., and Coady, D. P. 2007. 'Are the welfare losses from imperfect targeting important?'. *Economica* 74: 756–76.

Skoufias, E., and di Maro, V. 2008. 'Conditional cash transfers, adult work incentives and current poverty'. *Journal of Development Studies* 44: 935–60.

Skoufias, E., Lindert, K., and Shapiro, J. 2010. 'Globalization and the role of public transfers in redistributing income in Latin America and the Caribbean'. *World Development* 38: 895–907.

Skoufias, E., and Parker, S. W. 2001. 'Conditional cash transfers and their impact on child work and schooling: evidence from the PROGRESA program in Mexico'. *Economía* 2: 45–96.

Skoufias, E., Unar, M., and González-Cossío, T. 2008. 'The impacts of cash and in-kind transfers on consumption and labor supply: experimental evidence from rural Mexico', Policy Research Working Paper no. 4778. World Bank, Washington, DC.

Smith, W. J., and Subbarao, K. 2003. 'What role for safety net transfers in very low income countries?', Social Protection Discussion Paper no. 0301. World Bank, Washington, DC.

Soares, F. V., and Britto, T. 2007. 'Confronting capacity constraints on conditional cash transfer programmes in Latin America: the cases of El Salvador and Paraguay', Working Paper no. 38. IPC, Brasilia.

Soares, S., Guerreiro Osório, R., Veras Soares, F., Medeiros, M., and Zepeda, E. 2007. 'Conditional cash transfers in Brazil, Chile and Mexico: impacts upon inequality', Working Paper no. 35. IPC, Brasilia.

Soares, S., Ribas, R. P., and Soares, F. V. 2009. 'Focalização e cobertura do programa Bolsa-Família: qual o significado dos 11 milhões de famílias?', Discussion Paper no. 1396. IPEA, Rio de Janeiro.

Srinivasan, T. S. 2001. 'Comment on "Counting the world's poor" by Angus Deaton'. *World Bank Research Observer* 16: 157–68.

Stern, N. 1987. 'Comment on Kanbur's "Transfers, targeting and poverty"'. *Economic Policy* 4: 136–41.

Streeten, P. 1984. 'Basic needs: some unsettled questions'. *World Development* 12: 973–78.

Subramanian, S. 2004. 'Poverty measures and anti-poverty policy with an egalitarian constraint', Research Paper no. 2004/12. World Institute for Development Economics Research, United Nations University, Helsinki.

Sumarto, S., Suryahadi, A., and Bazzi, S. 2008. 'Indonesia's social protection during and after the crisis', in Barrientos, A., and Hulme, D. (eds.), *Social Protection for the Poor and Poorest: Concepts, Policies and Politics*, 121–45. London: Palgrave Macmillan.

Szreter, S. 2007. 'The right to registration: development, identity registration and social security – a historical perspective'. *World Development* 35: 67–86.

Tabor, S. R. 2002. 'Assisting the poor with cash: design and implementation of social transfer programs', Social Protection Discussion Paper no. 0223. World Bank, Washington, DC.

Takayama, N. 1979. 'Poverty, income inequality, and their measures: Professor Sen's axiomatic approach reconsidered'. *Econometrica* 47: 747–59.

Tanzi, V. 2000. 'Globalization and the future of social protection', Working Paper no. 00/12. IMF, Washington, DC.

Thomas, D., and Strauss, J. 1997. 'Health and wages: evidence on men and women in urban Brazil'. *Journal of Econometrics* 77: 159–85.

Thon, D. 1979. 'On measuring poverty'. *Review of Income and Wealth* 25: 429–40.

Thorbecke, E. 2007. 'Multidimensional poverty: conceptual and measurement issues', in Kakwani, N., and Silber, J. (eds.), *The Many Dimensions of Poverty*, 3–19. Basingstoke: Palgrave Macmillan.

Thurow, L. 1974. 'Cash vs. in-kind transfers'. *American Economic Review* 64: 190–5.

Timmons, J. F. 2005. 'The fiscal contract: states, taxes and public services'. *World Politics* 15: 530–67.

Todd, P. E., and Wolpin, K. I. 2006. 'Assessing the impact of a school subsidy program in Mexico: using a social experiment to validate a dynamic behavioral model of child schooling and fertility'. *American Economic Review* 96: 1384–417.

Townsend, P. 2009. 'Investment in social security: a possible UN model for child benefit?', in Townsend, P. (ed.), *Building Decent Societies: Rethinking the Role of Social Security in Development*, 151–66. Basingstoke: Palgrave Macmillan.

Tungodden, B. 2003. 'The value of equality'. *Economics and Philosophy* 19: 1–44.

Ulriksen, M. S. 2011. 'Financing social protection in Africa: status and implications', mimeo. University of Johannesburg.

UN. 1995. 'Report of the World Summit for Social Development', document A/Conf.166/9. UN, New York.

Usui, C. 1994. 'Welfare state development in a world system context: event history analysis of first social insurance legislation among 60 countries, 1880–1960', in Janoski, T., and Hicks, A. M. (eds.), *The Comparative Political Economy of the Welfare State*, 254–77. Cambridge University Press.

Vallentyne, P. 2000. 'Equality, efficiency, and the priority of the worse off'. *Economics and Philosophy* 16: 1–19.

Van der Berg, S., and Siebrits, K. 2010. 'Social assistance reform during a period of financial stress', Working Paper no. 17/10. Department of Economics, University of Stellenbosch.

Villa, J. M. 2008. 'Que familias estan en condiciones de salir del Programa Familias en Accion?', evaluation note. IPC, Brasilia.

Waldron, J. 1986. 'John Rawls and the social minimum'. *Journal of Applied Philosophy* 3: 21–33.

Wang, M. 2007. 'Emerging urban poverty and effects of the Dibao programme on alleviating poverty in China'. *China and World Economy* 15: 74–88.

Warlters, M., and Auriol, E. 2005. 'The marginal cost of public funds in Africa', Policy Research Working Paper no. 3679. World Bank, Washington, DC.

Watts, H. 1968. 'An economic definition of poverty', in Moynihan, D. P. (ed.), *On Understanding Poverty*, 316–29. New York: Basic Books.

Weigand, C., and Grosh, M. 2008. 'Levels and patterns of safety net spending in developing and transition countries', Social Protection Discussion Paper no. 0817. World Bank, Washington, DC.

Woolard, I., and Leibbrandt, M. 2010. 'The evolution and impact of unconditional cash transfers in South Africa', Working Paper no. 51. University of Cape Town.

Yap, Y.-T., Sedlacek, G., and Orazem, P. F. 2002. 'Limiting child labor through behavior-based income transfers: an experimental evaluation of the PETI program in rural Brazil', mimeo. IADB, Washington, DC.

Yaqub, S. 2001. 'At what age does poverty damage most? Exploring a hypothesis about "timetabling error" in antipoverty', mimeo. University of Sussex, Brighton.

Yeates, N. (ed.). 2009. 'Global social policy forum: conditional cash transfers'. *Global Social Policy* 9: 163–82.

Zeckhauser, R. J. 1971. 'Optimal mechanisms for income transfers'. *American Economic Review* 61: 324–34.

Zheng, B. 1993. 'An axiomatic characterization of the Watts poverty index'. *Economics Letters* 42: 81–6.

   1997. 'Aggregate poverty measures'. *Journal of Economic Surveys* 11: 123–62.

   2000. 'Poverty orderings'. *Journal of Economic Surveys* 14: 427–66.

   2007. 'Measuring lifetime poverty', Working Paper no. 07–01. Department of Economics, University of Colorado, Denver.

Zucco, C. 2008. 'The president's "new" constituency: Lula and the pragmatic vote in Brazil's 2006 presidential elections'. *Journal of Latin American Studies* 40: 29–49.

Index